365
Bedtime Stories

365
Bedtime Stories

By

Mary Graham Bonner

With illustrations in color by
Florence Choate and Elizabeth Curtis

DERRYDALE BOOKS
New York

Printed and bound in the United States of America

Library of Congress Cataloging-in-Publication Data

Bonner, Mary Graham.
  365 bedtime stories.

  Summary: A collection of brief stories coordinated
with the actual events in a calendar year.
   1. Children's stories, American. [1. Short stories]
I. Choate, Florence, ill. II. Curtis, Elizabeth, ill.
III. Title. IV. Title: Three hundred sixty-five bedtime
stories.
PZ7.B6422Aag 1987   [E]   87–13588
ISBN 0–517–63231–4

h g f e d c b a

This book was originally published in the first quarter of this century, and the modern reader may be surprised to discover
old-fashioned styles of punctuation and spelling, but these have
been retained in order to convey the flavor of the original work.

CONTENTS

[COLOR ILLUSTRATIONS FOLLOW PAGES 112 AND 208]

FOREWORD

There is a generosity of spirit in Mary Graham Bonner. It glows from every page and from every story in this remarkable collection. She has perched herself at the bedside of all children and done what turns out to be the most successful thing for tired little minds— she has made up stories as she goes along. Gathering her alert observations of what intrigues and interests young folks into a tidy pile, she carefully selects a tidbit for every night of the year; and then, graciously deferring, she lets "Daddy" tell them all.

Each little story begins with some indication of Daddy's participation in the bedtime ritual: "Commenced daddy," "Said daddy," "Daddy had a story . . ." The device adds a dimension of love to the book that it could not have achieved otherwise—the poignant sense of security which emanates from a gentle father's voice.

Generosity is also evident in the use Bonner makes of little stories to educate as well as entertain. With a wisp of a tale, she tells all one needs to know about oyster crabs; an extra paragraph or two brings adjectives to life in "The Words"; a cooking lesson is slipped in with "The Vegetables"; and the child learns about chipmunks in yet another. Science, natural phenomena, holidays, illnesses, all sorts of animals, insects, birds, and growing things have their day. And so do objects in the everyday world of the little child. Clothespins are important (and they certainly are!), keys, garden tools, umbrellas, elevators, pencils, newsboys, furnaces—for these things do loom large to little eyes. The author always deals with reality with charm and caring. Each object is made lovable, often by the use of personification, occasionally by simply stating its value. A carved chair is looked at a little more carefully, and through Bonner's eyes and words we once again become the transfixed child who stares and stares at what the grownups take for granted or overlook.

To entertain both child and parent on this journey through a year of bedtimes, we have the beautiful colored illustrations of Florence Choate and Elizabeth Curtis. It must have been difficult for them to select only some of the topics for their work from such a wealth of possibilities, but the finished products are perfect visualizations and manage to capture the spirit of Ms. Bonner's writing. Putting the child in "Mommy's lap" for the first plate completes the circle of the family which Bonner begins with father and child; and the fireplace emphasizes the warmth we feel at once from every little piece. The book was originally published in the first quarter of this century and the art portrays clothing, furniture, toys, hairdos, and decorative pieces from that period which have nostalgic charm today. The result for us now, viewing the illustrations and reading about a world that is as curious, unknown, and fascinating to a child today as it was then, is to take us back to a time when life was simpler. Without realizing what they would achieve, the artists created a serenity that increases, for readers, with each passing year.

Bonner knows that fantasy is as important as reality in a child's world; and she adds just the right amount of fairies, goblins, brownies, royalty, and, of course, Santa Claus, to delight the most active imagination of any little boy or girl. The artists are right there with her. Looking like little creatures from Max Reinhardt's masterpiece of a movie from the 1930s, "Midsummer Night's Dream" (which still appears on late-night television for those lucky enough to catch it), the figures in the fantasy illustrations have the magic of those in a Busby Berkeley musical scene. They are done on a grand scale and in a joyous manner; the colors make us happy and enchant us.

What a blessing that Mary Graham Bonner chose to share her love and talent with us all. What a blessing that she was aided in this mission by the artistry of Florence Choate and Elizabeth Curtis. And finally, what a blessing that this book has been reprinted now so that little children (and their parents) can once again enjoy the simple delights within its pages.

Baltimore, Maryland
1987

PATRICIA BARRETT PERKINS

Acknowledgment

The publisher of this edition would like to thank Rose Harrington for her consultation on this book.

365
Bedtime Stories

JANUARY 1: A New Year's Party

"JUST because it was the first day of the year," commenced daddy, "and because parties were about the nicest things in the world to the mind of a little girl named Ella, her mother decided to give her one.

" 'It certainly does seem like the first of the year, or the first of something,' said Ella. 'It's a new day, a new year and we have new toys and new games. We are even going to have supper out of new dishes.'

"For among the presents Santa Claus had brought to Ella was a fine set of dishes. They were pink and white and there were six cups and saucers, six little plates, a teapot, sugar bowl and cream jug. It was really a very complete set.

"They had thin bread and butter, hot chocolate with whipped cream and a cake which Ella's mother called a New Year's cake. It was pink and white on the top with pink sugared trimmings on the white frosting.

"In the center of the cake was one pink candle, for Ella's mother said it would be quite impossible to have a candle for the number of years there had been, and too, it would be nice to have a new way and just consider the year a day old.

"After the cake had been almost entirely eaten they played house. Each little girl took a corner of the room as her house and fixed it up with some of Ella's things. They all had their own dolls and many of their other toys so they really felt quite at home.

"Then they began calling on each other, dressing up in shawls and old hats which Ella's mother let them use. After a while they heard a flutter, flutter against the window pane, and then another little flapping sound.

" 'It's a little bird,' said Ella, as she looked out of the window. 'It's right on the sill, and I am dreadfully afraid it has hurt its wings. Poor little dear.'

"They opened the window and Ella took the little bird in her hands. Oh, how cold the little bird's feathers were!

" 'We'll take care of you,' said Ella. They gave the little bird some bread-crumbs and some water. Then he had a delicious piece of lettuce from the seeds which Ella had started in a box in her room.

"Pretty soon the bird began to grow much better and hopped and

I

chirped about the room, and then they let him out for he had simply been very hungry.

" 'We'll put some suet in that tree over there,' said Ella.

" 'Let's put some bread-crumbs,' said her friends, and then one of them added,

" 'And let's give some of the New Year cake crumbs too.'

"So the little bird was given a regular New Year's feast, and Ella and her friends were among other children who decided to look after the feathered people through the cold months of the winter and to give them bread-crumbs and suet which they love so well."

JANUARY 2: The Rhyming Years

WELL," said the Old Year, "I am going to make up a poem about myself. I feel quite poetical."

"And," said the New Year, "I will, too." For the New Year didn't want to have the Old Year think that he was unable to do anything like that, even though he was young. But he felt very much pleased when the Old Year said: "Though I have lived twelve whole months, I have not become a poet."

"I think age should be given the right to speak first," said the New Year.

The Old Year shook his white hair and smiled so that the wrinkles in his face all ran in together.

This is what he said :

> "Yes, it is true I was feeling old,
> Yes, it is true I was also cold,
> Yes, it is true I heard them cheer,
> Welcoming in the glad New Year."

Then New Year recited this verse :

> "Of course, you see I was out for fun,
> My life has only just begun,
> They said 'He is young and full of vim,
> No one can help but welcome him.'

"You mustn't think I am conceited," he added. "I say a lot to make my rhyme come out right."

"Of course," said the Old Year, "for I do too. Well, I will give my second verse. Don't believe it all, though!" Then the Old Year took an old harp he had and he began to play and sing, and this was what he sang:

> "And Poor Old Year—he almost wept
> As he packed up his things and left.
> But as he turned to say good-by,
> Something in him made him cry:
> 'Though my work is mostly done,
> I, have, too, had lots of fun,
> And 'ere I go upon my way,
> This I certainly would say:
> 'Happy New Year, big and small,
> Happy New Year, short and tall,
> Happy New Year, every one!
> May you all have lots of fun!' "

JANUARY 3: Naughty Wind

THE Clothes-Pins on the line," said daddy, "were having a very jolly time.
" 'I'll blow those clothes away,' said the North Wind.
" 'Oh, no you won't,' said the Clothes-Pins in chorus.
" 'You are only little wooden things,' said the Wind. 'I am strong and powerful and can do just exactly as I like.'
"Now the Fairies saw that the Clothes-Pins were doing their work so well that they thought they would like to help them, so they all perched on the line and began to sing :

> 'Heigh-ho, heigh-ho,
> Let the North Wind blow,
> The Clothes-Pins and we,
> Will certainly see,
> That the clothes will stay here.
> The day's nice and clear,
> The sun's good and strong,
> And the wind is quite wrong.
> To try such a trick,
> But the Clothes-Pins will stick.'

"The Clothes-Pins did stick to the line and the Fairies helped them, singing all the time. The Wind kept on blowing and tried his hardest to get the better of the Fairies, but he had no luck at all and the Clothes-Pins won!"

JANUARY 4: The Selfish Oyster Crabs

YOU know, I think oyster-crabs are perhaps the most selfish of all the sea animals," began daddy. "The oyster-crabs really belong to the crab family. They are called oyster-crabs, however, because above all things they love the juice of an oyster and absolutely live on it. And what I am going to tell you about now is the way they get it.

"First of all, the oyster-crab hovers around the oysters and then picks out a nice, fat, juicy looking oyster, saying to himself: 'You look as if you could feed me well without any effort. I think I will crawl into your shell.' So then he crawls right inside the oyster's shell and proceeds to enjoy himself. He prefers just to 'sponge' on others, as the expression goes!"

JANUARY 5: Brownie's Toothache

GOING to the dentist's always frightened Evelyn. "Dear me," said daddy, "I think I will have to tell you about the brownie's trip to the dentist, for I think his case was very similar to yours.

"This little brownie had had a toothache which had bothered him for some time, but he dreaded to go to the dentist's, just the way you do.

"One day, though, it got awfully painful and he felt he could stand it no longer. He went right off to see the brownie dentist. He was a very clever dentist and very kind and gentle. He got a pair of pullers, and after a moment or two Dr. Brownie said:

" 'Well, here's the old toothache.'

" 'What, my tooth already out?' said the little brownie. 'And to think of all I've suffered before I came to you.' "

JANUARY 6: The Pink Cockatoo

ON the morning of the birthday of a little girl named Natalie," said daddy, "a pink cockatoo was ready to greet her when she awoke. Well, you can imagine how happy Natalie was. And she kept saying over and over again:

4

" 'Oh, how lovely you are.' The cockatoo would raise up his pink crest on the top of his head at that—just as some people raise up their foreheads—only his crest went way, way higher. He did that whenever he felt like it, and he always felt like it when he was being talked to.

"And after a very short time the cockatoo was just as tame as could be and he seemed to grow more beautiful every day.

"Before long he began to talk just as a parrot will and follow Natalie around the house. He had his food out of special little pink dishes Natalie had given him to match his pink feathers, and every morning he took his bath in a pink soup bowl which he thought was very fine indeed.

"Maybe you will think he got spoiled by so much fussing and attention, but he just became tamer and tamer every day. He learned many tricks and would often perform them for Natalie's friends.

"And when it came time for Natalie's next birthday she gave a party. On the invitation it said the party was being given by Natalie and the pink cockatoo. And in one corner was a little colored drawing Natalie had made of her cockatoo. When the cockatoo saw it he put his crest way up in the air, and said in a funny voice:

" 'Goodie, Natalie,' which was his pet name for his Mistress.

"And this is a truly true story, you know."

JANUARY 7: The Pet Monkey

ONCE there was an old lady," said daddy, "who lived all alone. One day, though, she went to town and bought a pet monkey. She named him Niles. He was only seven inches long and had a curly tail. He was a very dark gray color. He proved to be a most expensive pet, for he liked all the most delicious fruits and would only eat his bread and rice when plenty of rich cream was poured over it. What fascinated him above all was the old lady's rings.

"When the old lady saw how fond Niles was of jewels she took out her jewel box. Niles had the most glorious time playing with its contents. He decorated himself with all the beads and chains and bangles and looked at himself in the mirror. He shook all over, for he liked the noise as well as the glitter of the jewels.

"So the old lady was very, very happy with her pet monkey. Niles was delighted with his new home and his new mistress, for he had never had jewels to play with in the animal shop."

JANUARY 8: The Bravery Medal

TWO children," said daddy, "were skating on a pond. It was a blustery, snowy afternoon, and they were the only ones on the ice.

"A big dog was taking a good run on this cold winter's day when he spied the children on the pond.

"He went down to the pond and ran across it a little way, but the ice had a bad way of creaking, and he was sure it was not so very firm. He decided that he had better stay around to see that nothing happened to the children.

"He had been there but a moment or two when a terrific crack in the ice sounded. It gave way, and the two children fell through. The sheet of ice broke rapidly, and the water was soon clear for some distance around them.

"Quickly the dog went to the rescue of the children and swam to the shore with them. He saw some people drive by in a sleigh on the road above, and he barked so frantically that they stopped to see what the trouble was. Then, of course, they drove the two children to their home. The big dog went along too. The hero simply said 'Bow-wow!' when later they fastened a medal on his collar. He wanted to tell them that he thought they were being very good to him, and he thanked them, but at the same time he was so modest that he didn't think he had been so brave. He felt any other dog would have done just the same, as he adored children.

JANUARY 9: The Jack-knife

THIS evening," said daddy, "I am going to tell you about the little boy who was given a jack-knife as a birthday present. He did so many things with his knife that I think it might give you some ideas and suggestions of things you might make with the help of the knife. He set up a little carpentry shop in his room with a workstand.

"He made little bird-houses, little squirrel houses, chairs, stands, boats, an express cart, and, oh, countless other things! In fact, he just made all the things that boys like.

"Before he had his jack-knife he was not at all interested in carpentry. But his knife helped so much. It was far more useful to him than his other tools."

6

JANUARY 10: The Brave Little Sister

THERE was once a little boy who had a sister just about Evelyn's age," said daddy. "He was much disappointed that his sister didn't care more for long walks and boys' games and that animals seemed to frighten her.

"He used to scold her about it instead of helping her to get over her fear. One day these two children were taking a walk. They went into the country along a quiet road. They passed a little house in which lived an old woman who had a great many cats. She was very queer and her cats seemed to be queer too. Anyway, it was said that they hated strangers.

"The little boy didn't believe this, and when his sister tried to hurry by he laughed at her.

" 'Oh, come and see this nice cat!' he said. And he tried to pick the cat up.

"The cat objected to strangers, as all the people had said, and she started to scratch the little boy. With a cry his sister rushed to him. She grabbed the back of the cat and got him off. Then she cried 'Shoo!' to the cat, which made him go right home, for he didn't care about hurting the little boy. He only would not be played with.

" 'I shall never make fun of you again, sister,' he said. 'You saved me by taking off that cat, of which you were afraid. I have not been at all a nice brother to you, and I don't deserve such a good sister, for it was love for me that made you forget about your fear. But you may be quite sure I will never make fun of you in the future, for really you are the brave one.' "

JANUARY 11: Baby Bears

IN the winter, at the start of the new year," said daddy, "Mother Bear was sleeping and dozing and dreaming in her home back in the hole of a big rock. Soon the little bears arrived. She taught them about the berries they must eat and about the things which would make them feel well and strong. She also told them of the bad things they must not touch—the things which would make their little tummies feel very miserable indeed and which would make them quite, quite sick.

"And when, at last, they went out of the cave, and saw the real world, the trees and the forest paths, they wanted to start off at once for adventures, for the world looked so mysterious and wondrous.

" 'Do you want to leave your old mother?' the black bear asked.

" 'We love you, mother, but we want to see the world,' they said.

" 'Bang,' suddenly went a gun, and Mother Bear received a slight wound.

"The baby bears were around her in a flash, but mother bear was safe, for the man with the gun had hurriedly gone when he had seen how near the old bear was. And he had seen her teeth and had almost been able to feel them!

"And the babies knew their teeth would never have done. They, too, had had a glimpse of their mother's anger and their mother's strength.

"And as they licked the wound they said,

" 'We won't leave you, Mother Bear. We don't know the world as yet.'

"And Mother Black Bear groaned with the hurt from the slight wound in her shoulder, but still more she grunted with pleasure, for her babies had seen that they still needed their mother."

JANUARY 12: The Snow House

AT night after the children had gone to bed and it had grown colder and colder Old Man Snow came around to see what the children had been doing," said daddy.

" 'Well, well, well,' he said as he saw a snow house and a snow fort and a snow man, 'this is fine. They appreciate me. They know what handsome things I can make. This is really gorgeous.

" 'Look, Prince Icicle, isn't this fine?'

"Prince Icicle appeared with a number of the other princes and princesses who hung down from the roof of the snow house and the top of the snow fort and from the shoulders of the snow man. Prince Icicle himself took a very fine place over the doorway of the snow house.

" 'Isn't this handsome?' asked Old Man Snow. 'Our fine king will be delighted and his royal majesty will be honored.'

"As Old Man Snow said these words along came King Snow. He wore a most beautiful crown of snow and he showed the Icicle family the compliment of wearing icicles from his beard and his crown and his locks of snow and from his hanging snowy sleeves.

" 'They stopped me as I went by the brook,' said King Snow, 'and begged me to have some of their jeweled icicles. Don't they sparkle beautifully? Yes, they asked me to have them, and the brook, which was beginning to freeze around the edges, begged me to listen to its story.

" 'It had so much to tell of its travels, how it ran down a long and winding hill and how it couldn't help trickling and laughing all the time with the jokes and merry tales it kept hearing.'

"So Old Man Snow, King Snow, Prince Icicle and the other princes and princesses talked all through the night and told wonderful stories as they sat in the children's snow house."

JANUARY 13: Peter Goblin's Trip

To think," and Peter Goblin looked as if he were going to cry, "to think," he repeated, "that children shouldn't like us. Why, children are the nicest creatures in all the world, and I love them, I do. That's why I am so unhappy when they talk about me."

The Fairy Queen had been listening to this talk and she felt sorry that so many untrue stories had gone around the children's world about Peter Goblin and the goblin brothers.

"I'll tell you what I'd do, Peter," she said.

"Keep on trying to tell as many children as you can how much you like them. Tell them that in years gone by people were far more nervous than they are now. They were afraid of the dark and things like that.

"Tell them that you never jump out at them in the dark, and that you only come to them when they are asleep. Explain as much and as often as you can that you never carry them far away from home, but that you simply sit on their bedposts and talk to them. I'll help you too, Peter."

"Thank you," said Peter Goblin, as he hopped and jumped away, for he felt far more cheerful now.

He went to call on his friends, the children. He had a very hard time with one little girl. "Good evening," said Peter, as he perched himself on the edge of the right bedpost of her bed.

She drew the clothes over her head. "Oh, don't do that," screamed Peter. "It will make you have bad dreams and maybe you'll smother."

"Oh, dear," thought Peter, "she will dream I'm horrid indeed if she does that." But after a moment she poked her head out again and looked at Peter.

She couldn't help laughing at him, for he looked so funny and yet so sad. But still she was frightened, until after she had looked again (for between looks she hid her face), when she saw two big tears rolling down Peter Goblin's funny little face.

"What's the matter, little sir?" she asked. She wanted to be polite

9

when he felt so badly and yet he seemed so small and tiny to be called just Sir.

"I'm blue and sad," said Peter, " 'cause children think I'm bad. They think I hide in the dark to catch them. And I love them, and want to tell them stories. Not a single goblin has ever hurt a child— no, no, no! Why, we would disown a bad goblin, we would." And the little girl promised Peter she'd let all her friends know this.

JANUARY 14: The Words

THE words Beautiful, Gorgeous, Glorious and Wonderful were talking. "You see," said Beautiful, "we've all been feeling rather sad that no one used us. We're always trying to live up to our names. We're always trying to be beautiful and gorgeous and glorious.

"We don't try to be mean or horrid or ugly. We haven't been jealous of you, Wonderful."

"Ah," said Wonderful, "I understand. You've never gone back on your names. You've always meant the same things. You've been fine to keep your names and to be beautiful and gorgeous and glorious.

"But you needn't feel sad because you haven't been given much attention and because you haven't been used much lately. People have got into the habit of saying everything is wonderful.

"Really and truly I've been worked to death. I don't like to be worked so hard. I really and truly don't. I get tired, and yet I have to be ready when they want me. I'm just jumping from one to another and sometimes I'm half with one and half with another at the same time.

"But you keep on being Beautiful and Gorgeous and Glorious, for you are three lovely words and Wonderful couldn't get along without you."

"Ah, Wonderful," said Beautiful, "you do cheer us up. Yes, you are Wonderful."

And they all laughed as they saw what a useful, fitting, wonderful word it really was!

JANUARY 15: The Medicine Bottle

IF you think my life is a pleasant one," said the Medicine Bottle, "I'll tell you from the start that it isn't.

"In the first place I was in the doctor's office. I saw the people quake and shake when they were told they had to take some bitter medicine. I don't suppose they really shook as much as I thought they did, but I was standing quite still at the time and they seemed to make a great deal of fuss.

"Then I heard some one say,

> " 'Doctors give us horrible stuff,
> When we think we're sick enough,
> But after all they make us well,
> And this fact, too, I think we should tell.'

"Then some one else said,

> " 'I wonder if the doctor has taken
> From the medicine bottle which must be shaken.
> It's hard to swallow it and be held by the nose
> While we get down the horrible dose.'

"Such are the things I've heard," said the Medicine Bottle.

"Did all the people speak like that?" asked the little White Pills.

"They didn't speak in rhyme like that," said the Medicine Bottle, "but those were the things they said which I've changed into rhymes.

"A medicine bottle must have something to cheer it up at times.

"Yes, I'll tell you my life is not a pleasant one. I'm never greeted with a smile. Fancy that, White Pills! I'm never greeted with a smile.

"Here I sit on the mantelpiece and three times a day I am taken down and shaken as though they'd like to kill me, I do believe, and then with groans or tears or complaints I'm swallowed. Or rather, some of the medicine from me is swallowed. It's a terrible life that I lead!"

JANUARY 16: A Loaf of Bread

ONE day in a baker's shop," said daddy, "appeared a very small-sized loaf of bread.

"A little girl named Lucy was shopping with her grandmother.

" 'Oh, look,' said Lucy, 'look at the tiny loaf of bread.'

"Now the loaf of bread would have smiled, only loaves of bread can't smile and if they should laugh they would crumble, so the loaf of bread kept a perfectly straight face.

" 'I thought I'd be noticed by a child,' said the small loaf of bread.

" 'You won't last as long as we will,' said a larger loaf of bread.

" 'Oh, who cares about the size,' said the small loaf.

" 'Of course you don't,' said another larger loaf.

" 'Now, now,' said the small loaf, "don't be mean and unkind to your little friend and relative, the small loaf of bread. I'm the only small one here, though I heard the baker say if folks liked me the size I am and if mothers bought me for their children he'd make a lot like me.'

" 'We didn't mean to be unkind or mean,' said the larger loaves, 'only we are a little envious. We've been the same size always. We have to follow our relatives who are baked ahead of us and are sold ahead of us. We always have to follow their example.

" 'But you have been made differently. You have been made a small size. You're cunning and different. You are just like us in taste and shape and kind, but smaller in size and that makes you very interesting.'

" 'Hush,' said the small loaf of bread, 'I am being bought. Hush!'

"And off went the little tiny loaf, in a paper bag, carried by Lucy. Just as soon as it got home, having been carried all the way, for Lucy knew it couldn't walk or run home, a nice fat crust was cut off and Lucy ate it with joy.

" 'My nice little baby loaf of bread,' she said, 'you are so cunning and so good to eat!' And the loaf of bread was glad it had been made so tiny and cunning and yet so good."

JANUARY 17: The Tame Canary Bird

DADDY had heard that afternoon the story of a very tame canary bird. The little girl who owned the bird, and who was a friend of Jack and Evelyn, had told daddy about her little pet. So when daddy got home in the evening he was ready at once to tell the story of the little bird.

"I am going to tell you about the little bird Elizabeth has. Her daddy gave him to her several weeks ago, and he is just as tame as tame can be," said daddy. "She has named him Bubsie, and he knows his name too, for whenever she calls 'Bubsie!' he replies with a little 'Peep, peep!'

"Every morning, bright and early, he wakes up and begins to sing the most beautiful songs. He sings so steadily that Elizabeth says it is a surprise to her that he doesn't burst his little throat.

"After Elizabeth gets up she always gives him a little piece of apple before she begins her breakfast. She puts it on her finger between two wires of the cage, and he hops right over on his little bar and takes it from her finger.

"The next thing is his bath, which he takes soon after breakfast. He loves that. He spatters the water about and has just the best time in the world. He acts as if it were the most wonderful game. After his bath he has a treat of delicious lettuce to eat, and then he sits in the sun and smoothes down his feathers.

"In his cage there is a swing, and he swings on it and hops from one perch to the other. In fact, he has a fine romp. He usually does this right after his bath, for then he feels so energetic.

"In the afternoon Elizabeth lets him out of his cage. Of course she sees first that there are no windows up or doors ajar before she opens the door of the cage. When the cage door is open Bubsie flies out and makes a tour of the room. How he does enjoy flying around and perching back of the different pictures and on the window-sill. The thing he likes more than anything else is to play with Elizabeth. He perches on her shoulder and walks around on her hand. And he loves to tease her too, for if there are any flowers in the room he will fly over to them, peck at them and begin munching at them. Then he won't let Elizabeth catch him. He thinks this a huge joke, and he always flies to some high spot in the room and begins to sing which is his favorite trick of all."

JANUARY 18: Little Carry's Birthday

CARRY was nine years old," daddy said. "A few minutes before eleven Carry's little brother came to her, ringing a large bell. 'Come to the celebration for the queen of the day!' he shouted and all the family joined the procession.

"In the center of the room was a table. And such a marvelously covered table! But, first of all, they seated Carry in a big rocking-chair at the head of the table. They were all dressed up in funny costumes which they always wore for birthday celebrations. The table was full of presents, and in the center was a cake with nine lighted candles on it. 'Many happy returns of the day!' they all cried together.

"She opened her presents one by one. She had lovely pink knitted bed-room slippers from her mother, a beautiful doll from her daddy, a workbag from her granny, a paint box from her auntie and a big box of candy from her brother, which he'd bought with his very own saved-up money, and which to Carry was the best present of all!"

JANUARY 19: Maggie's Meals

THERE was once a little girl whose name was Maggie," said daddy, "and how she did love meals! Now, one evening when Maggie had gone to bed along came a fine looking creature very handsomely dressed.

" 'Who are you?' asked Maggie.

" 'I'm the Dream King and I'm going to take you to a party.'

"So Maggie went with the Dream King and they visited such interesting and hospitable people.

"They went to a huge city which seemed to be made of delicious things to eat and which, as soon as people ate from the city, the food grew or was cooked back again!

"It was all very marvelous. And to Maggie's surprise she saw Duke Ice Cream take up a spoon and scoop a huge mouthful right off his very arm. And in another few minutes his arm was as before.

"The Duke told her he liked the cold weather and that he always lived in the coldest part of the city.

"Lady Lettuce was followed everywhere by her pages, the Vinegar and Oil boys. And sometimes she had friends to call on her like the Tomato Twins and the Cucumber Cousins and the Potato Pals. Maggie also met Apple, the queen of all the Pies.

"Maggie had the very best time in the world and when the Dream King told her he must be taking her back Maggie said:

" 'And you've not told me I was wrong to enjoy my meals so much.'

" 'I gave you a surprise, in not scolding you, eh?' asked the Dream King. 'Well, you're never greedy or selfish and if you like your food I think it is fine. Good-night!' "

JANUARY 20: Winter Trees

ALL the winter things," said daddy, "such as the cold Winds, the Snow and the Ice told the Pine Trees and the Fir Trees and the Spruce Trees how much they liked them.

" 'I will tell you a secret,' said the Pine Tree.

" 'Yes,' said the Snow, as it nestled closer to the branches of the big tree.

" 'Years and years and years ago, I talked to my family about dropping off in the Winter-time. We never got any further than talking about it, for just as I had said, "Well, and what do you think of the scheme?" some of the Snow Flakes came and rested on our branches.

"Oh," they said, "you're so much nicer than the branches without any leaves. There we have to fill up the corners, but with you we can nestle down."

" 'The North Wind told us,' continued the Pine Tree, 'that it was such a joy to have a good strong tree around that wouldn't feel hurt if he played about and had a good time. And so we discovered how much the North Wind liked us.

" 'Then,' said the Pine Tree, 'we heard the Grown-Ups. They said what a comfort it was to have some green trees in the Winter and they said how horrible it would be if every tree were quite bare and ugly. And then came the Children. They walked through the woods one snowy day and they stopped to look up at us. "Ah, how tall those trees are. And how warm it is in these woods. Our favorite trees are the Winter Trees—the Spruce Trees, the Fir Trees, the Pine Trees."

" 'Now do you understand how we have to be as fine looking in the Winter as in the Spring?' And the Snow understood."

JANUARY 21: Poor Prunes

"MY life is a sad one," said the stewed prune.

"How is that?" asked the orange, near by.

"Oh, dear, no one loves me. People usually eat me when they can't get anything else."

"But I saw them eat you, and buy you, of course I mean members of your illustrious prune family, when a member of my family was around."

"Once in a while that happens," said the prune, "but it is very, very seldom. One morning," continued the prune, "some one at the breakfast table apologized and said, 'I'm sorry, but we only have prunes this morning.'

"Wasn't that sad? Enough to break the poor heart of a prune."

"You haven't a heart, prune, dear; you only have a stone as your heart—heart of stone—that means hard-hearted, and so forth," said the orange.

"Ah, but that's wrong," said the prune. "I felt dreadfully to think that such a thing should be said of us. 'Sorry, but we only have prunes.' You'd have thought she had said. 'Sorry, but we only have bricks for breakfast,' from the tone in which she said it.

"And then what was our joy and a thing the family has never forgotten nor ever will forget when in reply the person at the table said she actually and really liked prunes.

"That event will be put down as the greatest event that has happened in a long time.

"And following that great event are a number of others, and we plan to erect a monument made of prune stones and made only of those stones left by people who've enjoyed the prunes!

"Isn't that a good idea?"

"Yes, indeed," said the orange.

Just then the orange was called for and the prune with its brothers and sisters stayed behind.

"Poor prunes," cried the prune who had been talking, "our great monument may not go up so fast as for a moment I had hopes that it would.

"Ah, well, we have the ever-ready prune juice to receive the sad tears of the prunes." And then they sang this ditty:

> "Poor prunes, poor prunes, how sad is your lot;
> Some people like you, but, alas, most do not.
> But you're really, poor prunes, you're really good food,
> And those who say not, are, I fear, very rude."

JANUARY 22: Molly's Piano Recital

M OLLY," began daddy, "was very musical and ever since she had been a little girl, so little that she had to be lifted to the piano stool, she had been able to play anything she heard.

"Her family were far from being well off, but they strove to give Molly a musical education.

"One day it was decided that Molly was so talented she could give a concert. So the evening for the concert was decided upon. Molly practiced and practiced the pieces she was to play.

"She was not at all nervous. She was very proud of her pretty new dress, for she had always before had the dresses of her older sisters cut down and made smaller for her. Unknown to her, Molly's teacher had invited an old friend of his to the concert. This gentleman was very rich and fond of music. He liked to help along any one he felt deserved it. He was so delighted with Molly's playing that he rushed up to the little girl, saying: 'I shall send you and your mother abroad. There you'll have the finest music teachers in the world. You will come back making us all very proud of you.' "

16

JANUARY 23: Goblins' Secrets

ONE night, not long ago, Peter Goblin went a-calling," said daddy. "From house to house he went, and in every house he went to the bedsides of the little boys and girls and invited them to go on the greatest coasting party of the year.

" 'We're going to coast,' said Peter, 'down the hill of Dreams.'

"They all put their sleds together and down the hill of Dreams they went until they reached the valley below.

" 'Down this valley all the dreams come,' said Peter Goblin. 'Then our Goblin Dream Workers must tie them up into little packages, for every nice dream must be saved. It must be made to come true some day or some time—that is, if it's all for the very best that is should come true. For the Goblins are wise little Creatures!' And as the Children watched the Goblin Dream Workers they certainly decided they looked very bright indeed.

" 'They tie the dreams into the little packages and then the Goblin Visitors take them back to the land of Children and drop them in their bedrooms at night as they sleep.

" 'But,' said the Boys and Girls, 'we've never seen packages like these.'

" 'No,' said Peter Goblin. 'In one of these packages a good many dreams will come true, and so the contents of the package are dropped, —some parts in the corners, some around the ceiling. And one by one they come out into the room later on when they're COMING TRUE!

" 'So on our way back to-night,' said Peter, 'a lot of us will lead you to your little rooms and we'll drop the contents of the packages of dreams which will sometime come true. But now we must be off for more coasting, hurrah, hurrah!' "

JANUARY 24: In the Fish Bowl

THERE was once a little girl named Susan," said daddy, "who had in her room a great big glass bowl which held some helleries."

"What are helleries?" of course asked Evelyn.

"They are fresh-water fish that live in climates where the water is sure always to be very warm. Susan also kept some snails in the water with the helleries.

"The helleries are about the size of minnows, but of a different shape, being more round than the minnows are."

"One day Susan saw the big hellery daddy trying to chase the mother hellery around so that she could not get hold of any of the little ones. Susan grabbed the mother hellery and put her quickly into a glass of water that was standing near by. The next thing Susan did was to count the little helleries and, to her delight, she found that all the twenty were quite alive. But they had evidently been very much frightened, for they were all in a corner of the bowl, as near to the daddy hellery as possible, and the big daddy hellery was quiet and seemed to be much relieved that the danger was over. The snails, as you can imagine, were only too glad to rest once more. Susan gave them all some delicious fish food to comfort them.

"And she kept the mother hellery in a separate bowl until the little ones were grown up, and then she was welcomed back."

"Why was she kept in a separate bowl?" asked Jack.

"Because the mother hellery doesn't care for her children until they are big, and she might harm them. But the daddy loves them, even when they are little bits of things!"

JANUARY 25: Mac, the Dog

THERE was a dog named Mac," said daddy, "a beautiful Airedale dog and he belonged to two young girls named Janet and Mildred. They were much excited for their daddy was to have a birthday.

"At last came the birthday.

"Mac thought to himself that he wouldn't be much pleased with the presents their daddy received, a pipe, tobacco, a necktie. Mac had been dressed up in a beautiful ribbon on a number of special occasions but he didn't think much of neckties. There were some candies, though, and they were all right. Candies were really a sensible present.

"Mac knew that there were going to be more festivities. He sat about and waited.

" 'It's time for the birthday cake,' they called at last.

"Up got Mac. 'It's rude to be late,' he said to himself, 'and I'll show them that an Airedale dog doesn't forget his manners.'

"After it was all over and Mac was about to go to bed, he smiled to himself:

" 'Well, it was foolish to have all those candles but the cake was good, mighty good!' "

JANUARY 26: The Three Horses

IN a barn there were three horses and their names were Danny and Fanny and Prince. Somehow Bobbie, who was the farmer's youngest son, always liked it when the horses had their ears up though he couldn't have quite told you why. They seemed to be so very, very friendly then.

Bobbie had been having a very fine day, and as he tumbled into bed he hardly had time to whisper to his old friend the Dream King. He used to say, just before he went off to sleep, "Please, Mr. Dream King, send me nice dreams."

If he did not feel so dreadfully, dreadfully sleepy he would make his little speech longer and would say, "Your gracious majesty, Mr. Dream King, will your royal highness do a poor, humble subject like myself the great and noble and wondrous honor of sending me most royal and noble dreams?"

This evening all he said was, "Nice dreams, please."

Soon, oh, so soon, it seemed as though he saw Danny and Fanny and Prince walking into his room. And then they stood at the end of the bed, all in a row.

"Hello, Bobbie," they said.

"Hello, Danny and Fanny and Prince," said Bobbie.

"We've come to tell you something," said Fanny.

"It's something you've always wanted to know," said Danny.

"And because I'm the oldest horse, they've given me the honor of telling it to you," added Prince.

Then the three horses neighed, looked at each other, smiled their horse smiles and then looked at Bobbie.

"You've always wanted to know why we put our ears straight up when you've come around," said Prince.

"Oh yes," said Bobbie, "I've always wanted to know if there was any special reason for it."

"There is," said Prince, "and I will tell it to you. When we put our ears up it's to tell you we're feeling pleasant and friendly. When horses put their ears way back it means they're cross and that perhaps they'll bite. But we have never put our ears back on our heads when you've been around, Bobbie, so it means we always, always like to have you with us."

And the next morning when Bobbie got up he went out to his three friends and kissed them and said, "I know a secret of yours."

JANUARY 27: In the Kitchen

O NE evening," commenced daddy, "when the house was quiet and still, and every one was sleeping soundly, the tins and pans began to talk in the kitchen.

" 'I think I am to be congratulated more than any of you,' said the egg beater. 'You see my name means that I beat eggs. But not only do I beat eggs. I beat cream and all other things they wish to whip into a fine fluffy state.'

" 'True enough,' agreed the other pans and tins.

" 'But you see,' said the egg beater, 'the wonderful part is that I am not cross. Imagine being used only as a beater. Imagine forever whipping everything that comes near you. Isn't that enough to make an egg beater cross? But am I cross?'

"And all the pots and pans creaked and said, 'No.'

" 'Then,' said the egg beater, 'it only goes to show that my disposition is quite perfect. Even whipping and beating everything that comes my way doesn't make me cross.'

" 'Listen to me,' said the cheese grater. 'Think of what my name means !'

"What ?' asked the others.

" 'It means I am greater than anything else. No other pot or tin or pan is named by my name.'

" 'Oh,' chuckled the gravy spoon, a big, good-natured, easy-going spoon, 'you don't understand at all.'

" 'What don't I understand ?' asked the cheese grater.

" 'You see I help the gravy at the table and I hear the grownups and children talk. They say that greater means something finer, bigger, stronger, more noble than something that is merely great. Now greatest means the best of all. You see the way they spell your name is quite different from the way they spell the word that means great.'

" 'And what difference does that make ?' asked the cheese grater, who was feeling sad.

" 'All the difference in the world,' said the gravy spoon. 'It means something quite different.'

" 'The very idea of making such a mistake,' said the cheese grater sadly.

" 'Never mind,' said the egg beater. 'I have a really bad name and I rise above it. I do the best I can and don't complain. You must do the same.'

" 'I will,' said the cheese grater. 'But I am so disappointed.'

"So the rest of the talk between the tins, pots and pans was not upon their names and the meanings of them."

JANUARY 28: The Little Needle

A LITTLE girl named Jinny in crossing the street one day saw a needle shining very brightly in the center of the crossing. She picked it up because, as she said to herself, some horse might get it in his foot and have it hurt dreadfully. She stuck the needle in her fur and walked on.

Soon after she was home she went to bed and soon she was sound asleep. The bright needle in the fur seemed to grow brighter and brighter. It looked like something alive, it was so bright, and, sure enough, it was talking!

"I came over from Italy with a very poor girl who was a sewer. She did most wonderful fancy work. Her beautiful work brought ever so much more money than it formerly did, and after a time she was never worried any more.

"Well, after a while she succeeded so well that she bought a little house and no longer had to work.

"To-day she was carrying her workbag to a friend's house to sew a little for amusement. But there was a hole in the bag, and I fell out. Then you came along and picked me up. I'll help you sew if you like, Jinny, for my kind mistress doesn't need me now."

When Jinny awoke there was the needle on her fur, and she put it in her workbag with such pleasure.

JANUARY 29: Real Dogs

L UCIFER and his mistress went for quite a long drive one day. On their way home his mistress stopped to make a call. Lucifer stayed alone in the wonderful carriage.

Some common dogs passed by. They were barking and playing and seemed to be having a very good time. Lucifer looked at them as if he sometimes longed to be a real dog and to play as other dogs did. But of course there was his family to be thought of and his background! He could not disgrace it. He must not try anything different. He must just stay at home, doing nothing but wear a big bow of ribbon and hear his mistress tell of what a fine breed he was.

But the other dogs did fill him with envy. He had a strange longing to be out playing, too. What a stupid life he led! No fun at all. And he would like to see more of the world. No matter where he went with his mistress, the world always seemed the same.

He wondered to himself if the dogs would play with him. He barked and they looked at the victoria and at the poodle dog with the blue bow.

They seemed to be laughing at him, and for the first time his family tree didn't seem of any use. It was simply that the dogs were judging him for what he was—they didn't care a bit about his father or his grandfather.

"Could I join you?" he asked.

"Well, you don't look as though you amounted to much," they said, "but come along. We'll try to be kind to you."

"Oh," said Lucifer, as he ran along, "I do amount to a great deal. You don't know. I have more of a background than any of you."

"What?" they all asked, with their ears and eyes showing that they could not believe what they had heard. "Tell us what a background is," they asked. "Is it another name for life-saving?"

"No," said Lucifer, "it means that I needn't do anything but live up to my family name. For years and years our family have been of noble, aristocratic line. I am a dog of wonderful breeding."

"You're only snobbish," they said, and Lucifer felt very badly. "Why, you poor little dog, we feel sorry for you," said one bright looking fox terrier. "Our friends have saved children from drowning this summer, some have saved lives in fire, and we all try to amount to something. Pooh, you can't be your grandfather. Try to be yourself and amount to something!" And Lucifer joined the dogs to be taken on a regular dog's trip.

JANUARY 30: The Little Old Man

THERE was once a very strange old man," said daddy, "who decided he would live at the top of the mountain. He liked to hear all the rumbling sounds and thought he'd like to help make them. He loved pine trees, too, of which there were plenty on top of the mountain. He told his family about his desire, and the next day they started off.

"At last they reached the top, and there were so many of them it did make a merry party.

"But it was almost dark, and they were all eager for supper.

"The grandmothers and mothers arranged the supper, and they had a most delicious meal too.

"They had moss soup, a salad of pine needles chopped up very fine, big berry pies and nuts, for they all wanted to eat mountain food at once. They sat on low stumps of trees while they ate.

"After they'd finished eating they all felt quite energetic, and so the old grandfather, who was the leader in everything, said:

"'Let's help with this storm which is coming on.'" And I should say they did!

"All the older ones bellowed at the tops of their lungs so that it sounded almost like roaring. The younger ones whistled and sang. The people who lived at the foot of the mountain shivered and said: 'Oh, what a terrific storm! Listen to the sound of the wind!'

"But the old man and his family thought it fine fun."

JANUARY 31: The Fussy Cat

A WHITE cat named Snow," said daddy, "and a black dog named Coal were the greatest of friends.

" 'I am so glad to-day is wash day,' said Snow. 'I saw the soiled clothes being scrubbed so hard and hung out on the line to dry. To-morrow they will iron the clothes and then put them back in the basket all nicely folded. Later they will go in the linen room! Ah, such joy.' And Snow purred happily.

" 'Now what in the world do you talk about wash-day and ironing-day for?' asked Coal. 'I can understand it when you talk about mice because I have never known any creature so fond of them. But what do you care for clean clothes? You don't wear them. You can wash yourself and comb your hair by yourself.'

" 'But I like to lie in clean clothes. Nothing gives me the joy that the basket of clean clothes does! At least it is one of the joys of my life. As for the linen closet—well, when they leave the door open I am happy. I love to lie among the white napkins and pillow covers and sheets.'

" 'That's the queerest thing I've ever heard,' said the dog.

" 'It's quite true, though,' said the cat. 'The mistress knows that. I've often heard her say that she couldn't leave the clean clothes in the basket a moment as I'd lie among them right away. And she never dared leave the linen closet door open. Of course they don't know how fond I am of such a bed,' added Snow, 'or they would enjoy having a bed made for me of clean clothes all the time.'

" 'Bow-wow-wow,' laughed the dog. 'You are a creature to love everything that is fine. How about soiled clothes? Wouldn't they feel the same?'

" 'You insult me,' said the cat. 'I only lie in clean clothes. Soft cushions, good food, especially cream and still more especially nice food from the table—all these things I like.'

" 'I'm glad to hear it,' said the dog. 'I knew you loved all comforts but this one of clean clothes I never heard of before.'

" 'That's why I am never talking to you when I see the clothes basket of clean clothes going upstairs,' said Snow. 'I am busy then!'

"And this," said daddy, "is a true story."

FEBRUARY 1: Mice are Discovered

T
HE Mice," said daddy, "had been enjoying a new pantry
they had found. They always found some pantry where
they could get good things to eat, and this pantry was full
of delicious cheese and all sorts of nice things.

" 'Really,' said Mr. Mouse, 'I don't think we could have found a
better pantry. It's one of the nicest homes we've had in a long time.'

" 'Yes,' said Mrs. Mouse. 'And there are no traps, and there is not
a single Cat in the House. That is what I call right. It's very wrong
to keep a Cat. They're such horrid creatures.'

"They would frisk about the pantry, behind the shelves and through
the drawers which were often left half-open.

" 'It is so stupid and inconsiderate,' said Mr. Mouse, 'for people to
close all the drawers and lock up their things in tin boxes. For my
part I hate tin boxes. They can't be bitten and they're so apt to cut
me when I try to get them opened.'

" 'Yes, they're horrid,' said Mrs. Mouse. 'We can't open them, no
matter how much we try. I like little cardboard boxes best that we can
nibble through.'

"Now one day the children who lived in the house had been out
coasting all the afternoon. It had been a glorious afternoon, and
they had coasted so hard they were very hungry.

"When they came in they asked their mother for something to eat.

" 'Go and look in the pantry,' said their mother. 'You will find
biscuits and jam, and quite a lot to eat in there. As it's a Saturday
afternoon you may have a little feast.'

"Off went the children to the pantry. Now, the Mice had not
been bothered all afternoon. They had seen the cook leave the kitchen
and the pantry was just off the kitchen.

" 'We'll have a feast this afternoon,' said Mother Mouse. And all
the little Mice had thought it was a wonderful scheme to have a
regular feast.

"They had been enjoying themselves and having a splendid time when
the children arrived.

"When they heard the door open and the children coming in, the
Mice scampered to their holes and to their hiding places back on the
shelves. They made a great deal of noise, and some of them squealed
in their hurry to get past each other.

" 'The pantry is full of Mice,' said the children.

"Meanwhile the Mice were saying, 'They heard us, and now they
know that we are living here. Well, we'll just have to move—that's
all. For somehow people don't like to have Mice for visitors. It's
very foolish of them, but they don't like us!'

"'Well,' said Mr. Mouse, 'we might as well make the best of it. Besides this has been a very nice home and perhaps we'll be lucky and find another.'

"'I hope it will be just as nice,' said Mrs. Mouse, as they all followed Mr. Mouse in his search for a new pantry!"

FEBRUARY 2: In the Sea

IN the sea," said daddy, "and far away in the tropics where the plants and birds and animals are very different from here, there are floating plant creatures known as Portuguese Men-of-War.

"The reason they've been given this name is because some one who was about to name them decided they looked like old battleships. The Portuguese Man-of-War is made up of many little creatures all joined together, just as though many of us were all fastened together in our villages or in our country places.

"Some of these creatures are very different from each other. The Portuguese Man-of-War is quite large, and when it is like this it is filled by a kind of gas which enters into it and which makes it look even larger than it is.

"It is beautifully colored and it floats on top of the water.

"These parts are the large members of the colony. The rest of them, or rather a second kind of members of the family, hang from under the side of these—many little creatures which form the largest part of the colony.

"Many of them are small and trumpet-shaped, and they are the ones who do the marketing and get the food for the rest.

"Then there are members of the colony who also hang from under the many members on top, and they are the fingers or the feelers for the community.

"There are still others who look like bunches of grapes, and they look after the baby creatures who come to form a part of this strange animal-plant.

"Still more of them are like great long ribbons and they are armed with cells which sting and slay young fishes down in the water. Then they bring up the food to the other members of the family.

"So, you see, this whole big community of many-colored little creatures, which are a kind of animal-plant life, all help each other. And they are all of many beautiful colors, and add as much to the beauty of the sea as anything else.

"But I want to make it quite clear that they are all together as a plant would be, and yet each has its purpose in life, whether it be to market or get the fish or look after the eggs.

"Lately I have seen in a great museum in one of the large cities a copy of one of these colonies made out of blown glass.

"There you can see the colors, for without the colors you can't half imagine how lovely it is. The little creatures are lovely lavenders, and green, and purples, and browns, and pinks—all like a lovely mass of soft and delicate colors.

"So that the Portuguese Man-of-War and its little inhabitants are becoming better known."

FEBRUARY 3: The Circus Dream

I WANT to tell you the story this evening," said daddy, "of a little boy named Jay Rial.

"Jay Rial was as nice a little boy as any one could ever hope to see. Every one liked him and he liked people, too. But the thing he loved above everything else in the world was the circus.

"He loved the sound of the train whistle which brought the circus to town, and he loved the old circus which used to travel by the road and not come by the train at all. He loved the circus band, the clowns, the animals. He loved the very tent itself, the smell of peanuts, the roars of the lions, the beautiful ladies who rode the beautiful horses.

"He loved the performers, and every time he went to a circus he wished his eyes were bigger so he could see more, and he wished that circus people didn't have to go to sleep at all.

"He used to follow the circus parade as it came through the town and he didn't mind if it was always late, for he could go to the circus grounds with some of the other boys and see them unpack, and maybe he could sometimes help a little, too!

"Once he had been allowed to stand in the middle of the sawdust-covered ring when they were fixing up the tent. That had been a great moment.

"There was only one thing about circus day which ever made him sad. That was that sometimes people couldn't afford to go to the circus. He had been very lucky. He was always able to do chores for his mother and daddy around circus time and he could make enough money for a ticket.

"But there were some little boys and girls who couldn't do that, or whose mothers and daddies couldn't afford to do that for them.

" 'If I ever get to be a big man,' said little Jay Rial, 'I'm going to take just as many children to the circus with me as I can.'

"Little Jay Rial called it his circus-dream. And sometimes he would really dream that he was taking hundreds and hundreds of little boys and girls whose faces had been sad and teary because they hadn't thought they were going to the circus. He had dreamed of how they would follow after him and would say:

" 'Me, too?'

"And he would smile at them and say, 'Yes, all of you!'

"It was a beautiful dream.

"Now there are many people who dream of doing something fine when they have more money or when they're grown up and who forget it when that time comes.

"They will excuse themselves by saying, 'Yes, I have more money than I used to have, but I find I need it all,' instead of doing more than they had been able to do before. There are little boys who say, 'When I grow up I'm going to see that poor children get ice-cream once in a while.' But when they grow up they forget and they don't realize that there are lots of children in hospitals and in homes who very seldom receive visits from the ice-cream man.

"Now Jay Rial was different. He remembered. When he grew up he went into the circus business. He was the one who would tell the newspapers in the different towns in advance when the circus was coming to town so every one could look forward to it.

"And he remembered his circus dream.

"So every year when the circus came to the very biggest city they visited, grown up Jay Rial arranged that every child in every hospital or home or any child who was crippled and not as fortunate as other children should come to the circus free.

"They arranged one afternoon when no one need buy a ticket but when every seat was free. And yet, that wasn't enough for Jay Rial. When the hospitals and homes sent in their lists of the numbers of children who would be able to go to the circus the lists grew so long that the place wouldn't hold them all.

"Do you suppose Jay Rial said, 'Sorry, but we've room for no more?' Not a bit of it. He had another circus party for those who couldn't come to the first.

"And Jay Rial's face was full of smiles as he looked at the thousands of children who were shrieking with joy over the circus, and he said, 'My dream has come true.'

"But," ended daddy, "Jay Rial is one of those people who help to make dreams come true."

FEBRUARY 4: Little Mildred's Muff

MILDRED had lost her muff," said daddy. "She lived in a small town near a big city. She went to school in the city. Every morning she took the train into the city and came back by train in the afternoon. When she got home that afternoon she told her mother and daddy what had happened. Mildred's daddy said that he would telephone to the railway station to see if anything had been seen of it. Mildred stood by listening.

"'Mildred,' said her daddy, 'they're asking me if your muff had a head on it. Did it?'

"'Oh, let me talk, daddy!' And Mildred grabbed the receiver.

"'Yes, yes,' she cried excitedly into the telephone; 'it had a black fox's head on it!' Then she heard the joyful words:

"'I think it has been found and brought here.'

"Mildred could hardly wait until the morning came. Then she went with her daddy to the lost and found department of the railway station.

"As soon as she got inside she cried, 'There is my muff over there with all those umbrellas and books!' And she jumped up and down with happiness."

FEBRUARY 5: The Coal-Bin

I'M proud, that is what I am," said a large piece of coal in the coal-bin. "There was a song written once about a king named Coal."

"But," said another piece of coal, "you have the idea, I believe, that his name was spelt as our name is spelt. I think that is wrong. The king spelt his name Cole. The song you mean goes like this, 'Old King Cole was a merry old soul.' Isn't that the one you mean?"

"Yes," said the large piece of coal which had spoken first. "That is the old song I mean. A fine one it is, to be sure. But what care I how the king spelt his name, or how the person who wrote the song spelt it? My grandfather once lived in a king's coal-bin in a great palace. That is, he must have. Of course he never told me about it myself for he was burnt before I came around. But one of my grandfathers must have been in a king's coal-bin and maybe he is still there. Kings must have coal-bins and be kept warm, mustn't they?

"Perhaps I've a little cousin this very moment crackling and sizzling and burning for a king, who knows?

"But, now I come to think of it I don't believe Old King Cole was good enough to belong to our family. He had to call for things all the time, whereas we are called for!

28

"Yes, people want us. They never knew before how much they appreciated us. They didn't know it until we became a little scarce."

"Yes," said the other pieces of coal, "we can now hold up our coal heads and say to all the world, 'Well, now what do you think of the coal-bin? You think a lot of it if we're within it, and if the coal-bin is empty—ah, you're sad!'

"Yes, that shows our importance. People talk about coal nowadays. They go around asking each other if they have enough coal. And people usually answer by saying that they are getting along all right but they would like to have more.

"They would like to have more of us, we, the fine pieces of coal, the coal which is at last appreciated, the coal which at last gets thanks for the warmth it gives, and the coal which is missed so sadly when it isn't around!"

FEBRUARY 6: In Dreamland

WE'VE got lots of work to do to-night," said the Dream King, and the Dream Fairies said, "What have we to do?"

"Well," said the Dream King, "in talking to the Fairy Queen this afternoon, she said that she had quite a lot to tell me and she looked very sad.

"It seems that there have been many children lately she has heard telling each other unkind things they have heard about each other.

"For instance, she heard one little girl say to another little girl, 'Oh, Sally, I heard Mamie say she thought you were awfully mean and selfish. I told her I didn't think so. I stood up for you. I was your friend.'

"Well, the Fairy Queen said that made her mad. She said it was far worse of the little girl who came and told such a horrid thing than it even was in the little girl who had said it.

"I am going to give dreams to lots and lots of children who have said mean things. I am going to show them a huge room full of children and all the children will be crying and sobbing, and there won't be enough handkerchiefs to go around.

"And I will tell them that these children are crying because of the mean speeches they have heard repeated.

"Hurry, Dream Fairies, tie up the dreams for me to take around. You know what I want now.

"And, Dream Fairies," continued the Dream King, "I'm going to tell each girl and boy how every mean speech she or he thinks of and doesn't make, or doesn't repeat, will come straight to Dreamland and every week we will have a great big bonfire of them. Then all the Dream Fairies will laugh and sing as the mean speeches are burnt up."

FEBRUARY 7: How the Inkfishes Protect Themselves

"INKFISHES," said daddy; "aren't black at all. In fact, they look very much like the ordinary jellyfish. But they are called inkfishes because when an enemy comes near them they drop ink out of an ink pocket they have near their mouths. You see, they can see perfectly through the ink, but the other fishes can't and so when they dive down again and again and try to catch the inkfishes, they can't do it. The water is so black they can't see anything and they flounder off into the clear water, while the inkfishes keep out of their way.

"The jellyfishes and inkfishes are great friends and often visit each other. Little Kitty Inkfish and Nelly Jellyfish were especially good friends, and one day Kitty Inkfish asked her mother if she could invite Nelly Jellyfish to visit her for a whole week. Old Mrs. Inkfish consented, so Nelly Jellyfish was invited. Such excitement as there was, and all sorts of entertainments and parties were planned. Nelly Jellyfish arrived at exactly the hour she was invited to commence her visit. That afternoon the first party in her honor was to be given, and, of course, a number of other jellyfishes were invited for the party.

"But a great big, dangerous fish was hovering near. He saw all the nice fat looking jellyfishes, and he said to himself, 'Here's where I have a supper party too.' So he dove through the water toward little Nelly Jellyfish. Oh, how frightened all the jellyfishes were, but as quickly as possible the inkfishes had dropped ink into the water and made it so black that the big fish couldn't see. They all got out of the way, pulling the jellyfishes with them, and watched, with great amusement, the great big fish trying to find his way out.

"He coughed and sneezed with the ink in his face and made very wry faces at the taste of the ink, which made the inkfishes chuckle.

"At last the big fish had left, and all the jellyfishes congratulated the inkfishes on their wonderful means of protection, and they said they felt pretty sure that Nelly Jellyfish would be well looked after on her visit as well as have a wonderful time."

FEBRUARY 8: The Vegetables

THE vegetables on the stove were talking," said daddy. 'I insist upon being well-cooked,' said Mr. Leader Potato.

" 'To my mind, that is nonsense. The cook arranges the heat and puts us on the stove when she wants to,' said one of the String-Beans. 'She takes us off when she sees fit. And she gives us just what she wants in the way of salt and pepper and butter.'

" 'Yes, can you imagine her saying, "Mr. Bean, have you enough salt?" '

" 'Neither would she say,' went on the Stewed Corn, "Are you quite warm enough, Mr. Corn, or are you too warm? I will open a window if you wish." No! We do exactly as we're told. Mr. Potato, you are wrong. Yes, I grieve to admit it, but you are quite, quite wrong.'

" 'I insist upon being well-cooked because if I am not well-cooked, I am extremely horrid to eat,' repeated Mr. Leader Potato; 'I am hard and not "done" at all. No one likes me then. So they find it is well to cook me properly.'

" 'We all should be cooked properly,' said the others.

" 'You all should, it is true,' said Mr. Leader Potato. 'But it is absolutely important that I should be well-cooked. A half-cooked potato is so extremely disagreeable.'

"But as he was talking, along came the cook to mash Potato and his family, for dinner was almost ready.

" 'How much fussing over I require!' said Mr. Potato proudly."

FEBRUARY 9: The Life Saving St. Bernards

ONCE there was an old man who owned a number of St. Bernard dogs," said daddy. "One night they camped near a small settlement. The old man had found sticks and wood, and the dogs had carried it along on the sleds. So they had a huge fire. They got nice and warm and had a supper of the provisions they'd brought and which, too, the dogs had carried.

"But a storm could be seen coming, and the snow was flying so fast it was almost blinding. The old man rolled the dogs up in warm rugs, and then, rolling up in a sleeping bag, he went fast asleep.

"He had not been asleep long before he was awakened by one of the biggest St. Bernard dogs, who was tugging at his sleeping bag.

" 'What is it, my beauty?' asked the old man. Still the dog tugged at the bag. The old man was so sleepy at first he was half dazed, but he opened his eyes. Slowly he realized that some one must be suffering near-by, for he heard a strange wailing sound as of some one in distress. He got up, put on some warm things, and, hitching some of the dogs to a sled, they started out into the blizzard.

"They went toward the place where the sound of the wailing came from, and there, half buried in the snow, they found a man almost frozen to death. The old man, with the help of the dogs, put him on the big sled and dragged him back to their camp. There the old man rubbed him, and by the fire he began to recover. He said he had started out for another settlement to find food and had become blinded by the snow until he could go no farther. He was so grateful to the old man for saving his life. But the old man told him that the dog had been the rescuer."

FEBRUARY 10: The Birthday Goblin

A LITTLE girl named Polly," said daddy, "could hardly wait for her birthday to come. She had been thinking about it for a long time, and at last there was only one more night and the birthday would actually be here.

"It was bedtime and Polly was ready for bed.

" 'I'm going to stay awake for ages,' she said to herself, 'and try to guess what mother and daddy are going to give me, and what we'll have to eat at the party. I do hope it will be ice-cream. I am a little afraid it won't be, though, because when I asked mother about it, she said that perhaps it would be nice to have a change. Nothing is so nice as ice-cream for a birthday party.'

" 'That's true,' said a jolly little creature, who suddenly appeared before her.

" 'Who are you?' asked Polly.

" 'I'm the birthday Goblin. That is, I am one of the birthday Goblins, for there are a good many of us needed for our work. There are such lots of birthdays,' and the Goblin tossed his head and laughed.

" 'And,' continued the Goblin, 'I tell mothers and daddies not to forget the good, old-fashioned way of putting a ring, a thimble and a button in the cake. I have to see about the presents, too. For how well I know what the girls and boys like as presents! That's our business, you know.'

" 'Are we going to have ice-cream to-morrow?' asked Polly.

" 'Yes,' said the Goblin. 'Your mother took my suggestions so

32

quickly. I didn't have to coax her at all. But your birthday is here and the sun has been up some time. Good-by, happy birthday!' And as Polly opened her eyes, her mother was by her bed, whispering that always wonderful birthday wish of:

" 'Many happy returns of the day!' "

FEBRUARY 11: A Make-Believe and Real President

YOU have heard," said daddy, "how Abraham Lincoln pretended the cabbages which he grew in his garden were real people and how he named them. The straightest and very best-looking one he named General Strong, and another he named Captain Brave. One more he admired especially and thought it an exceptionally fine looking cabbage. He called it Mr. President, and little did he then think that he, the little boy, would be President when he grew up."

FEBRUARY 12: Abraham Lincoln

I HAVE one little story to tell you to-night which I don't think you've heard before," said daddy. "When the present King of Siam was a little boy and his governess was teaching him American history he became so impressed with Abraham Lincoln and his freeing of the slaves and the tragedy of his death, that he said,

" 'When I become King I will free the slaves of the palace.'

" 'Will you promise me that?' his governess asked, and the little boy promised. And when he became king all of the wives and slaves of the royal palace—four or five hundred—were freed and were given money and assistance to get fresh starts as free people.

"That story came to me," daddy continued, "from my own mother who knew the governess, and I have never told it to you two children before.

"And while it is splendid to think of a little boy in far-off Siam loving and following the great example of our splendid Lincoln, still I've been thinking to-day that the greatest thing of all is that we all know Lincoln so well that we can hardly find a new story to tell of him.

"He was so simple, so human, so real a person that we have all grown to know him—not only as a President and a magnificent figure in history—but as Abraham Lincoln, the man of the people."

33

FEBRUARY 13: The Boy Who Cried "Wolf!"

THERE was once a shepherd-boy who kept his flock at a little distance from the village. Once he thought he would play a trick on the villagers and have some fun at their expense. So he ran toward the village crying out, with all his might:

"Wolf! Wolf! Come and help! The wolves are at my lambs!"

The kind villagers left their work and ran to the field to help him. But when they got there the boy laughed at them for their pains; there was no wolf there.

Still another day the boy tried the same trick, and the villagers came running to help and were laughed at again.

Then one day a wolf did break into the fold and began killing the lambs. In great fright, the boy ran for help. "Wolf! Wolf!" he screamed. "There is a wolf in the flock! Help!"

The villagers heard him, but they thought it was another mean trick; no one paid the least attention, or went near him. And the shepherd-boy lost all his sheep.

That is the kind of thing that happens to people who lie: even when they do tell the truth they will not be believed.

FEBRUARY 14: Isa's Valentine Party

A LITTLE girl named Isa had been very ill in a large city hospital," said daddy. "But at last a joyful time came when Isa really seemed to be on the road to getting well, and very happy her mother and daddy were.

" 'Oh, little Isa,' said her daddy, 'we're going to have a surprise for you. You know to-day is St. Valentine's day, and I have an idea my little daughter may be going to have all kinds of bright, heart-shaped presents!'

" 'Oh, daddy!' said Isa, 'instead of giving just me a valentine party couldn't we have one for all the children in the hospital? I'm well enough to be moved into the big ward, and all the children who are able to be there can have a party with me, and we can have a huge valentine party. Oh, couldn't we do that, daddy?'

" 'Yes, indeed,' said her daddy.

"So in the afternoon the big ward was bright with red hearts strung from the ceiling and hanging over the beds. The lights were covered with red paper shades, and in the very center of the room was an enormous big heart, and what do you suppose was in the heart?"

"What?" asked Evelyn eagerly.

"Why, for every child there was a red ribbon. Each child pulled one ribbon attached to the heart and at the end was a beautiful present."

FEBRUARY 15: The Desk and the Ink-Well

I MISBEHAVE most frightfully if children don't pay me attention," said the Ink-Well.

"Yes," said the desk. "And then you make me suffer."

"Do you really know what I mean?" asked the Ink-Well.

"Of course," said the Desk. "If, for instance, a little girl or a boy is pouring from the great big grandfather Ink-Bottle and is giving you something more in the way of a nice Inky fluid or drink, and if the little girl looks the other way, you spill."

"I don't spill. I turn a somersault, or I trickle down the desk."

"Yes, down me," said the Desk. "And do you think it is very nice to make me suffer?"

"Ha, ha," laughed the Ink-Well, "as if you cared whether I trickled down over you or not. You are made of wood and you don't care."

"That's so," agreed the Desk, "but even if I am made of wood I like to be varnished and made over nice and fresh every little while. It's just like having one's face washed."

"But people who have their faces washed," said the Ink-Well, "(though I do believe they always wash their faces themselves) do so far more than once a year. That is as often as you get your face washed or varnished."

"Well, I'm made of wood, you see," said the Desk, "and so I don't care. Once a year does quite nicely for me. Besides it would be quite utterly useless any oftener for you'd only spill over me and I'd get quite horrid looking."

"That's polite of you, I'm sure," said the Ink-Well, "to say you'd look horrid with some of my nice ink on you. It adds a lot I think."

"It may add ink," said the Desk, "but it doesn't add beauty."

But the school bell was ringing and so the Desk and Ink-Well were silent.

FEBRUARY 16: Dr. Sun

FOR over two weeks a little boy has followed me around,"
said the Sun.

"Whatever do you mean?" asked the Sun Rays.

"He has been ill. He has had a very, very bad cold. Oh, he has
been so wretched and he has not felt like doing anything. A little boy
is pretty ill when he doesn't feel like doing anything and wants to stay
quiet."

"That's true," said the Sun Rays. For how often they had seen
small boys scampering and playing, and sometimes they had danced,
too, for joy.

"The doctor comes every day," continued the Sun. "Sometimes he
comes twice a day, and once he came three times. But every time he
comes he tells the little boy always to sit in the sun! And he has been
following me around. When I am shining into one window in the
morning, there I see the little boy sitting by the window. In the afternoon when I choose an entirely different part of the house to shine in
the windows, there is the little boy again. And for two weeks he has
been doing this. Just following me around. I do feel so honored.
And you, my good Sun Ray children, you should feel honored too."

"We do," said the Sun Rays.

"Listen now!" said the Sun. And they all stopped talking to listen.

There was the little boy sitting by the window, and by him stood
his mother and a big man with a low voice. The man was carrying a
little black satchel and he was talking.

"Well, how are you to-day, my boy?" he asked.

"Oh, much stronger and better," said the boy. "I almost feel like
getting out again."

"You'll be able to in a very few days now."

"Oh, doctor," said the mother, "you have saved my little boy's life.
He was so sick." But the doctor shook his head.

"I did not save his life," he said. "The Sun did that. The Sun
fights germs better than medicines or doctors. We are needed to tell
the people to take advantage of the Sun and use it, and we have to tell
them what the trouble is. For the Sun can't talk. If he could he
would be one of the greatest doctors in the world. For he always
carries his cure with him. Ah, now he helps me drive away the colds,
the many horrid sicknesses that come when little boys have to stay in
the house."

"Dear father," said the Sun Rays, "you are really Doctor Sun."

"And you my little assistant nurses," said the Sun.

FEBRUARY 17: Mr. Moon Hides

WHAT'S the matter?" asked the Earth.
"I'm tired," said the Moon.
"All right," said the Earth. "My shadow is always ready for you to hide behind when you want it."

"You don't mind, do you?" asked the Moon.

"I'm highly flattered," said the Earth. "It is a great honor. Lots of people come out and look at us both at such times. For people call it an Eclipse."

"What do they mean by that?" asked the Moon.

"They call it a total eclipse," said the Earth, "when there is no Moon to be seen at all."

"My! And they use words like that—total Eclipse—just to say that the Moon can't be seen. Well, well, well, they do pay me a great compliment."

The Moon talked to the Earth for a long time and the Earth's shawl or shadow kept the moon from sight for several hours.

Before long the Moon grew a little restless. "I think I must be leaving," he said.

"Sorry to see you go," said the Earth. "You call on me so seldom. Your visits are so rare."

"Oh," laughed the Moon, "you are so nice to me, but where did you pick up that last word? Was it running around down on the earth where you heard it as it walked over you?"

"Words don't run around," said the Earth, " but the people who use them do. That word means that your visits are so few. I'd like to see you oftener."

"Thank you," said the Moon. "Perhaps because I come only now and again it is better, for you see it is more of a treat."

"Maybe that is so," said the Earth. "I always enjoy looking at you from afar, but I do thoroughly enjoy your calls."

"Then I'll come some time again," said the Moon.

FEBRUARY 18: A Careless Master

A HORSE," said daddy, "was very thirsty.
'I don't know how I can go on working so hard without a drink,' he was trying to tell his master. But his master paid no attention.

"On and on they went. The horse's tongue became so dry. He hung it out of his mouth, but the master didn't notice—not even when

37

he gave him a pat as he came out from a house where he had left a package.

"Now, a little fairy was hovering near-by. The fairy was the Princess Joy and she was in her long dress of mist-fog material. For the day was misty and there was a light fog. But not enough rain had fallen for the horse to wet his tongue. He had tried to hold his mouth open and get a drink that way but the rain-drops were not coming down. They were feeling shy and not like a trip to the earth.

" 'I'm so thirsty,' said the horse again to himself.

" 'Thirsty,' said the Princess Joy. 'Why doesn't your master give you something to drink? You're a good horse. You go wherever he wants you to go—and so willingly, too. You're so loyal and you are nice with his children and let them play with you whenever they want to. Can't he give you a drink?'

" 'He has forgotten,' said the horse. 'He doesn't mean to be cruel. He has just forgotten—that's all.'

" 'Well, we'll attend to that,' said the Fairy Princess Joy.

"Now she knew that the horse's master and the ice man did not like each other. 'I'll attend to this,' she said to herself.

"The ice man was delivering ice from house to house along the same street where the master was delivering his parcels. The ice man had his ice in a little hand wagon he was pushing along himself.

" 'You shall have some fine ice water,' whispered the fairy to the horse. 'The best of ice water.'

"The Fairy whispered to the ice man, and though he didn't know that the fairy had told him to leave his wagon in just such a place, he did so.

" 'Now walk up a little bit,' she said to the horse.

"The horse began to lick a fine piece of ice. Ah, such a drink as he had. The ice melted so fast against his dry tongue, and there was a great deal in the side of the wagon. He licked the ice until half of a piece had gone.

"Just then the ice man and his master came out at the same time. There the horse was having his drink.

" 'You owe me for a piece of ice,' said the ice man. 'I can't sell that piece now. Why don't you give your horse some water? What are you—cruel to animals, eh?'

"This made the master feel very badly. 'I forgot,' he murmured. 'I shall pay you for the ice and I'll never forget again.'

" 'The first good speech I've heard you make. You've always been too careless and thoughtless before, but now we'll be friends, and I do believe you'll never forget your fine animal again.' And the master agreed."

FEBRUARY 19: The Cat Show

THERE were cats at the Cat Show," said daddy, "such as are never seen in any kitchen. Cats on velvet cushions who looked far too haughty ever, ever to crawl under a good old stove on a torn cushion. For at this Cat Show there were cats whose families were old and noble in the history of Catland. And cats of all colors! They were even lavender and so many other queer colors for cats to be!

"And such wonderful fur they had! It was soft and silky and combed so well. They wore bright ribbons, and their cushions matched! And they were fed the most delicious bits of meat and fish—and drank cream, real, real cream!

But two cats were talking. One was named Royalty and the other Nobility.

" 'What do you think of the Show?' asked Royalty.

" 'It's about the same as most,' said Nobility, with a yawn.

" 'How dull they are!' snarled Royalty. And some passer-by said,

" 'That cat is so highly bred, you see. Did you notice how he snarled?'

" 'Isn't that too absurd!' said Royalty. 'As if it were something very fine to be cross. I'm cross because of these people. They make such a fuss over me. They spoil me, and then some of my poor little sisters and brothers are left by these very same people to starve in the city all summer, while they go off and shut up their houses!'

" 'What do you mean?' asked Nobility. 'You haven't any sisters or brothers who live in kitchens, have you?' And Nobility's back rose in surprise.

" 'Indeed, I have,' said Royalty, 'and I'm proud of it! Do you for one moment think that my family were born in Egypt or India—or Malta—or wherever they say the family came from? Do you know where my family came from? From the alleys and side streets where they used to hunt for scraps of food—almost any kind of food.

" 'Then, you see, the family were ambitious, and somehow we became kitchen cats, and we lived on milk and good food.'

" 'But how did you ever come here?' asked Nobility.

" 'Because my little master wanted to make some money to buy a bicycle. He thought perhaps I'd win a prize at a small Show which was given at that time. He fed me up, put a ribbon around my neck, and had me sit on a purple cushion. I won a prize and I've been winning them ever since. I was bought for a great deal of money, and I make a lot! But what does that mean to me? Nothing! All I want to say is that if only I knew Grown-Up talk I'd say to all these people that they could admire me if they wished but to please remember my sisters and brothers when the summer comes again.' "

FEBRUARY 20: The Queer Pets

A FUNNY old woman," commenced daddy, "lived all alone. Her chief delight in life was to have all the chickens, geese and ducks she could, and let them walk anywhere they pleased. They could go right into the parlor or into the kitchen, whichever suited their fancy. Luckily, for the good of the parlor, they really preferred the kitchen. All the food was there, and they liked to eat better than anything else.

"Now, this old woman was very peculiar, too, and she looked it. But the funniest thing about her was that all the animals she had were queer looking too. The geese seemed to be a little different from any other geese. The ducks had even more hideous feet than most ducks have, and they were all of rather strange colors.

"One day not very long ago there flew around the neighborhood a strange looking bird. He seemed to be quite alone.

"But soon, to every one's surprise, they saw him playing with the strange looking geese, ducks and chickens that belonged to the old woman. He never wanted to fly in the house, but they saw that she brought out water and crumbs to him. And the old woman welcomed with joy one more strange creature."

FEBRUARY 21: Harry's Composition

H ARRY was a very clever little boy," daddy said. "The teacher of the class to which Harry belonged had had all the pupils write original compositions to recite at the Washington's Birthday entertainment.

"The day before the entertainment (at which, of course, all the mothers and daddies of the children were to be present) a rehearsal of everything was to take place. It was Harry's turn to recite his composition. As he got up on the platform his legs were shaking, and every one saw how nervous he was.

"He began, then he faltered, and then he broke down and sobbed. Harry, the hero of the school, was crying. Could it be true? The pupils looked at him with pity. What could be the trouble, they asked themselves.

" 'Teacher,' he finally said between his choking sobs, 'I didn't write that composition. I cheated. I copied it out of an old book I found. I'm not worthy to recite on Washington's Birthday.'

"And then he rushed from the platform down to his seat, and, putting his head in his hands, he cried and cried.

" 'You've done a thing worthy of George Washington's Birthday, Harry,' said the teacher. 'You're not able to act a lie, and because you are truthful you will still recite the composition, giving the name of its real writer.' "

FEBRUARY 22: Father of His Country

WE all know the old answer to the question of "Who was George Washington?"

Many a time have we gaily answered the question as we've pounded fists on the table:

"First in war, first in peace, first in the hearts of his countrymen." And at the end of that we've had a nice little winding up of pounding.

There is hardly a place, it seems, that in some way is not connected with Washington. Perhaps at one time or another he had made his headquarters there, or a chair is preserved carefully because Washington sat in it!

At Mount Vernon, where Washington lived, one can see the very rooms through which Washington walked, his bed-room, and the very four-poster bed in which he slept. And around the house are the grounds which Washington loved and through which he wandered, down to the banks of the Potomac River.

Time and time again George Washington faced difficulties of a bitterly hard nature. But he never flinched.

Time and time again Washington saw his men suffering or deserting. But Washington suffered with them and he never lost courage.

Time and time again Washington was doubted; jealous groups tried to work against him. But Washington went straight on, doing as he should and not stooping to "play favorites" or to be a "favorite."

There was the time, too, when the country he loved doubted him, and showed him cruel ingratitude. But Washington did not turn from his course. It was the hardest of all to bear but he was the Father of his Country and—his children did come back to him.

And then—when everywhere people were singing his praises, shouting them, exclaiming them, Washington never lost his head.

He never let his own little inner feelings of likes and dislikes keep him from being fair.

Always fair, always just, always true to the country whose government he really made, he is the Father of his Country in truth.

After the Revolutionary War, as after all wars, the country was in a frightfully upset state and the people were the same. Then it was that Washington held together the country, made its government, and slowly but steadily brought order out of the most frightful disorder.

In those days people traveled by stage-coach; cities were small and far apart, the country was spread out and rumors and prejudices were hard to overcome.

But all of these tangled threads and oh, so tangled were they, Washington unraveled!

His Christmas Days, too—often how unlike Christmas they were! One was spent at Valley Forge when everything was frozen and the men went forth seeking food. Another was spent at New Windsor where the suffering from the cold had been intense, but there was brightness that day because of the arrival of a great wagon filled with shirts and warm clothing for Washington and his men. And yet another Christmas was that when the famous crossing of the Delaware River took place.

Washington—whom historians all call very great.

Washington—the Father of his Country!

FEBRUARY 23: The Stamp Traveler

I AM very superior," said the Airmail Stamp. "I travel all over the world. My family have always traveled. We don't stay in one place—of course sometimes we do—but more often we go away. Now and again our little domestic brothers go about the town, but we, the noble airmail stamps, how we travel."

"You don't travel any more than we do," said the Envelope upon which the stamp was stuck fast.

"I disagree with you," said the Stamp.

"That makes no difference to me," said the Envelope. "But if you disagree with me, why don't you leave me?"

"I can't," said the Stamp.

"Of course you can't, you poor dear," said the Ink which had made the address on the envelope. "You're stuck to the Envelope, and no matter how hard you quarrel you still have to stick."

"Well, I'd like to know if you don't have to stay on too," said the Stamp.

"Ah, but I have fun when I'm being put on. Sometimes I make a nice smudgy spot, and then the Creature who has been writing with me does not know what to do.

"The Creature will argue like this, 'Now shall I let the Envelope go as it is, or shall I address a fresh one? There is something queer about this Ink.' Then it is that I chuckle. 'No,' the Creature continues, 'I think I will not notice the smudgy spot. Maybe the persons getting it will think that the rain has made it look so badly—rain often gets at a letter.'

"And so the Creature blames it on the rain, and I go off quite free."

"That's not to your credit when you're guilty," said the Envelope.

"We mustn't quarrel," said the Postage Stamp, "as now we're off for a trip. The man is putting us in a bag. Then we go on a train—then to a new Post Office, and at last we reach the place for which we started."

"Yes," said the Ink, "the place I have marked with my ink!"

FEBRUARY 24: How Rowdy Shared His Home

ROWDY was a beautiful and very handsome bulldog. He had a lovely white throat, too, and when he went out into the street he wore a fine big collar, which made him look very distinguished," said daddy, "and he belonged to a little boy named Alfred. Alfred's mother was a very rich lady, and Rowdy had all the comforts that any dog could possibly ask for. He slept in Alfred's room in a beautiful basket.

"Alfred and Rowdy were really inseparable companions. Alfred was not a very strong little boy. He couldn't join in all the sports that other little boys enjoy. Because of Alfred's ill health he and Rowdy were all the better companions.

"Alfred had a phonograph, which he used to play a great deal. Rowdy would sit before it, so delighted at the music. He'd put his head first on one side and then on the other. Of course Alfred would talk to him and ask him how he was enjoying the music. Rowdy would wag his tail to show he thought it was fine.

"In the afternoons Alfred and his mother used to take drives in a lovely big open Victoria. One afternoon it was beautifully bright and sunny. Alfred's mother said:

"'We'll go for a nice long drive to-day.'

"'Rowdy!' called Alfred, for Rowdy was fast asleep on the sofa.

"Rowdy jumped up eagerly as if he knew something pretty nice was going to happen.

"'Rowdy, how would you like to take a drive? Speak and say if you would like it.'

"So Rowdy wagged his tail and gave a bark as if to say, 'Charmed!' Rowdy's best collar was put on, and off they started. They had not

43

gone far before they passed a poor, pathetic little waif dog. Rowdy was not snobbish and proud as some dogs might have been, brought up in all the comforts he had always had. Instead he seemed to feel very sorry for the little waif dog and whined sadly. Then he tried to jump out of the carriage.

" 'Do you want to take the little waif dog driving?' said Alfred to Rowdy. And Rowdy showed as well as he could that he would like that tremendously.

"They took the poor little homeless dog back with them and gave him good food and a nice home. Rowdy seemed to be glad to give such happiness to a little friendless dog, and he seemed to feel that it was giving the dog rare pleasure to have a master like Alfred."

FEBRUARY 25: The Tired Eagles

IN the house where Kenneth lived there was a chair which had always fascinated him. It was a very, very old chair, and Kenneth's mother and daddy were very proud of it," said daddy to Jack and Evelyn. "Kenneth's daddy had bought it at a sale of old and curious things. It was a Roman chair, and on either side were two heads of eagles. These four heads in all always made Kenneth wonder, for they looked so very life-like. He used to imagine that even little wooden eagles must get very tired of always being just the same. And late one afternoon, sitting in the chair he fell asleep.

" 'You're terribly tired, aren't you?' said the first eagle, who suddenly seemed to be looking at him.

" 'Yes, I'm a little tired,' Kenneth admitted.

" 'Well, you're not as tired as we are,' said the second eagle.

" 'No, indeed!' said the third eagle. 'You're only tired because you've played so many games. We're tired because we're always still.'

"Kenneth listened eagerly, because he'd so often thought just what he was hearing. 'Yes,' said Kenneth very sympathetically, 'I should think you would be very dull. I've often thought that. Have you been there a long time?'

" 'Oh, ages and ages!' replied the fourth eagle, who up to this time had not spoken. 'We were very old before your daddy got us. We've been on this chair so long. We can't remember how long. And what makes us feel so sad is that we are called eagles and should fly and yet are forever glued to this chair.'

" 'Kenneth, Kenneth,' cried Kenneth's mother, 'it's long past bedtime!'

" 'Oh, I am not so tired as the eagles are!' said Kenneth. And Kenneth's mother wondered if he was talking in his sleep."

FEBRUARY 26: The Squirrels' Peanut Hunt

A LITTLE girl named Polly," began daddy, "lived near a park. In this park were a great many squirrels. They were principally gray, with great, long bushy tails, and they were very tame. Polly had often fed them peanuts, but she thought it would be lots of fun to have a real peanut hunt. So she ran around as quickly as she could, hiding the peanuts from her bag.

"First one very old fat squirrel found three peanuts hidden under a rock.

"He called to the other squirrels and waved his bushy tail in the air, trying to say, 'There are peanuts if we will hunt for them!'

"The squirrels didn't stop to eat the peanuts after they discovered that there were so many hidden. They just kept on getting more and more until finally they had succeeded in finding them all.

"Then they began to carry the peanuts to their little homes, and they looked so happy, just as if they were free from cares or worries for days to come, for, of course, they didn't have to worry about meals for ever and ever so long with the wonderful supply they now had on hand."

FEBRUARY 27: The Game of Manners

I MUST tell you a story about the game of good manners which they play in a large public school in a big city," said daddy. "They are let into the secret that it's a lesson, but it is a play-time lesson and they have it in connection with their gymnasium and play-time work, though it doesn't take the place of recess.

"And they grow to understand their teachers better, who are teaching them the game of manners and they get on so much better when both teachers and pupils understand each other and really like each other.

"For example, they hear a story of a little boy who didn't want to wash his hands or face and who became so dirty that he found himself without any companion except a pig.

"After they have heard such a story they all act it out, one taking the part of the dirty little boy, and the others of the people he met who wouldn't play with him or have anything to do with him, or invite him into their homes, or anything nice like that.

"And they take turns in having the story about a boy and about a girl.

"They hear a story of a very rude boy or girl and of how he grew up into a cross man or woman, and they hear of his adventures and what horrible times he had making others miserable as well as himself.

"Then they act out these stories in their classes where they have dramatics and different ones take the parts of the bad child or the unmannerly child or the unmannerly grown-up, and of all the people whom these met with in their adventures.

"And oh, what laughter there is when a boy makes a mistake in acting his part of the teacher and in being very unlike the teacher and more like himself which of course is quite natural. Yes, the game of good manners is a great and successful game in this school where there are three thousand and six hundred boys and girls."

FEBRUARY 28: Naughty Julius

THERE is nothing more dreadful to my mind," said daddy, "than a little boy who is mean to other children not so big and strong as he is. I once knew a little boy like that and will tell you about him this evening.

"The little boy's name was Julius.

"A family came to live one day in the house opposite where Julius lived. The house had been vacant for a long time, so Julius was delighted when he found he was to have neighbors. What was his disappointment, though, to find that the family opposite consisted only of a mother, daddy and a little sick boy named Hugh. He was cross when he saw Hugh's little pale face at the window opposite. He would laugh at him until he saw the tears trickle down Hugh's face and he would turn away from the window.

"One day Julius' mother came to him and said, 'Julius, it is very cruel to make fun of a little sick boy, and I will tell you what is the trouble with Hugh.

" 'Hugh does not have the good, strong legs that you have. When he was born, his legs were crippled. But to-day he is going out for the first time in a while on his crutches,' concluded his mother.

"Julius kept very quiet, but inwardly he was planning something very mean to do. He waited around for some time, and still no sign of Hugh. At last he saw him, so he shrieked from the window, 'Hello, tenderfoot!'

"Hugh was bound he would be brave, so he beat back the tears. Julius rushed downstairs and out into the street.

"Just at that moment a fast motor-car came along. Julius did not see it, but Hugh did, and as his little voice was too weak to rise above

Julius' laughter he hobbled on his crutches and pulled Julius out of the way just in the nick of time. Oh, how frightened Julius was! And his escape from some terrible injury seemed marvelous.

"In a flash he saw what it would have meant to him to have no football, no skating, no sports, and the little crippled Hugh he had laughed at and who had so much to bear had saved him.

"Hugh forgave Julius, and they became fast friends from that time, and Julius never forgot that Hugh had saved his life."

FEBRUARY 29: The Whistling Boy

I AM going to tell you a story," said daddy, "about a whistling boy. It is a true story too. The boy was asked to a party and he went.

"All the children were playing games—follow the leader, prisoner's base, blind man's buff, hide and go seek, still-pond-no-more-moving, and many other games.

"They asked him if he wanted to play and he put his hands in his pockets and whistled. Then they had supper and they asked him if he liked creamed chicken and he whistled.

"They asked him if he liked ice-cream and he whistled. And as he whistled the same three notes whenever he was asked anything they didn't know whether he liked ice-cream or not.

"They gave him some supper when everything was passed around and he whistled when he took his plates and his cup of cocoa. When he had finished, without saying a word to any other children he got up, put his hands in his pockets once more and whistled.

"The children began to giggle, for they thought he was such a funny boy, and a funny boy he was. He had been rather spoilt and he hadn't really learned to play with other children.

"'They felt very sorry for him, but still he wouldn't say a word or do anything. They had asked him to the party because he had just come to the town to live and they thought he must be lonely.

"Well, when he got home he felt very badly, as many shy people do who have been rude because they were so shy they didn't know what to say, and so did the wrong thing.

"He cried when he was going to bed. And he was much ashamed of himself, for he thought it was a dreadful thing for a boy to cry.

"After a while he went to sleep, and in his sleep the Dream King came to him.

"'I'll help you,' said the Dream King, 'and I will not let you behave as badly as you did this afternoon if I can help it. For listen,

Boy. If you whistle again instead of talking and playing I will take away your speech for a whole week and you won't be able to make any sound.'

"And the dream seemed so real to the boy that he tried his best to act as other boys, and he succeeded too."

MARCH 1: Two Verses from *Mother Goose*

Come hither.

COME hither, little puppy dog;
　I'll give you a new collar,
If you will learn to read your book
　And be a clever scholar.
No, no! replied the puppy dog,
　I've other fish to fry,
For I must learn to guard your house,
　And bark when thieves come nigh.
With a tingle, tangle, tit-mouse!
　Robin knows great A,
And B, and C, and D, and E, F, G,
　　H, I, J, K.

Come hither, pretty cockatoo;
　Come and learn your letters,
And you shall have a knife and fork
　To eat with, like your betters.
No, no! the cockatoo replied,
　My beak will do as well;
I'd rather eat my victuals thus
　Than go and learn to spell.

Come hither.

With a tingle, tangle, tit-mouse!
　Robin knows great A,
And B, and C, and D, and E, F, G,
　　H, I, J, K.

Come hither, little pussy cat;
　If you'll your grammar study
I'll give you silver clogs to wear,
　Whene'er the gutter's muddy.
No! whilst I grammar learn, says Puss,
　Your house will in a trice

Be overrun from top to bottom
  With flocks of rats and mice.
With a tingle, tangle, tit-mouse!
  Robin knows great A,
And B, and C, and D, and E, F, G,
  H, I, J, K.

Come hither, then, good little boy,
  And learn your alphabet,
And you a pair of boots and spurs,
  Like your papa's, shall get.

Come hither.

Oh, yes! I'll learn my alphabet;
  And when I well can read,
Perhaps papa will give, me, too,
  A pretty long-tail'd steed.
With a tingle, tangle, tit-mouse!
  Robin knows great A,
And B, and C, and D, and E, F, G,
  H, I, J, K.

I like little Pussy.

I LIKE little pussy, her coat is so
    warm,—
And if I don't hurt her she'll do me no
    harm;
I'll not pull her tail, nor drive her away,
But pussy and I very gently will play.

MARCH 2: Lucy's Visitors

L UCY had been sick in bed with a sore throat for several days,
    but finally she woke up in the morning to find that the sore
    throat was almost all gone.   You can imagine her delight to
find the nice visitors that came to see her that same day.

A most attractive little toy wooden bunny came.   His ears could be
moved up and down and a most roguish look he would have when one
ear was up and the other down.

Lucy gave him chicken broth and he was extremely pleased.

If he had not been afraid his wooden face would have cracked he
would surely have smiled.   For it was pleasant indeed when one was
only a little wooden bunny rabbit to be given chicken broth.

It was most superior chicken broth, too. Oh, yes, for it had been made for Lucy and was made so as to give her lots of extra strength.

Besides the toy bunny a rag doll came to see Lucy. Yes, a very lovable sweet rag doll came to visit her.

She wore a little knitted hood on her head and a little sweater and a knitted scarf to keep her warm.

And she had a pair of warm knitted shoes. She wore her outside jacket, too, over her sweater, and she took along her little apron, so she could wear that when she played, so as not to hurt her good dress.

Oh, yes, the rag doll was going to play with Lucy and have an excellent time.

Then many members of the game family came to call on Lucy. They, too, came ready for play. Yes, there is nothing in the world that a game is more ready for than a good play.

Then people came to see Lucy, too, and congratulate her on the fact that her sore throat had gone away for good.

A lovely gray felt bunny and a brown felt monkey always were with Lucy. They had always belonged to her and, though new visitors came, they did not leave her. The monkey put his arm around the bunny and with his other arm on the pillow by Lucy he looked most comfortable.

He hadn't left her all the time that she lay sick in her bed. He had been such a comfort. While she drank her soup, and when the doctor came to call, and when Mommy told her comforting stories to help her get well, the monkey was tucked as neat as you please under Lucy's arm.

"Well," he was saying to the gray rabbit, "I'm laughing up my sleeve."

"How can you do that?" asked the rabbit. "You haven't any sleeve and you aren't laughing up your arm. You're not even turning your mouth in that direction.

"What do you mean by saying that?"

"Oh, it is just an expression," said the monkey. "When Creatures say they're laughing up their sleeve it does not really mean that they're holding open their sleeve and saying:

" 'Ha, ha, ha,' up it. But it means they're laughing inwardly or to themselves or so no one can see their laughter. That is what the expression means.

"So, you see no one can see my laughter, but I'm laughing all right because even though that mean old sore throat would have liked to stay, he couldn't, because Lucy wanted to get well.

Just then there came another visitor. This time it was the prince of desserts—Prince Ice-Cream. Proudly the Prince came in on the best and most royal of saucers. Hurray!

MARCH 3: The Homesick Puppy

DADDY had a story about a little dog that he knew would please both the children.

"Would you like to hear of a little dog who was homesick?" he asked.

"Yes," said Evelyn, "we would love to hear about it—that is, if he didn't die of homesickness."

"No, indeed," said daddy, "this little dog didn't die of homesickness, for he was sent home again and then was perfectly happy.

"He was the pet puppy of his mother, and he had told the man who had sold him to a little girl that he didn't want to go.

"The man who sold him thought that the little girl would give him such a nice home, and so she did, but the little puppy wanted more than just a nice home. He wanted his mother.

"Of course the little girl hadn't hesitated a moment about buying him, for he was a beautiful little Boston bull, and she promised him that she would make him happy.

"Now, when the little girl reached home with her puppy she gave him a great big bowl of the most delicious warm milk and a good puppy biscuit. But the puppy wouldn't touch the milk and biscuit.

"At bedtime the little girl showed the puppy his basket, which was nice and soft and comfortable. She thought that after a good night's rest he would be hungry for his breakfast and feel better.

"But morning came, and the puppy still refused to eat. And, would you believe it, hours passed, and the puppy still would not eat.

"Then the little girl decided that the only thing to be done was to take her beautiful puppy back to his mother.

"She ordered her pony cart to be ready for a certain hour, and off she started, holding the puppy by her side.

"When the puppy came near his home and began to see familiar sights it was all she could do to keep him in the cart, and when they were right by his home she could not hold him, for with a bound he was out and frisked and jumped over his mother, and she did the same, looking as if they would almost kill each other with joy.

" 'I guess he had better stay home,' said the man.

" 'Yes,' answered the little girl, 'this is where he belongs.' "

MARCH 4: Lady Ethel

I WANT to tell you a story this evening of the horse called Lady Ethel," said daddy.

"One time Lady Ethel's master took a long ride far out into the country away from where people lived.

"He felt quite ill after he had ridden a long way, and all of a sudden he got quite dizzy and fell.

"Lady Ethel pulled him out of the road and off to one side so no one taking the same road would go dashing over him by mistake.

"And then she went back home, all the distance alone, and neighed so that the people came out with her and found her master.

"He was quite ill after that, for he had been feeling poorly when he had started out on his ride, but if it hadn't been for Lady Ethel he wouldn't have had the chance to have been taken home and put back to bed and nursed back to health.

"He said he was grateful to all who helped him get well, but the one he was most grateful to of all was the faithful Lady Ethel.

"And every day while he was ill they led her under his window and she neighed happily after he had called out with as much strength as he could:

" 'Hello, my faithful, fine Lady Ethel!' "

MARCH 5: The Soup

WE'RE going to be mixed together, I hear," said the tomato. "You don't say so," said the milk. "Well, we will be chummy, won't we?"

"Yes," said the tomato. "They're going to make cream of tomato soup. It's supposed to be quite delicious. And when we're both well cooked they will mix us together and season us up very fine and we'll be eaten as the first thing at the meal. Yes, soup is very apt to take the lead. It's a leader, soup is."

"Good," said the milk. "But how silly to call it cream of tomato soup, if they're going to use me. I'm milk, I am."

"Oh, well," said the tomato, "let them have their little airs and graces. And maybe when you're mixed with me you're every bit as good as cream. Who knows!"

MARCH 6: Elephant Ways

WHY did you have your toe-nails cut, your skin oiled, and your feet sand-papered?" asked Sally of an elephant in the Zoo. "One question at a time please," said the elephant. "I can't answer all three at once, for then the answers would be all jumbled up. Besides, I don't know how to say more than one word at a time.

"My nails were cut because they needed it. And, come to think of it, I can answer all your questions at once. My feet needed to be sand-papered and my body needed to be oiled. My skin required it, and so the keeper looked after me, as he did after my friends here." This he said waving his trunk.

"But what do you do when you are not in the Zoo?" asked Sally. "They don't have sandpaper and nail scissors in the jungles, do they?"

"Ah, that is where you do not understand, and where the keeper does. In the wilds I can cut my nails on the great rocks. They keep them short. Here I cannot do it myself, and so the keeper has to do it for me. And I get the oil for my skin in the swamps when I'm free, and my feet are kept hard by the ground and rocks. We do not need the keeper's scissors and so forth when we are free, for old Mother Nature looks after those things for us."

MARCH 7: The Marbles

THE Marbles," said daddy, "were very proud because they had been used so much by boys and girls—especially by boys.

"Then, too, the Elves had played marbles, as years before they had found out about them and thought they were lots of fun to play with.

" 'You are nothing but an ordinary Marble,' said one large and very blue Marble to a little Marble.

" 'But I am useful for playing. And I joggle along and roll much better than you do. You are so big. You are quite awkward!'

" 'I'd feel pretty badly,' said the big Marble, 'if I were as cheap as you. You cost next to nothing. In fact, you didn't even cost a cent. Not one whole cent!'

"The Marble rolled along a little way as if it couldn't be too near the cheap Marble.

" 'But a cent bought me,' said the little Marble.

" 'Yes,' said the big Marble proudly, "it bought you and also a number of other marbles, too. You were one of five for a cent. One cent bought you and four others! Now, as for me! well, it took the whole of five cents to buy me!'

" 'I know it,' said the little Marble sadly.

" 'My Master only bought me yesterday,' said the big Marble. 'His friends have not seen me. They'll trade everything for me! Gracious—they'd trade dozens of little Marbles just for me! I cost five cents!'

"The children had arrived, but they did not seem to want to trade everything for it! One of them said,

" 'It is a beauty, but then it is not nearly so nice to play with as the smaller ones; besides, if I gave up a lot of small marbles for that big one I'd never be able to have a real game.'

"And all the other children said just the same thing.

"They played and they played. But the big Marble was so mad that it rolled away crookedly and no one thought so much of it.

"After the children had finished playing and had taken their marbles, and after the Master of the big Marble had put it away with the smaller ones, the little Marble which had been bought with four others for a cent said,

" 'Well, you may be handsome and big. But you are not nearly such fun as we are. Sometimes the cheap things are the most fun. It doesn't mean because you cost five cents that you can give more pleasure.'

" 'I'm glad I can't be used all the time like you all are,' said the big Marble. 'I am too fine for little Marbles, anyway.'

"But all the little Marbles were happy because they were the best for the children's games."

MARCH 8: Tomatoes' Advantages

THE Vegetables," said daddy, "had been put into the pantry to keep. There were the Potatoes, the Apples for cooking, Carrots, the Squash family and many others. As they were talking mother came into the pantry. 'Well,' said she to herself, 'it's nice to get something from the hot-house once in a while. I get so sick of these everlasting winter vegetables and apples that we keep in the cellar. It's nice to have a few Tomatoes for a change.'

"Down she put a box with bright red Tomatoes—just from the hot-house.

" 'Well, Vegetables,' said the Tomatoes, 'how do you do?'

" 'We're quite well,' said the Vegetables and Apples, who were rather quiet right now.

" 'I don't see why I shouldn't talk to you, though I'm pretty different from you,' said the biggest Tomato of all.

" 'And why shouldn't you be?' asked Mr. Potato. 'You have been in a hot-house, spoilt and petted. You'd be queer if you weren't superior. With sun and warmth of course you have a fine color!' And the Tomatoes agreed that they had had unusual advantages."

MARCH 9: The Old Woman and the Pot of Daffodils

A LITTLE girl named Laura," said daddy, "had been quite ill. One day she was wondering if she would ever feel like herself again, able to do things and to play around. She was sitting up by the window in a big chair. She was looking out, feeling very sad and forlorn, when suddenly she saw a funny old woman who looked just like a witch stop by the window and then walk right into the room.

"The funny old woman spoke at once.

" 'Don't be frightened,' she said. 'I'm not going to hurt you. Instead, you see this pot of daffodils I am carrying?'

" 'Yes,' exclaimed Laura. 'Aren't they beautiful?'

" 'I am so glad you like them,' continued the old woman, 'for they are for you.'

" 'For me?' repeated Laura. 'For me?'

" 'Yes,' said the old woman. 'When the spring comes I take a walk each day, carrying with me a pot of daffodils. When I see some one sitting in the window of a house looking sick and longing to go out I just go right in and leave my pot of daffodils, for they are better than any spring tonic, to my mind.'

"And the yellow flowers smiled at Laura and bobbed their pretty heads, saying, 'We'll make you well.'

"And, sure enough, they really did more toward making Laura well than anything else. How could she help but feel better with the bright flowers smiling at her and cheering her up?"

MARCH 10: The Tick-Tock Twins

H ELLO, twin Tock," said Tick, and Tock answered, just as quickly as anything:
"Hello, Tick."
They never got tired of saying to each other "Tick" and "Tock."

They were the two clock twins, as you may have guessed, but sometimes between their words to each other, sometimes between saying to each other "Tick" and "Tock," they talked.

Of course they would only say a few words at a time and those would be said so very quickly we could not understand them, and anyway Tick and Tock only talk for each other.

They just speak to each other all day long, as the time goes on.

And they don't stop at night, but as it would be very hard to understand their story without leaving out all the ticks and the tocks we will hear it with those left out.

Really it was like this.

"Hello, Tick."

"Hello, Tock," and the "Hello" would be said very quickly so no one else could hear it.

"Nice-Tick."

"Nice-Tock."

"Day-Tick."

"Day-Tock," and so on and on, never forgetting the tick and the tock.

"We're such happy twins," said Tick.

"Yes," said Tock, "and we never forsake each other. If one of us can't go on, the other won't go alone. There is never a tick without a tock following right on behind."

"Ah, you're so loyal, Tock," said Tick.

"And so are you," said Tock.

"There are many clock twins," said Tick.

"Many," agreed Tock.

"Every clock has us," said Tick.

"Every one," said Tock.

"And if the clock stops, they stop too."

"Of course," said Tock.

"One would never go without the other," said Tick.

"Of course not," said Tock.

"It's nice," said Tick, "to be so loyal, very nice and very unusual. Think of how we can always wait for the other, and then follow after!"

"We're each always following the other," said Tock.

"I'm glad," said Tick. "We're not people. If we were, when we grew up, we might have to go our different ways. Dear me, it's much nicer to be the clock twins. We'll never be separated."
me, it's much nicer to be the clock twins. We'll never be separated."

MARCH 11: The Fig

I'M mad," said the Fig.

"What are you mad about?" asked the Apple.

The Fig and the Apple were in the fruit dish together, along with an orange or two and a bunch of grapes.

"What are you mad about?" the rest of the fruit asked.

"Yes, you'd better tell us," said the Apple. "I'm sure it will make you feel much, much better."

"I don't know whether it will or not," said the Fig.

"Why don't you think it will?" asked the Apple.

"Because it might make me cry, and some one might call me a cry baby."

"My dear Fig," said the Apple, "no one could ever call you a cry baby, because even if you cried you're not a baby."

"But I've heard big boys and big girls called cry babies, and they weren't babies," said the Fig.

"All very true," said the Apple, "but they behaved as babies and once they had been babies. That is, each one of them had once been a baby. It would have been impossible for them to have been more than one baby I suppose."

"We suppose so, too," said the rest of the fruit, as it moved in the fruit dish a little.

"And," continued the Apple, "they were behaving as though they hadn't grown up into boys and girls by crying over some silly little thing.

"You see, Fig, you have never been a baby. You have been a little fig, but never a little baby. So you couldn't be a cry baby, though you might be a cry fig, or a cry little fig. I'm not sure about that."

"That wouldn't sound so badly," said the Fig. "I will have to tell you what has made me mad, and what may make me cry at any moment."

"Tell us," said the Apple.

"Imagine," said the Fig, "I heard people speak of a person they knew was mean and horrid and unfair and all that was dreadful as not being worth a fig. Oh, that was cruel, cruel."

"I am so glad you told the story," said the Apple, "for you are being unhappy for no reason at all. When any one says that a person isn't worth thinking about and he wouldn't give a fig for that person, it doesn't mean an insult to the family of figs, but is simply an expression people have used for a long, long time." And the Fig was happy again.

But the Fig was more delighted when a lovely child came by the fruit dish and taking the Fig said, "I simply love figs."

MARCH 12: Happy Compton

I N the first place," said Happy Compton, "I'm a dog. I'm not any special breed. I'm not what is known as a thoroughbred, but they say I'm brighter than a great many thoroughbreds. I'm glad they think I'm bright, and that they like me.

"I was a little waif dog first of all. Louise and Ada had been promised a dog. Their daddy had told them that the first chance he had he would go and buy them a dog. Then I came along, a lonely, homeless little waif dog.

"They took me in and fed me and loved me and made me warm and happy.

"When their daddy asked them about the dog he was to buy for them Louise said:

" 'Such dogs as those, in kennels, which are for sale, will get homes, for they will be in good condition, but this is a homeless little dog and I'd rather have him. He will be happy here and he will be loved here. No one could love him more than I do.'

" 'Except the way I love him,' said Ada, and to prove how much she loved me she put me down by her on the pillow and covered me up and then Louise stroked my head and I went off into the dreamland of dogs.

"They both loved me so right away and they still love me so, and I know how much they always will love me.

"Because they could see how happy I was to be no longer homeless and miserable they called me Happy. It's such a nice name, and they have given me their last name, too—Happy Compton. Isn't that fine?"

MARCH 13: Freezer and Furnace

N OW the furnace and the freezer were both in a big cellar. The freezer was some distance away from the furnace, but still they were in the same cellar. The freezer was near a door, which was by some steps. These steps led up to the kitchen of the house and every one came down to the freezer to get out the food which was going to be used and the meat and all such things which belong in a freezer.

Of course, half of the year the furnace wasn't doing anything, and in the winter time the freezer did not have nearly so much to do.

"I feel sorry for you," said the furnace. "Here you are so cold and you haven't even enough warmth about you to make the ice melt quickly as it does in the summer time.

"You have to be so cold always; even in the winter you have to be cold. That is the saddest of all. In the summer I'm not so hot myself but as soon as a cold day comes I am ready to be warm."

"Ah, furnace, you mustn't boast too much," said the freezer. "I've heard the family having great trouble with you. There are days, sometimes the cold, cold ones, too, when you won't burn. I've even known you to go out sometimes.

"And oh, how you have made the family shiver. You have made them fuss over you."

"And why shouldn't they fuss over me?" asked the furnace. "I'm the furnace, I am; the great and warm and powerful furnace. I keep the whole house warm. I keep all the people in it warm."

"But you don't keep them warm when you go out and when you go slowly and when you won't burn nicely," said the freezer.

"That is to show that I won't let any one think I'm so unimportant that I don't have to be noticed and fussed over."

"It shows that sometimes you are very mean, furnace. Important and great and wise and clever creatures don't have to be fussed over. They're above it."

"Look here, young freezer," said the furnace, "I don't want any rules from you. You are a fine thing to talk about a creature keeping warm. What warmth do you ever give to any one, I'd like to know?"

"You're right, furnace, I don't give any warmth. But I am not supposed to, and you are. I am supposed to keep the icecubes to make folks cool in the hot summer and make the food keep nice and cool. I do my work, I do. And you should do yours, you should."

"I do it all right, never fear," said the furnace, though it knew that many a time it had behaved badly. But now it was mad and it went for all it was worth and the freezer chuckled and said to itself, "The poor people have been saying how cold they were and how badly the furnace was behaving. Now the furnace is mad and will behave by burning and raging for all it is worth."

And the furnace burned angrily and furiously and how nice and warm the people kept on that cold winter's day!

MARCH 14: The Pet Dogs

THERE were five dogs," said daddy, "who belonged to a boy who was named Jack.

"Brutus was the largest of all. He was a big Newfoundland dog. Next came Bogi, another Newfoundland dog, but not so large as Brutus.

"Third came Patty, an Irish terrier. Then came Ouji, a cocker spaniel, and last came Susy, a little fox terrier. When they all stood together they looked like a flight of stairs, and just as though one could walk from Susy right up to Brutus.

" 'Ah,' said Patty, 'I see something coming my way.'

"All the other dogs looked and Patty said, 'There is a bug and I'm going to catch it.'

"But the bug said to itself, 'I'll play a joke on that dog.' And the bug did play a joke, a very mean joke.

"Patty snapped at the bug and then was about to swallow it when she had gotten the bug on her tongue, when what should that mean bug do but turn itself over so that it attached itself to Patty's tongue, and so Patty couldn't swallow it or eat it or anything!

"Then Brutus had a fine idea. He ran for Jack, for he had seen Jack go to a near-by field to play baseball.

"He ran just as hard as he could and when he reached the field he didn't even notice the baseball which had just been hit with the bat.

"The boys were awfully frightened for a moment as they thought Brutus might get hit by accident with the hard ball, and they called out to him, but Brutus wasn't thinking of being afraid of anything.

"But luckily the ball didn't hit Brutus, and Brutus went right on up to his master, barking, and showing by his eyes that he wanted to have Jack follow him.

" 'I guess Brutus wants me for something,' said Jack, 'for he wouldn't come to the baseball field if it weren't for something important.'

"So Jack ran quickly home, following Brutus. There he found Patty with the bug on her tongue and feeling most uncomfortable.

"Jack quickly took the bug off and then Patty no longer looked sick and miserable.

"She jumped up on Jack and wagged her tail and her eyes looked very glad and happy as she tried to thank her master. And then she did quite the sweetest thing ever a dog did. She suddenly seemed to know that Brutus was the one who had done everything.

"Jack had come quickly when Brutus had called him, for Jack was always so good to his pets, and Jack had been able to take the bug off her tongue because he had nice useful hands.

"But Patty knew that it was Brutus who had gone for Jack, and Brutus who had brought him back so quickly.

"And Patty went over to Brutus, looking so small beside the great big Newfoundland dog and she licked Brutus' paws and rolled over on the grass, saying to Brutus that she was a very grateful, happy, little dog.

"And then, for a special treat, every one of them had a bone, and Jack gave himself a piece of cake!" ended daddy.

MARCH 15: Biddle's Trick

BIDDLE the cat," said daddy, "was very thirsty and he wanted to get a drink of milk.

"Look," one of the family suddenly exclaimed. And from the study they could see a light in the pantry.

"When they went into the pantry there was Biddle on the pantry shelf and he had just pressed with his paw the electric light button—so the light had gone on!

" 'Do you want something, Biddle?' one of the family asked, after they had all exclaimed at the wonderful thing which Biddle had just done.

"Biddle purred, and looked at the refrigerator, and they got some milk for him.

"But don't you think it was clever of him to get the family into the pantry by turning on the light? This is a true story of Biddle Birdsall, the clever gray pussy-cat."

MARCH 16: The Naughty Colds

MR. and Mrs. Cold were having a very good time. Now, when most people have a good time it means that they're playing or singing or laughing or dancing or reading or hearing music. Perhaps it means they're having a party of some sort, or perhaps it may mean they're in swimming or having a picnic. Oh, there are lots and lots of ways of having good times as every one knows.

But when Mr. and Mrs. Cold have a good time it is something very different from what we mean by a good time. In the first place, Mr. and Mrs. Cold are very disagreeable people. They have always been disagreeable. Their daddy and mother were the same way, and as for Aunt Grippe and their Uncle Bronchitis—well, they're horrid old creatures, I can tell you.

Mr. and Mrs. Cold have very mean children, too. There is Sadie Sneeze, for example. She has the worst sort of a disposition! She just loves to plague people and make them as uncomfortable as she can.

Then there is Charlie Cough. He likes to hurt creatures. You can just imagine how mean he is. And there is Susy Sore Throat, and Hatty Headache. They are all children of Mr. and Mrs. Cold.

"Let's go on a trip," they said to the children.

"All right," said the children. They always agree to go a-traveling, and the worst thing about them is that they have many cousins and relations, and their cousins and relations are just as busy a-traveling as they are!

"I think," said Mrs. Cold, "we'll go and call on a little girl named Annette. She is such a nice little girl, I'd like to make her feel uncomfortable. Let's give her a good dose of us."

And the Cold children clapped their hands.

"Is she nice?" they said. And when their mother and daddy said:

"Oh, she is wonderfully nice," they were just overjoyed. That is how mean they are. They love to be horrid to nice, nice boys and girls and grown-ups!

So they picked up their suitcases with plenty of Sadie Sneeze's best frocks, and plenty of Charlie Cough's extra neckties, and lots of Hatty Headache's hair ribbons and Susy Sore Throat's collars and off they went. Their hair ribbons and collars and dresses aren't like nice children's, for they are mean like themselves!

"Oh, please," said Annette, when they all arrived, "I didn't ask you to come and see me. I don't need you. I have a nice daddy and a nice mother all of my own. I don't want Mr. and Mrs. Cold, and I have two nice brothers, and I don't want any others, or even any sisters. Please go away."

But the Cold family paid no attention. They were so mean they liked being where they weren't wanted.

But the time passed and the dream king found out that Annette had some horrid visitors. The dream king hurried to tell the fairy queen about it.

"Did you ever hear of such rudeness and such unkindness as that horrible Cold family show?" he said.

"We'll put a stop to this, Dream King," said the fairy queen. "Thank you for telling me. I know that little girl Annette. Yes, I know her well. She has golden hair and fair skin and blue eyes. And she lives in a city house. Ah, yes, I know her Just like that horrid Cold family to go and bother some one who is nice!"

The fairy queen set to work. She called together all her assistants and they hurried to Annette's house when she was fast asleep.

They gave the Cold family a good talking to and they waved their wands over Annette so that the Cold family were driven away.

And in the meantime the old dream king had told the dream fairies about Annette and they made up the most wonderful package of dreams, lovely dreams sent to her as she was getting all, all well again. But the dream king himself made up this poem for her:

"Annette is so nice, Annette is so sweet,
Just Annette herself is a great big treat!"

62

MARCH 17: Why the Shamrock is Worn on St. Patrick's Day

"IT is said," daddy told the children, "that the shamrock keeps away the snakes which St. Patrick drove out of Ireland, for they cannot live and thrive where the shamrock grows.

"But there is a legend about St. Patrick which I think I'll have to tell you to-night.

"What are said to be St. Patrick's footprints can be seen on the rocks off the shore by the Skerries harbor. The story goes that once a chieftain named Dichu drew his sword to strike St. Patrick. When he was about to do this cruel deed his own arm became perfectly stiff until he said he'd be obedient to St. Patrick. Then St. Patrick taught him to be good and kind.

"Still another interesting story is that of the idol worshipers. St. Patrick went into the place where these people were and found them worshiping the idols. There was a huge pillar of stone with the chief idol on top of it. It was covered with slabs of gold and silver, and around it in a circle were twelve other idols. St. Patrick smote the chief idol with his crozier and the idol crumbled to dust at once."

MARCH 18: St. Patrick

"DADDY, do tell us this evening more about St. Patrick," asked Jack and Evelyn.

"He was born in 372," said daddy. "When he was only sixteen years old he was stolen by pirates. They did not treat him at all well, and he was sold by them into slavery in Ireland.

"His master had him look after pigs in the mountains. But Patrick had a strange dream in which the Lord told him to run away and set out for a far-away country. He had been seven years in Ireland, so he was used to its language and all its customs and manners. After a time he was ordained a deacon, then a priest, and finally he became a bishop. At this point the pope told him to return to Ireland to preach the gospel to the Irish people. Since then he has always been known as St. Patrick. One story is that on a bitter cold morning St. Patrick and a number of his followers found they could not possibly build a fire. They had had no breakfast and were half frozen. St. Patrick listened to their complaints for a while, and then he told them to gather up the snow in a pile. This they did. St. Patrick breathed on it, and it became a fire.

63

"Another tale is that St. Patrick beat the drum so loudly when driving the snakes out of Ireland that he knocked a hole in it, but that an angel appeared and mended it, so that the drum was afterward kept as a relic.

"It is told that in one part of Ireland from which St. Patrick drove the snakes and toads he chained one huge serpent by a lake called in Irish Lough Dilveen and told him to stay until Monday. The people around the district still claim that every Monday they hear the serpent calling out in the Irish dialect, 'It's a long Monday, St. Patrick!'

"St. Patrick is said to have died on the 17th of March, 493, aged 121. His grave is at Dunpatrick, Ireland, and a tombstone now bears his name cut in Irish characters."

MARCH 19: The Clocks

I THINK I shall tell you the story of the talking that went on one day in a clock shop when the old clock mender had gone to his lunch," said daddy.

" 'My master is so lazy!' said the Eight-Day Clock. 'He keeps saying: "Oh, dear, I must wind up that Clock." And then he grabs a newspaper and sits down and reads. He quite forgets about me. He should wind me up when it is time. Gracious, I strike so he can tell I need to be wound up. But he doesn't pay much attention. He just winds me up after I have had to stop for days. And such a fine Clock as I am, too.'

" 'You may be a fine Clock,' said the little Watch with the broken mainspring, 'but I don't see as it does you any good. You are always being brought here.'

" 'I can't help it,' said the Eight-Day Clock. 'You see, I get so upset over not being wound up and I get so tired and worried wondering if my master will remember, that I get feeling run down. Then I weep a Clock's tears, which only we Clocks and Watches know about. We feel so badly when we are not treated right. And then when we feel badly it upsets our works and we have to be brought to the clock mender's shop. But I wish we could teach our masters a lesson,' said the Eight-Day Clock.

" 'We will,' said the Cuckoo Clock.

" 'What will we do?' asked the rest.

" 'We will be so hard to mend,' said the Cuckoo Clock, 'that we will make the clock mender charge great big prices. And then our masters will look after us.' And all the Clocks at once looked happier."

MARCH 20: A Party and Polly

"POLLY want a cracker, ha, ha," laughed the parrot.

"No, Polly doesn't want a cracker, ha, ha," the parrot continued. "For there is no one in the room to give me a cracker, and I've eaten up the one I had in my cage. I have some seed and some water, but not a trace of a cracker."

Polly, the parrot, stepped out of her cage and looked about the room. She flew this way and that, and she had a good-sized room in which to fly—a room with very high ceilings.

"Polly doesn't see a cracker," she said to herself. She couldn't talk to any one else, you see, because there was no one else in the room. And she knew perfectly well that the pictures on the walls and the rugs on the floor didn't care about being talked to. She had never heard them say anything or fly about or walk about—and she knew very well why they couldn't.

Because they weren't live things. They weren't people, nor were they animals, nor birds. They were nothing but rugs and pictures and extremely, extremely silly.

She hadn't been looking about long when her mistress came in all dressed up in a most beautiful manner.

"Well, Polly," her mistress said, "we are having a party to-day."

"Polly have a party, Polly have a party," said the parrot.

And when the guests arrived Polly looked down from her perch and said: "Polly have a party, Polly have a party." How every one did laugh and admire the nice, cheerful, friendly Polly Parrot. And her mistress was very proud of Polly!

MARCH 21: Salt, Pepper and Sugar

"CREATURES and things aren't to be admired who won't take the trouble to go out of their way to do nice things," said Sugar of the Sugar Bowl. "And as the Sugar Bowl can't go walking around looking for nice things to do at least it can admire the Salt Cellar and the Pepper Shaker for the work they do in seasoning and making things have a good taste."

"Ah, Sugar Bowl," said the Salt Cellar, "I am glad to hear you talk this way. For some time I have been afraid that you didn't have enough character. I was very much afraid that you were becoming too sugary and too weak!

"The Pepper Shaker would tell you, too, how much he thinks of you, but if he comes about too much he is apt to make people sneeze. He doesn't like to do that. He can't help it if too much of him is used, but he hates to be used like that. He likes to add to the taste of things, but not to be made out a cruel creature.

"Yes, he had a terrible blow once. He was treated so badly! It wasn't fair to him at all.

"Some very mean boys and girls thought it would be fun to put sneezing powder in the flowers which they would give to their friends to smell. Then as their friends began to sneeze they would laugh.

"Well, a great deal of my Pepper friend was used then. He made those people sneeze and he didn't want to in the least. Oh, he did feel so badly about it. It wasn't funny, he said, it was mean, out and out mean! The people who sneezed were miserable. Their noses hurt, their throats hurt and they couldn't sleep for several nights.

"One little girl who had sneezed so hard and so much lost her voice for several days, for the sneezing powder got down in her throat, and her throat has never been quite so strong since.

"So I think we should all be used in our places and not too much of any of us, for if too much sugar is used things will be sickish and if too much pepper or salt is used the poor pepper and salt creatures are taken a mean advantage of!"

MARCH 22: A Sun Parlor for Birds

THERE was once a grown-up lady," said daddy, "who had loved the stories of the fairies and of birds and flowers when she had been a little girl. She had so loved to read of all the kind deeds of the fairies that she had made up her mind that when she grew up she would do something kind too.

"Well, this lady had the roof of her house made into a Sun Parlor. There were trees all round, and moss, and little pools of water which she had fixed to look as much like out-of-doors as possible. The Sun Parlor she had enclosed in glass. Of course the glass made the sun shine through all the brighter. And she had little wee doors so the birds could get in and out, but so small that a cat could never get into this bird home.

"But still more wonderful was a big cellar where all kinds of good apples, bread crumbs, more water and countless goodies were kept."

"But how could the birds get from the roof to the cellar?" asked Jack.

"I don't wonder you ask that," said daddy. "The lady had all that part beautifully arranged. In the Sun Parlor were tunnels which led down into the cellar, and the birds used to love going through these dark passages into the 'Goody-shop' as it was called in Bird language —and it sounded the same to them as it would to you in Boy-and-Girl language.

"At first the birds were tempted into their winter home by the bread crumbs that were in the Sun Parlor. For, of course, as you can imagine, it took the birds some time to get used to a beautiful summer home in the winter that was really just for them. Soon, though, little birds know when people are being kind to them.

"Of course the lady let all the birds who wanted to come in have just as good a time and stay just as long as they wanted to. But she especially wanted little sick birds who had perhaps fallen out of their nests.

"One day the lady came across a baby Robin whose family had arrived before the warm weather. The baby Robin had fallen from its nest, and very gently the lady picked him up and took him to the Sun Parlor. The mother was crying near-by for she saw her baby being taken away from her and she couldn't help at all.

"But she saw from the top of a tree where her little sick baby was taken. How happy and relieved she was—for, of course, she had to be in her nest with all the other little Robins. But she sang every day the most wonderful songs for the lady who watched over her baby Robin until it was quite strong and able to fly."

MARCH 23: The Automobiles

HONK-HONK, it seems a pity," said one automobile to the other. "I know I seem like the rudest sort of an old thing. I scare folks, and children just run when they see me coming. But it does seem a pity. Yes, it seems a shame that I can't help it.

"One day I was resting. My owner had gone inside a building. I heard a little girl and an old lady talking. The little girl said, 'I've been quite ill and my heart is just beginning to get strong. I have a horrible time crossing the street, for I simply cannot walk across. Those old automobiles make me run.'

"The old lady said to the little girl, 'I know just how you feel, my dear, for I have been ill too, and I am not supposed to run fast. It hurts me when I run fast and yet I have to hurry to get out of the way of the automobiles.'

" 'I don't see why they have to make people run, when they're not going to fires and they're not going after accidents,' said the little girl. 'It does not seem fair in the least.'

" 'It doesn't,' said the old lady. 'But I don't suppose the people who run automobiles are ever sick. They don't know what it means to have a horn tooted at them when they feel they cannot run.

" 'And it seems a pity that folks should be in so much of a hurry, as they run along in their automobiles, that they can't give those who are walking a fair chance, too.'

"Sometimes I wish I weren't an automobile."

"Sometimes I wish I were one with a different owner," said the second automobile.

"Maybe we will be sold and nice people will own us, who will consider those who are walking," said the first automobile.

"Let's hope so," said the second automobile.

"There's the first star of the evening," said the first automobile. "We'll make a wish."

So the modern automobiles wished in the old, old way, their wishes!

MARCH 24: The Trailing Arbutus

WE mustn't waste any more time," whispered one of the trailing arbutus family to another.

"No, we mustn't. We must awaken for we are first to awaken every year. And all the families in this part get up soon.

"Years ago," continued the second arbutus, "some children came here to look for trailing arbutus flowers. They said to each other:

" 'It must be too soon. There aren't any.' But they looked under some of our leaves and several of us were trying to peep out as fast as we could, so we would not disappoint the children.

"Many of our sisters and brothers were picked and I believe they came out later in water.

"But those same children have come back every year, and now they are almost grown-up. They always say,

" 'Here is the first place we find these lovely spring flowers.' And so we know what is expected of us. Our roots always hand on this story to all the arbutus flowers.'

And now along came the grown-ups and some children.

"We hide our heads under the leaves because we're shy, but we love children and the whole beautiful world, so pick lots of us, and we'll be bright and gay," softly whispered the flowers.

But the children only knew that the flowers were very, very fragrant, and oh, so very sweet!

MARCH 25: The Telephone Dog

THE telephone always seemed very important to Rogue, the collie," said daddy. "He had known his mistress to rush out after the telephone had rung and she had answered it, as if some one were ill, or something had happened which she had found to be of very great importance.

"She was working in the garden one day when Rogue heard the telephone ring. Evidently she didn't hear it, for she stayed out in the garden and didn't come in to answer it. It rang and it rang, and Rogue didn't know what to do.

"Finally he thought up a scheme, and this is what he did. He ran out in the garden and he stood before his mistress and barked and barked without stopping. First she stroked him and didn't seem to think anything special was the matter, but that, perhaps, he wanted to play.

"He kept on barking, and after a few minutes she said: 'What is the matter, Rogue?'

"He started to go towards the house, barking, and turned around to see if she were following him. When she didn't he went and pulled at her skirt. Then she went into the house, following Rogue, and he stopped before the telephone which was still ringing.

"She answered it and found that it had been ringing a long time, but it was so important that they had kept on ringing to see if she wouldn't hear it after a while.

"Then she knew that Rogue had let her know the telephone was ringing and wanted her to come to answer it, for that was something he couldn't do. But he could let her know that it was ringing, now that he had found a way of doing so.

"And now Rogue always lets his mistress know when the telephone is ringing. She works in her garden a great deal but she never misses a telephone call because Rogue hears it, barks for her, and leads her in before the telephone."

MARCH 26: The Kettle's Trouble

I'M not angry," said the kettle. "I'm hurt. My poor porcelain feelings are most dreadfully hurt. A child tried to move me and in so doing she spilled some of the boiling water over herself."

"I wasn't quite boiling," said the water; "very nearly boiling I was, though."

"Don't interrupt," said the kettle. "You've caused me enough trouble. Well, the child got quite badly burned. It hurt awfully, for burns always do."

"Yes," said the butter, from the refrigerator in the corner of the kitchen, "I too know how it feels to be burned."

"But she blamed me for burning her," said the kettle. "She said that 'the horrid old kettle burned her,' and it wasn't I at all."

But the water, fire, gas, and match each in turn quickly said they were not to blame but only the cook, for starting the fire in the first place!

MARCH 27: Mr. Measles' Puzzle

"GO away, go away," said Peter Goblin. "You mustn't come around here. No, you mustn't. I won't have it, not for a moment will I have it."

"May we talk to you, then?" asked Mr. Measles, as he hurried off.

"Yes, I will come and talk to you, but you mustn't stay around here. Goblins don't get measles, but children do, and I won't have it. Hurry off. Hurry off."

"Wouldn't they like to have us?" asked Mr. Mumps. "Just think how we'd make their faces puff up and look so fine and fat."

"Yes," said Peter Goblin, crossly, "and make it hard for them to swallow. No sir, no sir, you get right away from here."

"How about me?" asked Mrs. Croup.

"You go away, too," said Peter Goblin.

"Can't I have just one little look at a nice little boy or a nice little girl?" asked Master Chicken-Pox.

"You most certainly cannot," said Peter Goblin.

"I don't see why not," said Mr. Measles crossly. He had come back a little because he had heard the others talking to Peter Goblin and he thought perhaps Peter had given in. Of course he had never known him to, but he might—one could never tell.

"I thought I'd told you to start off," said Peter Goblin. "Now I won't put up with any more of this nonsense. Be off—all of you. Be off, right away."

"You promised to talk to us," said Mr. Measles. "You will, won't you?"

"But we'd rather have a little chat with a child first," said Mr. Mumps.

"Maybe you would like to," said Peter Goblin, "but you're not going to. And so, one, two, three—go! Every one of you. I'll follow along."

"Now, what is the use," Mr. Mumps muttered, "of being able to make some folks fat when one isn't given the chance?"

"You don't want to make them fat and well," said Peter Goblin.

They had all wandered quite far away from the children and so Peter Goblin felt they were safe. He would get many of his goblins right to work to keep an eye on them, for goblins cannot get measles, mumps, chicken-pox or croup.

"Yes, I make them fat," said Mr. Mumps. "I never bother about more than their cheeks. They grumble so after I've made them fat that I get disheartened."

"Good thing you do," said Peter Goblin. "You're certainly mean enough."

Mr. Mumps knew Peter was right, so didn't say another word. Mr. Measles spoke next.

"We wanted to have you talk to us," said Mr. Measles, "because we cannot understand you."

"Why not?" asked Peter Goblin. "I try to protect the children from getting measles, mumps, chicken-pox and croup. Of course they have to help me by trying to keep as well and strong as they can so as to escape you. Whenever one of you gets past us, how badly we do feel. You often do, but we try our best to keep you out. We can't keep you out entirely but we can help.

"And then good, kind doctors drive you away."

"We hate doctors," said Mr. Measles.

"Well," said Mrs. Croup, "we shouldn't hate them so much, because we give them a lot of trouble, and we love to give trouble."

"That's so, we do," said Master Chicken-Pox.

"But," said Mr. Measles, "people say, 'oh, don't catch the measles. And be careful not to catch the mumps. Don't go near any one with chicken-pox or you might catch it."

"Now, to catch a thing," continued Mr. Measles, "means to chase after it or try to get it in some way. If they don't like us why do they talk about catching measles? They say 'Be careful not to catch Mr. Mumps.' It's very silly, for if they really don't like us, they should say, 'Don't let Mr. Mumps catch you.'"

"It's rather an absurd expression," admitted Peter Goblin, "but stay away from children and talk about it for a good long while. That's what you must all do!"

71

MARCH 28: Winter's Exit

WHEN we speak of a person making an exit," said daddy, "we mean that the person has gone out, and so when we speak of the winter's exit, we mean that the winter has made his departure. The winter was quite angry that Mr. Sun was so eager to see the spring.

" 'I'd think,' said the winter, 'you'd be a little scrap more polite, anyway. It always makes me so mad that I just hang around and hang around, and laugh when I hear folks say: "Isn't the winter ever going?" '

" 'Are you going to make your last bow soon?' asked Mr. Sun.

" 'To-morrow,' said the winter. 'Yes, by to-morrow I'll really have to go. And after this last little snow-storm there'll be no more until next year. Ah, what a sad thought that is to me, though it's not such a sad thought for others. They seem to be so absurdly fond of young spring. They spoil him frightfully.'

" 'And you won't really send any more blizzards?' asked Mr. Sun.

" 'I can't," said the winter, 'because you *would* cross that old Equator.'

"Mr. Sun smiled and the winter said: 'I'll take a rest now and fool the people! They'll think it's really spring, and then I'll give them my fine farewell to-morrow.'

"And sure enough on the morrow there was a light fall of snow. The spring hardly knew what to make of it at first, until he found it was so light a storm.

" 'That's the winter's bow as he makes his exit,' said Mr. Sun to the spring.

"And the spring sent out the early Breezes and said: 'Whisper to the birds, the buds, the children that I've really, really come, and that winter has made his exit!' "

MARCH 29: Another Biddle Story

I MUST tell you another story about the gray cat, Biddle Birdsall," said daddy. "His mistress Gertrude was away at school. His mistress' mother and daddy were out, and the cook was out. It was a very sad household for a cat who wanted a drink of milk.

"Then he had an idea! He went into his master's study and emptying the waste-paper basket in a pile on the floor, he pushed the waste-paper basket towards the pantry door.

72

"When he had finished pushing the basket and when it was right up by the door he turned it upside down and climbed upon it.

" 'There,' thought Biddle, 'now I have it.'

"And he had! He opened that door with his two front paws, turning the knob until it was undone and he could push the door open.

"Then he moved the basket away, opened the door wide, and purring delightedly to himself, he walked inside the pantry.

"There was the milk in the saucer, and then, as you can easily guess, Biddle had the milk which he wanted. When he was drinking it the family came home and saw Biddle and the waste-paper basket and saw just what he had done. And this is another true story of the cat, Biddle Birdsall," ended daddy.

MARCH 30: The Squirrels' Spring Work

A LITTLE girl named Gwen had fixed a squirrel house on a pear tree near an old apple tree," said daddy. "Now, the apple tree was near Gwen's bedroom, and the squirrels could jump from the apple tree to her window-sill, where they were very likely to find nuts waiting for them.

"When the days began to get a little warmer Gwen hung just outside the window sill a little hammock and waited to see if the squirrels would dare to swing in it. Having all the nuts Gwen put on her window-sill and seeing her do such kind things so often made them pretty tame. And, too, they appeared to realize that it was Gwen who had seen to the building of the little house.

"But the hammock seemed very strange to them at first. However, one very brave squirrel thought he'd try it and jumped into the hammock. Gwen was watching back of a curtain, and it was all she could do to keep from crying aloud with joy, for she was so pleased that one of the squirrels was actually using her little hammock. After a while the other squirrels tried it.

"Before long one of the old squirrels began to scold for all he was worth. Oh, he was very much annoyed, and all the squirrels stopped swinging in the hammock. They seemed to be paying great attention to the old squirrel, and Gwen wondered what it was all about.

"The old squirrel was the leader, and he was the one who always gave the directions and did all the managing. This, in squirrel language, was what he said:

" 'Now, don't you know you can't spend all your time idling! You are the laziest lot of squirrels I have ever known. Don't you know that you must get to work? This is the season for us to tap the sirup from the maple trees, and you are spending your time swinging in a hammock. It is all very well to play, but then there is work to be done. We don't want to waste our time and let all the good sap go, do we? And you really do want the maple sirup, don't you?'

"Off they started to scamper to the nearest maple tree. Gwen put on her hat and coat and followed along to see what they were going to do. They got all the sap they wanted and smacked their lips over it. They enjoyed the work really, for it meant good times to follow, and they were glad the wise old squirrel had told them about it in plenty of time."

MARCH 31: The Bunch of Keys

THE keys were all talking in their jingling way. "I open a drawer in which birthday presents are locked up before the birthday has come," said one of the keys. "I know so many secrets, all about presents and nice things for celebrations."

"I open the cake tin," said another key, "and there is going to be a birthday cake to-morrow all decorated with candles. There is going to be a party."

"So I'll be used too," said the candy drawer key.

"And I will too," said the birthday drawer key.

"And I will too," said the key which opened the money box, "for some little treats will be bought."

"We'll jingle to-morrow, all right," said the keys in chorus, "for we are going to open up secrets and pleasures and treats for a birthday celebration."

And the keys all sang:

> "If you're a key, a key,
> You can see, can see,
> The opening of joys,
> For girls and for boys."

APRIL 1: Marketing

IT is surprising," said Mr. Robin, "how many creatures forget that they're not the only ones who go marketing.

"Ladies go to the shops and they think they're the only ones who see that their families are fed. But they're not at all. Now, all of the robins go a-marketing. We are very good at it. And most of the gentlemen birds do the marketing when the mother birds are watching over the eggs and the little birdlings."

"That is so," agreed Mrs. Robin; the dear father birds are splendid about looking after the food for the home when we're busy guarding the nests and seeing that the eggs hatch out into dear little birdlings.

"And you always know where to get the best worms."

"To be sure," said Mr. Robin, "and that is what I meant when I said that though we did not go to the same markets as people we went marketing, too.

"What a horrible thing it would be if people did come to the lawns and began digging up all the worms! Gracious, the poor birds would have a dreadful time!

"But they don't do that any more than we go to the grocery stores and tell the grocer to please do us up a package of potatoes and another of onions, and one more of meat which we'd order at the meat shop.

"It is fair the way things are divided up. In this way the lawns don't run short of worms as they otherwise might do."

APRIL 2: The Buds' Secrets

SOME of the tree buds," said daddy, "were talking about themselves softly. 'We do so enjoy being liked,' said the little bud which had grown the most. 'We love to be encouraged—helped along.'

" 'But how can any one help a bud?' asked a Fairy who happened along then.

" 'The Sun encourages us by shining and smiling at us. The South Wind whispers secrets to us and we are helped so much by the secrets—for the South Wind tells us such lovely things. And she promises us more sunshine, more warmth, more brightness. And then there are the Clouds and their promises. They tell us they will not forget about the April showers. They never have, and I don't believe they ever will.'

" 'And,' the bud continued, 'it is so glorious to burst into bud and bloom again after a long winter when the branches of the tree are bare that we like to do it slowly and enjoy every second of it. Besides, the tree has been so used to being lonely that it would be too much of a shock if we came forth all at once. We just peep forth first of all and tell the tree that we are coming, for spring is here.'

" 'Ah, how young I feel,' said a very little bud.

75

" 'We all feel so young, too,' said the other buds.

" 'You are all wonderfully young,' said the Fairy. 'You are buds, wonderful spring buds, and you'll soon be leaves !'

"The buds came forth a little more and smiled gently at the Fairy to show her how pleased they were at the kind things she was saying to them, and when they smiled a little more green showed.

"The grown-ups that day said, 'How far the buds came out to-day. They'll soon be leaves if they keep coming out at this rate.'

"But the little Fairy knew the secrets of the buds."

APRIL 3: The Clock and the Watch

NOW when I say," the watch began, "that I have to hurry and catch up—or rather try to catch up—I mean that my master has a foolish way of trying to hurry me up at the last moment. He waits and fusses and wastes his time, and then he wonders how he can reach somewhere on time—reaching there almost before he starts if he wants to be on time. Then I hurry and try to catch up to him as he seems in such a rush. And the trouble is I'm way ahead of the time he wants me to be. I try to keep up with his hurrying—for after he has wasted a great deal of time he does try to hurry. In fact he runs around all day trying to catch up with himself, and I run around with him. But it's of no use. He tried putting me way ahead of time one day not long ago, but it was senseless when I disagreed with every other watch, and every one said to my master, 'Your watch is fast.' We watches must agree, you know, and so I just get nervous trying to catch up with the lost moments for my master, and the only thing, I think, for him to do is to expect less of me and to start off everything ON TIME !"

APRIL 4: Billie's Springtime

I'D like to tell my story," said Billie to the Fairy Wondrous Secrets. "People are always wondering what babies think about and what they are planning to do when they grow up—if they are planning to do anything or not. They wonder so much about us, and so I'd like to tell my story. I don't know about other babies. But I would like to tell about myself, if no one minds."

"I'd like to hear," said the Fairy Wondrous Secrets.

Now Billie was in a baby-carriage which was out on the front porch of a little house in the country. Billie's mother was busy and so was Billie's daddy, but Billie, they knew, was quite safe in the carriage on the porch where the soft spring air was blowing.

No one was around but the Fairy Wondrous Secrets and if any one had come around the Fairy Wondrous Secrets would have vanished quickly.

"I'm really a little girl," Billie began, "though my name is something like a boy's name, I believe. You see my great big daddy's name is Bill and my mother wanted to name me after him. She couldn't have my real name Billie, but she had every one call me that, so it's my daytime every-day name, and my best, dress-up name is Mary Ann, or Marion or some such fine name after my mother.

"I came to the world in December," said Billie. "You see, Fairy, I thought it would be fun to arrive in the world when everything was so exciting. Christmas was coming on and it was very gay and merry.

"I've had a nice winter, but now is the best time I've known, for it's springtime. And I'll tell you, Fairy Wondrous Secrets, I feel as though it were all my own springtime.

"I feel the soft, warm wind blow over my little pink cheeks which every one admires so much and I smile and I croon and I make soft little singing sounds as the trees do. And I look around to smile at the trees and the bushes, too, and to let them see my blue eyes. I ask them if they think my eyes look like the blue sky, for the bushes and the trees are always looking up at the sky, so they should surely know.

"I can see the yellow forsythia upon the bushes, and how gay and lovely it is. The lilacs are in bud, and there are white blossoms on the bushes. Back of our house there are some waterfalls and they laugh and gurgle as they dash over the rocks, something the way I laugh and gurgle.

"I believe it is their way of kicking with fun. I kick with fun when my mother puts me in the wash-basin every morning. The wash-basin, Fairy Wondrous Secrets, is my bathtub, and I splash and kick and laugh and have such a good time! I don't care if the water spills over the floor any more than I imagine the waterfalls care that they spill water over the rocks. They enjoy it! So do I!

"I can see the ducks and hear them quack, quack. I hear that some-times they lay seven eggs a day. The chickens and the hens and the roosters walk about and chatter, and one day a lady passed and said 'Hello,' to a chicken and the chicken got up from the ground most politely as a mannerly person would do, I'm told.

"The pussy-willows are out and the skunk-cabbage is in bloom. There are red flowers and yellow flowers and little star flowers. The trees are full of buds or little leaves or blossoms of different colors.

There is a little turtle who is sunning himself by the brook near-by and who is an interesting creature, I have heard. He wears a shell over his back as I wear a little knitted jacket.

"At night I hear the crickets when I wake up for my bottle. And I believe these creatures all like the country, too. The chickens and the ducks say that in the cities they aren't wanted and they wouldn't be allowed to wander about, so they wouldn't leave the country for anything.

"And one evening I saw a moon in the sky. My daddy told me it was a moon and surely he knows! And over the moon there was a bright gold star, and I made a wish. This was my wish: that other babies might have happy homes as I have, where they don't want to cry, because there is no reason to cry. I'm well looked after, I'm never spoilt and they love me; so why should I cry? But what I'm thinking about mostly, these days, is of how lucky I am to have such a daddy and mother and to see the beautiful springtime in the country."

APRIL 5: Brenda's Easter Visit

"HER name is Brenda," said daddy, "and when I saw her yesterday she told me that every year at Easter time she went to the head nurse of the big hospital and found out the names of all the children. Then she went shopping, and it took her a long time to pick out things for little sick children. She picked out for each child a big round chocolate egg which rattled, for inside it there were little sugar candies; also a chocolate chicken and a chocolate bunny. She always picked out ones that had lots of expression too. Around the egg she tied a big red ribbon, around the chocolate chicken's neck she tied a bright green ribbon, and around the bunny's neck she tied a bright purple ribbon. Then she put them in a little box and wrote on the box the child's name.

"Last year Brenda went to the hospital the day before Easter. It was far from being a pleasant day. There was a cold wind in the air and no sun.

"She arrived at the hospital just as all the little children had had their wounds dressed. They were lying in their little white cots trying to keep back the tears that wanted to come.

"Brenda asked the nurse if she could go inside with the gifts.

" 'Yes, indeed!' said the nurse. 'The children would love that. The child's name in the first cot,' continued the nurse very softly, 'is Elsa. She has hurt her back, and no one knows how long she will have to lie there.'

" 'Elsa,' said Brenda, 'happy Easter. A little chocolate bunny, a little chocolate chicken and a big chocolate egg all said they wanted to wish you a happy Easter.'

"Elsa opened her half shut eyes and clutched the box. She opened it eagerly. There they all were! And the chocolate bunny did have the funniest expression! He would have made any one laugh, and his purple ribbon bow was sticking way up on one side with such a saucy expression. Elsa burst out laughing. Afterward the nurse told Brenda it was the first time she'd seen Elsa laugh since she'd been brought to the hospital.

"Then Brenda took the rest of her boxes around to all the other little sick children. And such happiness as there was in the ward!"

APRIL 6: An Uninvited Guest

THE children were just finishing their lunches which they had been eating in the school yard and were going back to their classes when what should they see but a bear!

"Oh, oh, hurry, scurry, run, run," they all cried.

"Oh, what an escape!" some of them panted, when they were safe in a nice big barn down the road.

But the bear was having the time of his life.

"Well, well, well," he growled, "I really don't understand it at all. Children come to the circus and gaze and gaze at us, and tell their mothers and their daddies how nice they think we are. But how they did run! And I had come to pay them a nice call.

"Sniff-sniff, what is it I smell?" continued the bear. And then he jumped around for joy. "Goodies! Food! Wonderful, wonderful food! How kind of the dear little children. They really expected me to lunch—for they've left lots of food—and when I came they didn't want to make me uncomfortable by watching me eat.

"Ah, now, I have had a fine meal, a luxurious meal, fit for a king— no, fit for a bear!" And the bear rubbed his front paw over his well-filled tummy and again growled delightedly to himself some more, saying over and over again: "Delicious; such a meal!"

But along came the keeper of the animals of the circus and led the bear back to his cage. For a circus was traveling through the country and when they had stopped for a rest this bear had escaped. But what a tale he had to tell when he got back to the circus again!

APRIL 7: The Tired Honeysuckle

"I'M very tired," said the Honeysuckle, "and I'd really almost rather not come up this spring."

"But you are supposed to come up every year," said the Hyacinth. "You are like me, my dear: your roots are good and lasting. We don't have to be replanted from seeds every spring."

"Yes, what you say is perfectly true," said the Honeysuckle. "But then I am old, so very, very old."

"How old are you?" whispered the Hyacinth in a very low voice which the Wind carried on his shoulders.

"I am so many years old I can't remember. This garden I've heard people say has been kept just like this for over a hundred years, and the house near-by is just as old—in fact, it is older. I've been here a very large part of that time."

"Well," said the Hyacinth, "then I don't blame you for feeling tired. I should think you would want to rest. Let them start another Honeysuckle growing. You've worked hard enough."

"Ah," said the Honeysuckle, "that's just what you don't understand. I am tired, very tired. But ah, I must blossom because of the people."

"What people?" asked the Hyacinth.

"The people in this house. You see, I am just outside a window, growing on my vine, and my sweet fragrance can be carried indoors. Of course yours can, too, dear old Hyacinth, though you aren't so old, are you? But I last all through the summer, and you are just a glorious spring flower."

"Then it's no wonder you get tired out. And you have to give the bumblebees honey. Your honey is very fine, I have heard."

"And don't forget the humming-birds," said the Honeysuckle. "They love me every bit as much as the bumblebees do. And I love them too! The little dears! But I must tell you the reason why I come up each year, even though sometimes it seems so hard.

"Years and years ago I was planted by a little girl—a little girl, Mary Alice, who loved flowers and who could always make them grow. And above all the flowers she loved her red Honeysuckle best of all. She watched over me. She gave me drinks. She dug up the earth around my roots. She made me so comfortable. And for a very special occasion she would pluck off a spray of my red blossoms and wear them.

"Now Mary Alice grew up to be a big lady—though she was never very big. She always seemed like a little girl to me, for she was so dainty, so small and so lovely. Her eyes were very blue and her hair very golden. But as the years went by each spring I noticed that silver was growing in her hair, and then one spring I saw that it was quite white.

"During all this time there were other little children growing up —and now there are some more. And I always saw my little girl— for I thought of her as that even when she was quite, quite old—smiling at all the little faces, and the children would smile at her—never scowls—always smiles. Somehow no one could have scowled at Mary Alice, and I don't believe she ever scowled at any one. For when her hair was white, her forehead had no wrinkles.

"Every spring she would be waiting for me. 'There comes my honeysuckle,' she would say. The last few years it has been very hard to come up. My roots have lost their strength, but I have come along as best I could, for I have thought of Mary Alice and her smiles.

"Last year she was sitting by her window and looking out at me. 'That honeysuckle is as old as I am,' she said.

"And not long after that I missed seeing dear little old-young Mary Alice and her smiles when I wafted my fragrance through her window.

"But one day I saw the other people of the house and the children, too, looking at me. 'The honeysuckle that she loved,' they said. 'Oh we hope it will keep on coming up each year, for it reminds us so of her. But it looks pretty old now.'

"So you see, little Hyacinth, I must come up, even though I am so very tired and old!"

APRIL 8: The Flower Parade

WE'LL tell you a story," said the white lilac bush while the purple and Persian lilac bushes listened as did the garden flowers.

"We'd like to hear a story," the fairies said.

"You see," said the white lilac bush, we are all a part of the great Flower Parade. When the snow leaves the ground the crocus flowers appear and take the lead in the parade. They are like the drum-major who leads the procession, but instead of tossing a fancy stick into the air, they lift up their little heads and tell the world that spring has come.

"Next follow the hyacinths, the tulips, daffodils, narcissus flowers, garden violets, pansies, and little daisies. They all are about in the same part of the parade. And when they come we appear too, as well as the flowering almond shrubs and many others.

"But the pansies, little daisies and garden violets blossom all through the season, so they're like the small boys who run along by the side of the parade—almost anywhere, at any time.

"And after we go the flowers will still keep on parading. The lilies-of-the-valley are marching now, and soon the dear forget-me-nots with their blue, blue eyes will come.

"The rockets, peonies, honeysuckles and roses all will follow along, making a very handsome part of the parade. And later on the phlox, larkspur so blue, and foxglove will follow.

"These are the flowers that come up year after year and they are the ones which belong to the great Flower Parade. It takes a whole spring and summer and early autumn to see the whole parade. But it's worth seeing, and though we can't be here all the time, we're glad for our part of the parade—we are."

And the fairies knew that the lilac bush was right and a parade of gorgeous garden flowers would continue all summer.

APRIL 9: The Big Parade

I WANT to tell you of a parade which took place some time ago," said daddy.

"After many bands had gone by, many soldiers, and many sailors, a wagon drawn by four big horses came along, and upon the wagon was an enomous cage. In this cage were homing pigeons.

"On the side of the wagon was written a little story about the pigeons, telling how they had taken messages through all sorts of dangers, how brave they had been, how clever, and how they had thought of their duty and not of themselves.

"And when that wagon passed along carrying the homing pigeons every one clapped, for here were little dumb creatures who had shown a wonderful understanding and had done all they could for the country, and the little pigeons were so modest that they actually wondered what all this excitement was about!"

APRIL 10: The Alphabet Letters

MY story is a very sad and sorrowful one. If I tell it to you it will make you cry," said the letter Z.

"Alphabet letters don't cry," said the letter S. "Tears are shed over us, but we don't cry ourselves. So tell us your sad and sorrowful story, Mr. Z."

"Tell us the sad and sorrowful story," repeated the other alphabet letters.

"It shows I have a good disposition," said the letter Z. "I'm neither angry nor cross."

"There, there," said the letter S. "You used me twice in that last word, which was all very well, but you need not have brought in that word angry, for angry and cross mean the same."

"All right," said the letter Z. "I do so little work these days that I really feel as if I didn't know anything."

"Poor letter Z," the other letters all said.

"Tell us your story," said the letter S.

"I will," agreed the letter Z.

"Pray do," the others urged.

"It's the letter S which has caused the trouble," said the letter Z.

The letter S wiggled and wriggled and twisted and turned and said:

"I beg you pardon, letter Z. I am sure I have meant no harm."

"None at all," said the letter Z. "I know you have meant no harm. And you needn't beg my pardon, for it isn't your fault. You can't rule teachers and parents and writers and students. You do what you can for them, that is all.

"But think about it, letters, and you will understand. Just think of the number of words which used to need my letter in them and now they have put the letter S in instead."

"Yes," said the letter M, "that is true, and we can think about these things now, for it is recess time."

"Think of all the words which end with the letters 'ise.' They used to end with the letters 'ize.' "

"True," said the alphabet letters; "perfectly true."

"You're sure you are not angry with me?" asked the letter S, wriggling nervously.

"Quite true," said the letter Z. "As I said before, it is not your fault. But isn't my tale a sad and sorrowful one?"

"It is," said the other letters.

But just then up spoke the letter S and the letter I and the letter E.

"Letter Z," they said, "come and join us or we won't be a word. We need you, letter Z; we must have you."

So the letter Z joined these three letters and they all jumped around as the word SIZE appeared, as you have doubtless already guessed.

"You're all very good to me," said the letter Z as it played around with the letters S and I and E. Each one kept its own place in the word, but sometimes they made themselves look very big and sometimes they made themselves look very small and sometimes they made themselves look just about medium size. For, as they made up the word size, and as size can be small—small size, you know—or big, they did everything they could and played all the games they could.

Then other letters formed other words and they played around, just as they should have played to show folks what they meant. You can imagine what a wonderful time the letters F and U and N had.

"Hurry, hurry," said the letter S. "All the big S letters and all the little S letters. Hurry now to the class rooms."

"I don't have to hurry much," said the letter Z, "but I will either live to a very old age from being lazy and doing nothing to tire myself, or else I'll be forgotten entirely."

"Oh, no, you won't be forgotten," said the other alphabet letters.

"We'll see to that," said the letters A and B and C. "We have a great deal to do with schools and lessons, you know, and we will keep you with us, never fear."

"Thank you, thank you," said the letter Z, as it twisted itself slowly back into the school rooms.

And the letter S said: "Thank you for not being angry with me. You're a good sport, letter Z."

APRIL 11: The Scissor-Tailed Flycatcher

T HE Scissor-Tailed Flycatcher," said daddy, "is known by such a name because he has a very long tail which is very much the shape of a pair of scissors. In fact, his tail is like two tails which open and shut as one would open and close a pair of scissors.

"He opens and closes his scissor-like tail when he does his marketing just as ladies would open and close their purses after they had bought something.

"His home is a very large nest, and it is made of anything at all— grass and bits of cloth and strings and bits of twigs. In fact, he is very good natured.

"Mrs. Scissor-Tailed Flycatcher has a happy time with such a pleasant mate and she is pleasant herself which makes them both happy.

"The event of her life is hatching time. When she is sitting on four whitish-brown eggs which will soon be little scissor-tailed fly-catchers she is as happy as a bird can be, and that is pretty happy, as you can imagine.

"I am going to tell you now about Mr. Scissor-Tailed Flycatcher and his talk to an insect.

" 'Little insect,' said Mr. Scissor-Tailed Flycatcher, 'I am very well named. I am called a flycatcher and I catch flies. But I don't only catch flies. I catch other insects as well.'

"But the insect heard no more for he had scampered away from the Flycatcher."

APRIL 12: The Woodpecker Band

COME on, come on, join the band! Rehearsals to begin this morning! Get in practise! Lose no time! We're ready, and we hope you'll be ready too. First practise to start in half an hour."

Now the woodpeckers were the ones who had been talking. They were already starting to practise by drumming on the bark of the trees. The trees are the drums and the woodpeckers all beat the drums. Of course a great deal of the time they work hard at the trees, burrowing for insects, and they help to destroy many bad ones.

But some time before Mr. Hairy Woodpecker had suggested they should start a band. The drums were played by Mr. Hairy Woodpecker, Mr. Red-Headed Woodpecker, Mr. Downy Woodpecker, Mr. Sapsucker, Mr. Crested Woodpecker and Mr. Flicker Woodpecker.

Those who sang and helped along the chorus and played little mouth-organs and various instruments made out of twigs were the warblers, the vireos, goldfinches, mocking-birds, bobolinks, chickadees, pewees, phoebes, orioles, thrushes, song-sparrows and whippoorwills. And of course, almost the most important of all were the robins!

Mr. Robin Redbreast was the leader of the band. He waved a little stick in front of the band-stand, which was up in a tree.

How they all did play and sing. Now in a great many bands, in fact in most bands, they do not have singing, but in the woodpecker's band it is entirely different.

What would a band be like in birdland without singing? They would miss all the beautiful songsters who would add so much music, and that would be such a pity.

So the woodpeckers were wise indeed when they asked the song birds to join in the band.

They practised all that day for the coming concert. And before they went to bed that night and before they even thought of putting their heads under their wings, they sent around notices to all the birds to be on hand, and this is how the notices read: "First concert of the season to be given by the Woodpeckers' Band to-morrow at sunrise. Mr. Robin Redbreast will conduct."

The concert was a huge success and the people said, "It's really and truly the springtime when we have a concert such as we were given this morning!"

APRIL 13: The Tease

"G RACE," said daddy, "had a brother named Edward, and Edward was a tease; not a nice, good-natured, funny sort of a tease, but he was the kind who hurt people's feelings. He would see some one who had a suit on which was not new, or which had been patched, and he would try to make the one who was wearing it feel very uncomfortable.

"Edward would also see boys wearing their older brothers' suits, and he would say with a mean look: 'Where did you get that suit?'

"And—he also liked to tease Grace by making fun of her doll Gracie and by tossing her up in the air, and playing with her as though she were a ball, and he could bat her in a game of his own mean making.

"Oh, how she would feel when Gracie was lifted up into Edward's hands, and then he would toss her up and say:

"'What's the difference? She's only made of rags. Why do you care? Gracie doesn't.' One day he left the doll high up in a tree out in the yard, and Grace was afraid that more snow would come in the night and that it would spoil her beloved Gracie, for there had been a late snow-storm that day.

"But a boy, a friend of Edward's, who didn't think Edward was really much of a boy for teasing Grace in that horrid way, had found Grace crying. He found out what the trouble was, and he got Gracie from the high limb of the tree.

"Edward didn't know that his friend had brought down the doll, and at night when he slept, lo and behold, Gracie seemed to come and stand at the end of his bed.

"But no longer was Gracie a little rag doll. She had grown, oh, she had grown. And she was wearing instead of a painted wig, great icicles which were so heavy and cold looking.

"Her body seemed very stiff and straight. It seemed very strong, and as if she were made of steel or of iron instead of rags.

"'Edward,' she said, and her voice seemed harsh and terrible, 'Edward,' she continued, 'you left me out in the snow to-night, so as to tease your little sister. But now I will show you what it is like to be abused. Even if you don't actually hurt me, you hurt your sister who loves me. Wait and I will show you.'

"'Oh, don't,' shrieked Edward. He was very cowardly when he was going to be teased, you see. 'I'll be good. I promise,' and his voice sounded thoroughly frightened.

"'I'll have to show you first,'" said the doll. She took Edward in her arms, which had grown so big and so hard, and she tossed him up in the air and around and about, so that he was frightened any moment he might land on the ground.

"And Edward thought of the doll outside—he thought she still was there, and oh, he was so sorry, but he never again made Grace miserable by teasing Gracie."

APRIL 14: The Onion's Speech

THE vegetables were talking in the cellar," said daddy, "and I must confess that they were boasting a great deal. But still one can forgive a vegetable for boasting very often, for if we lived so near the ground—or in the ground as they do—we'd probably like to pretend we were higher up! The onion was now talking. 'I came from the Land of the Pyramids originally. My ancient home was in Egypt, far, far across the water, in a wonderful, ancient part of the world that is full of history and interest and beauty.'

" 'Hear! Hear!' said all the other vegetables.

" 'I myself have never seen that far land,' continued the onion, 'but my family came from there at first, way, way back where the family tree first starts from.'

" 'How can you have a family tree when you're an onion and not even a branch?' asked a very plain little potato.

" 'People,' said the onion haughtily, 'have family trees, and they aren't branches, nor are they leaves. Family trees mean ancestors, noble grandfathers and aristocratic grandmothers, high-up great aunts, and snobbish great uncles. A family tree is something every one and everything can't have. Now you, poor potato, haven't a family tree at all.'

"But the potato didn't seem to mind in the least. However, the onion went on talking. 'Now my young friend, the radishes came first from China—an interesting history has the Radish family. The Horse-Chestnut family came from Asia, and the Mulberry trees from Persia. The Cucumbers came from the East Indies, and the Spinach family came first from Arabia.'

" 'How very fine,' said the potato in a very sarcastic tone of voice.

" 'You're right,' said the onion, not noticing the sarcastic voice; it's very fine to have a family tree. It's something, as I said before, that every one can't have. You never came from afar, Mr. Potato. And neither did the oats, corn, pumpkins and other plain creatures who don't know what aristocracy and grandeur mean.'

" 'What does it mean?' asked the potato.

" 'You weren't paying attention,' said the onion. 'It means a family tree and noble grandparents.'

" 'Pooh!' exclaimed the potato. 'If a vegetable isn't good itself it makes no difference where it came from nor what its grandparents were. It's what a vegetable is itself. Suppose I were a bad potato, which I'm not, I'm thankful to say, would it make any difference because my great-great-grandfather had come from some interesting land across the sea? Not in the least. I'm a good useful vegetable and can be cooked in many ways. That's what counts in this world. To amount to something yourself. Be a real vegetable! Do what you can to nourish the world! Don't boast!'

"The onion felt very badly. It had been so proud of its fine history, and often it was unhappy because it was so unkindly talked about.

" 'I try to be good,' said the onion. 'I season things and I make many good dishes. I do the best I can.'

" 'Of course you do, little onion,' said the potato. 'But next time you make a speech, tell us all to do our best and not boast about what others have done or have been.'

"And the onion always made speeches after that which were not about family trees, and when it was finally cooked every one said: 'What a nice onion must have been put in this soup.' "

APRIL 15: A Bookworm

I TRIED cork biting once," said one bookworm to another bookworm.

"And yet," said the other bookworm, "you are known as 'The Bookworm' by some people who don't know much."

"That is not a great complaint," said the first bookworm, "to be called 'The Bookworm' by people who don't know much. I love books, but I don't care for reading. That might sound strange to some folks, but the bookworm families know that being a bookworm doesn't mean reading words. Once I went through each page of each book along on the shelf in just the very same spot, so that they could have put a ribbon or a string or anything they might have had near at hand through all those many holes and hung the books up instead of standing them on the shelves. I thought they might care to change the books a little, so I did my best to help. That certainly makes me deserve my name!"

APRIL 16: The Wild Black Cherry

"THE wild black cherry tree is very handsome," said daddy. "Its foliage is something like that of the willow, drooping and looking very dainty and lovely. Its bark is rich and soft, but best of all, is the fruit which is used for making all sorts of delicious goodies, especially wild cherry juice!

"Then medicines and tonics have been made from the fruit and bark and roots of the wild black cherry.

"Cherry-wood is considered by many people to be almost as handsome as rosewood and mahogany, and the old wild black cherry tree is the tree which is used to make beautiful cherry-wood furniture.

"Its cousin, the wild cherry, is greatly enjoyed by birds who simply love to eat the little fruits.

"Another cousin, the choke-cherry, is a tree filled with very bitter fruit but the birds like the choke-cherry trees almost as well as any other and flock about any they may find. The fashionable and rich cousin is the sweet cherry which is cultivated in this country. And these are the cherries which we all like to eat best."

APRIL 17: Spring Blossoms

"HOW do you feel?" asked the first apple blossom of a pear blossom on one of the other trees in the orchard.

"Splendidly," said the pear blossom. "How about yourself?"

"Never better," said the apple blossom. Now when the other pear blossoms and apple blossoms heard these two talking they all wanted to see what was going on.

And before long they were all out talking and chatting while some of them were having games with the Breeze Brothers who blew them to the ground and made it look as if the snow had come again.

"Did your tree have a secret to whisper to you?" asked the first apple blosssom.

"Yes," answered the first pear blossom. "I was just about to ask you the same question."

"It's this way with us," said the first apple blossom. "You see the farmhouse is very shabby. It has been needing a coat of paint for so many years. And the people who live inside are so poor they can't afford anything they don't actually need.

"They feel badly that they cannot afford to have their house painted for it would look so much brighter and prettier.

"Well, it has been this same way for so many, many years, as I said before. And they have had bad luck with the potatoes and the corn every year. Something always happens. Bugs eat up the potatoes and a storm is likely to come and hurt the corn just when it would be growing quite perfect.

"All these things my tree whispered and said, 'Little blossoms, all of you must be beautiful so for one season in the year the people in the farmhouse will think they have the loveliest of homes. Make their dingy home look like a fairyland.'" And once again the blossoms gave joy to the people in the dingy farmhouse, who every year had the most beautiful place owing to the blossoms.

APRIL 18: The Button Bag

IN a work bag," said daddy, "there lived a button bag. The button bag was made of blue and white cambric, I believe you call it, and it had a blue silk ribbon around it at the top—I suppose a sort of neck-tie, one might say.

"At any rate, in this bag were loads and loads of buttons. The button bag was a very large button bag, and the work bag was a very large work bag.

"Whenever any one wanted a button, or whenever any one said they had lost a button or that a button was off, the work bag was taken out and then a button was found—always a button for everything that needed a button.

"And when any member of the household wanted to do a little mending, for everything that lacked a button there was always found to be one.

"What did the buttons and the button bag have to say to all this? Were they pleased they were so useful? We shall hear.

" 'When is the party going to be?' asked the big, white button, with the shining face.

" 'Pretty soon,' said the little green button, 'pretty soon.'

" 'I've been to lots of parties,' said a button with a funny little face, a face of some old, old knight or lord or something very noble!

"He had two sisters and a brother and the four of them were all just alike. They had never been used, as nothing had ever come up that needed their time and their presence. They had been in the button bag for years. But, of course, they were kept, for there might be a time, no one knows when or how soon, when the buttons with the faces might be just the ones wanted.

" 'It's so nice,' said the one who had just spoken, 'that we are always sure of a home. It's so nice. Some would throw us away and would say they had no use for a lot of old buttons taking up roon when they were about sure we'd never be used.

"'But we don't have to worry, for the mistress of the house who owns the work bag and the button bag and all the buttons, always says that we don't eat or drink, meaning we don't cost her any money, and we might be useful some time.

"'She's a sensible lady, yes she is. And we're sure of a home, quite sure of one.

"'But as I said I have been to a great many parties. Although I have lived in the button bag such a long time, once I lived on a handsome dress, oh, such a handsome dress, and then I went to great balls and parties and all.'

"'Ah,' said a big black button, 'I've had a nice life, too. I've lived on fur coats. I've been on several, and I've been out on glorious bracing winter days when the snow came in my face and body all at once!

"'I've been for sleigh-rides where bells jingled and where my button heart leaped for joy!'

"'And I,' said a little brown button, 'have on the other hand been about in the summer. I belonged to a lovely bathing suit which belonged to a little girl, and I used to see the sand made into castles and bridges and rivers, and all sorts of marvelous things, and the lovely ocean would go over me—oh, it was so cool and refreshing!

"'And all about me were happy, smiling people. Every one was shrieking with delight. If I had known how to shriek I would have called at the top of my voice, if I had a voice:

"' "Oh, the button is happy, too, the button is so happy!" '

"'Well,' said the tan button, we must get ready for the party, as we must frolic all night and then be back in our places by morning, so it won't confuse or mix any one up who may sew in the morning.'

"'Right,' said all the buttons.

"So they all borrowed old pieces of ribbon from the bag and little pieces of thread, and they dressed themselves in fine array, and then they danced and sang in their little button voices, which, of course, aren't real voices, but only make-believe ones. This was their song:

"'The buttons are we, happy, gleeful and glad;
We are of all kinds and we never are sad.
We love those who use us and even those who do not;
Ah, yes, indeed, we're a merry, merry lot!'"

APRIL 19: The Patient Chimpanzee

CHARLIE was the name of a chimpanzee in the Zoo," said daddy, "and he was ill. The keeper went to Charlie with a medicine bottle, carrying a glass and a spoon, too.

" 'I am sorry, Charlie,' said the keeper, and from the look Charlie gave him he knew he understood.

" 'Good chimpanzee,' said the keeper. 'You fine, patient animal. You teach us all a lesson—all of us—for none of us take medicine well, neither children nor even grown-ups.'

"The chimpanzee swallowed the medicine. He tried very hard not to make a face as he did so, but he took it all—every drop—and then he tried to lie quite still. For it was such horrid tasting medicine.

"The keeper still stood by Charlie with the empty glass and bottle in his hand. Then he put them down and took Charlie's head and stroked it again and again.

"Charlie nudged up against the keeper.

" 'You will make me well, keeper,' he seemed to say. 'It is not your fault you had to give me the horrid medicine. Dear keeper, you know that by to-morrow I will be feeling like my old self again.' For monkeys and chimpanzees are the most patient creatures when they are sick."

APRIL 20: The Toad

A TOAD," said daddy, "was once sent all the way in a little box from one side of this continent to the other to be the pet of a little sick boy named Paul.

"He was a horned toad, and he was the kind of a toad that needs little else beside air to live on.

"Now, the toad seemed to know he must behave on the journey and he was carried in a little box with air holes punched through it. Of course he needed the air more than anything, and wasn't he happy when at last he arrived, and could have all the air he wanted. And when Paul saw him he knew from the toad's honest, ugly face he would be loyal and good, and a real pet.

APRIL 21: The Pine Needles

I MUST thread my needle before I begin my work," said a little girl as she sat under a big pine tree, with another little girl. "What's that I hear?" asked one of the pine needles. "She speaks about threading her needle? Am I her needle, or are you her needle, or who in the world is her needle? And what is thread?"

The poor needles were very nervous. And the other little girl spoke next: "I like to knit better than I do to sew because then I can use four needles."

"Oh, dear, oh dear," said the pine needles. "There's a child who needs four needles. Do you suppose she threads us too?"

They watched for a long time, trying to move away from the children so they would not be used. They whispered to the pine tree saying:

> "Blow about and move us away,
> Sway, swing, swing and sway.
> For we've just this minute heard it said,
> That into needles they will put thread."

And the pine tree whispered to the breeze:

> "Blow, blow, make me sway,
> So I can move the needles away.
> Please, Mr. Wind, would you mind
> Doing this act so very kind?"

So the wind blew the pine tree and the pine tree's branches swayed and blew about the little pine needles. But no sooner had all this happened than they saw that the children had other things called needles. They hadn't wanted pine needles at all!

APRIL 22: The Cat's Mistake

A S I don't think you will be able to guess right away and as I want to tell you what really happened, I will tell you the place Blackie the cat chose for his nap one Sunday.

It was in the church organ! Well, he had a fine sleep. And he was still asleep when the organist came in and began to play.

Then poor Blackie woke up with a start! At first he didn't know whether he was having a nightmare or a bad dream, or what was happening.

He moved to one side and the organ gave a curious rumble and a very funny sound and the organist looked as if he didn't know what the trouble could be, and the people stopped singing and then tried to go on singing without any music.

The organist tried to play again and this awfully queer rumble and burr and buzz was heard once more. So the people went on finishing their singing without any organ.

Of course Blackie tried to move when he felt the pedals moving and he jumped over the inside stops and pedals and made these very strange sounds as he did so.

The organist looked inside the organ and saw nothing. Then, suddenly, he saw two big green eyes staring at him.

"It's a cat in there," he said to himself.

Poor Blackie was very much frightened. This was altogether too much. He liked adventures and he liked to explore but this was going too far.

"Yes, that is a cat," said the organist to himself, and Blackie's green eyes shone back at him when he said this.

"Come, pussy; come, nice pussy," said the organist in a whisper. Poor Blackie was so frightened he did not know what to do. Still the organist kept on coaxing and begging Blackie to come out. And after a while Blackie felt less frightened and the soft whisper of the organist sounded very kind and Blackie came out from inside of the church organ.

Oh, how happy he was when he was out and the organist got a little boy to lift him quietly and take him out of the church.

And what joy it was for Blackie to be back home again, to rest and have a nice sleep after his adventure, which had turned out to be such a mistake!

APRIL 23: The Butterfly Who Loved the Sun

I SAW a little boy to-day," said daddy, "named Robert who has a collection of cocoons. He keeps them on little twigs in a great big box punched full of holes.

"Then he waits to see the butterflies come out. After they have come out he never kills them or tries to keep them, for he thinks that is dreadfully cruel. He knows well that they love to see the sun and be out in the fresh air among the flowers, and he wouldn't deprive them of that pleasure for anything.

94

"But one day about a week ago out from a cocoon came the most beautiful pale blue butterfly Robert had ever seen.

"He at once took it out of the box, and off it flew into the warm sun's rays and lighted upon a small bush which was covered with plum-blossoms and the butterfly acted as if it thought, 'Well, this may be my first party, but it certainly won't be my last.'"

APRIL 24: The Horse-Chestnut

I'D like to know," said Fairy Ybab, of a magnificent tree which was one mass of huge blossoms, "why you are called the Horse-Chestnut tree? You aren't eaten by horses, are you? You don't look like a horse."

The Horse-Chestnut gave a funny low, whispering laugh.

"I will explain," said the Horse-Chestnut. "You see, there are some creatures who have engagements all the time. They have to meet a friend at such and such a time or they have to be back for dinner at such a time or they must be in bed at such another time.

"Now, the trees are different. We haven't any engagements like that. We trees don't have to go anywhere at all. In fact, we can't go anywhere. We're perfectly satisfied, too.

"You've never heard of a tree pulling itself up by the roots and crying out in a hoarse, leafy way:

"'Dear me, I do want to go to a birthday party.'

"In the first place of all I am called a Horse-Chestnut tree because I have marks between my leaves and twigs which look like horseshoes with nails in them.

"That is the answer to the first question. And the answer to the second question is this: No, I am not eaten by horses. My nuts are much too bitter. Children like to play with them, for they're big and handsome, but they're not good to eat.

"There are your two questions answered."

APRIL 25: The Loving Mates

A LITTLE bird had lost her mate," said daddy, "and was very sad. A sudden storm had come up when she was out, but when the storm blew over she found her way back to the dear mate who was looking for her.

95

" 'T-r-i-l-l, t-r-i-l-l,' her little mate cried, and trembled with joy.
" 'My little mate, my loving little mate,' she said in her bird language as she gave him a kiss with her little beak.
"And then such a song! Such a song as has seldom been heard before was sung by that happy bird to his little loving mate."

APRIL 26: The Dandelion

TWO children were walking," said daddy. "One of them stopped to pick some dandelions.
" 'I love these yellow flowers,' said the little girl. 'No one scolds when you pick them. I've never owned a garden. But I always get these flowers every spring. And, oh, how I love them! Dear, soft, yellow posies,' she said.
"This was many years ago but from that day the dandelion's family have always come up in the spring."

APRIL 27: Butterfly's Growth

A BUTTERFLY lays an egg on a leaf," said daddy. "In a little while the egg becomes a caterpillar. And what do you suppose the caterpillar has for its very first meal?"
Both the children shook their heads.
"It eats some of the shell from which it came. It's a little like moving out of a house and before leaving it entirely, eating it up!
"Then the caterpillar becomes a chrysalis and soon a butterfly. It's a happy day for the caterpillar when it becomes a beautiful butterfly. No longer will people call it a horrid caterpillar. They will say, 'Look at the beautiful butterfly!'
"And as the butterfly sips from the little flowers and enters right into the hearts of many of them, it whispers:
" 'I've been a long time coming to you, flower, but the hard crawling journey had a wonderful ending.'
"And though the flower does not altogether understand, it partly does, for it whispers: 'Eat all of my honey and sip my sweetness, for you are my beautiful butterfly visitor!' "

APRIL 28: The Tack and the Nail

I HEARD something far from pleasant about you, little Tack," said the big Nail.

There were many other tacks in the box, but there were also many nails. They were all together in one big white box, and whichever size was wanted could be picked from the lot.

But the Nail which was the biggest of all, or about the biggest, was talking to the Tack which was about the smallest of all the tacks in this big box.

"Well, I suppose you want me to ask you what it is," said the Tack, moving a little in the box.

"You needn't ask me if you don't want to," said the Nail haughtily.

"But of course I want to; that is only natural," said the Tack.

"I thought you would want to," said the Nail, in a hard, metallic voice. Now a metallic voice is a voice which sounds as hard and cold as any metal could be. Of course that was the natural sort of voice for a nail to have—still it was not a very cheerful voice to hear.

"The Master said that he had kept forgetting things all day long. And then he said that he had a head like a tack."

"Well, what of it?" asked the Tack. "Is that all?"

"That's all, little Tack," said the Nail. "Isn't that enough?"

"I don't think that was so dreadful," said the Tack.

"Perhaps you don't understand," said the Nail.

"Perhaps not," the Tack agreed.

"I'd better make sure you understand and so I will tell you. The Master meant that his head was so small and stupid that he couldn't remember anything, and when he said that his family told him he mustn't talk so about himself. There, little Tack, you see you have a little stupid head. No head at all, and because it's such a poor head they've made that sad saying about it. There was never such a thing said of a Nail."

"Maybe not," said the Tack angrily, "but I can hang just as many pictures as you can. Maybe you are used for big pictures but I am used for small ones—nice little favorites, photographs and so forth. I'm just as useful in my way. Just as useful," the Tack repeated.

"But what is more," the Tack continued, "I have very little use for you in saying such a thing. You are supposed to be a friend of mine. A nail is a sort of relation of a tack. I don't blame the people for saying such things. In their opinion my head is very small, and quite rightly too, and I have not the things they call brains—neither have you. So I don't blame them in the least.

"But I blame you, Nail, for coming and telling me something to make me unhappy. It's not doing me any good. I can't change my head.

You're just like a creature who wants to be praised because you didn't say the mean thing yourself; but you did worse than that—you repeated it. Bah!" The Tack moved away disgusted, and the Nail moved far to one side of the box, feeling much ashamed.

APRIL 29: Moon's Misunderstanding

A RE you sad, Mr. Moon?" asked the Fairy Queen. "I feel that something is the matter with you. You don't seem to be yourself to-night. Won't you tell us the trouble?"

"I heard you say that once in a blue moon, you liked to have a banquet, and I thought perhaps you knew of another moon, and wanted him to shine for you. I'm not blue—that is I'm not really blue, though now I do feel blue, blue and very sad."

"Oh, Mr. Moon," said the Fairy Queen, "I am so glad you told me what the trouble was, for if you hadn't told me we might have had a very sad misunderstanding.

"Of course we didn't want another moon, and there is no other moon but you, dear Mr. Moon.

"When people say, 'Once in a blue moon,' they mean 'Once in a great while.' They don't mean that they want a blue moon, and can only give such a party when there is a blue moon, or whatever they are planning to give or do.

"Now we are going to have a banquet, and I meant that I thought it was nice to have a banquet once in a great while. That was a silly saying I used, that's all."

"I'm so relieved," said Mr. Moon, smiling once more. "I never heard of another moon, but of course how was I to be sure? Such wonderful things happen all the time. People fly up in the air in planes, and behave just like birds. So I wasn't sure whether there was another moon or not, and thought perhaps this fellow was blue. Being blue in color and feeling blue in spirits are different— eh?"

"Quite different," said the Fairy Queen. "You don't feel blue now, do you?" And as the moon grinned happily the Fairy Queen knew that everything was all right, and a banquet took place in Fairyland that night.

APRIL 30: Marion's Fern Garden

MARION had a little shady flower bed. Every spring at just about this time she would go into the woods with a trowel and basket and pick out the loveliest ferns. These she would carry home in her basket. Then in the shady afternoon she would go to her fernery with a watering pot. First she would dig a little hole, then she would put some water in it to see that the roots of the fern got plenty of moisture, for that is what ferns love. Then she would put the root of the fern in the hole and put soft earth firmly around it. After she had planted her ferns she watered them some more, for she was very careful that her ferns should be planted just right, and that is why she had such good luck with them.

Every spring she would add to her fernery, and the ferns that she had planted the year before came up more beautifully than ever.

She would get interesting looking rocks and stones and put them between ferns here and there in the little fernery. It was very delightful to see the plants come up in the spring and then go to the woods and get some more beautiful ones. She was very particular, you may be sure, to get nice young ones, for they are the best to transplant.

MAY 1: The Tree Swallows

THE Mr. Tree Swallows are bluish green above and white underneath. The Mrs. Tree Swallows are gray and white beneath," said daddy.

"Sometimes they build their nests out of grass with feathers for the lining; in fact, that is the way they usually do, but they sometimes like to find bird homes already made for them.

They sing or make a little chirping sound as their other swallow cousins do. They usually build their nests in hollow trees and like to sit on old branches, so they have been called the Tree Swallows, for their cousins, the Barn Swallows, build their homes around barns.

"These swallows like to fly high in the air, and they also love to sit on telegraph wires. They say that they wish to be modern and up-to-date, and that as they can't answer the telephones or call their friends up, they can sit on the telephone wires and feel they are part of a nice world!"

MAY 2: The Pig Who Took a Walk

THERE was once a little fairy, who was named Fairy Sunrise, because every morning she got up just at the same time as Mr. Sun did.

"She had a great love for nice little pigs, as she thought they were very cunning, and not at all the horrid little creatures some people think they are.

"But one little pig worried her a great deal. He put on airs and was very proud of himself. The little pig's name was 'Gink,' and he was the pet pig of a little girl who lived on a farm.

"Gink had overheard some city people who had visited the farm talk about their figures. For a long time he couldn't imagine what they meant. Then, after listening for some time, he heard one of them say that it was quite all right to eat everything any one wanted to, but every one must exercise, walk and play games so as not to grow fat— for it was so ugly to be fat!

"Gink had never thought it was ugly to be fat, but then that was because he had never really thought about it at all. And yet when he did think about it, he decided that he would much rather keep just 'plump' as he now was than grow as fat as his mother was. For he said that his mother was a little bit old fashioned, and he wanted to be a very modern pig.

"The next day he went for a walk. He went through the little village, just managing to escape from under horses' feet, and the little boys' bicycles. He went as far as the lake, where he saw some boys starting off on a camping trip.

" 'Don't you want to come with us?' asked one of the boys.

"The little pig was just about to start off, thinking in his vain way that the trip would do him good, when he heard a second boy say:

" 'Won't he make wonderful bacon?'

"Then you should have seen little Gink run home to his mistress. And after that awful fright and narrow escape, Gink stayed on the farm outside the village, and decided fashions were very silly, and apt to be dangerous. He also lost his love of walking!

"And little Fairy Sunrise who had been around just in time to whisper to the little boy (though of course he didn't see her) the word 'bacon' which had frightened Gink so much, was delighted that all her schemes had worked out so well, and that she had cured the vain Gink."

MAY 3: The Fairy and the Kangaroo

I MUST tell you a story to-night," commenced daddy, "of the sick kangaroo in the Zoo.

"To tell the truth the kangaroo wasn't sick at all. He simply thought he was but he succeeded in making the keeper think so too. This pleased the kangaroo as all he really wanted was to have a fuss made over him.

"The strange thing about his illness was that the keeper couldn't imagine what was the matter with the kangaroo. He had a perfectly good appetite for he couldn't give up eating just to pretend he was sick, for really and truly he knew he was just 'pretending.'

"Now, this puzzled the keeper, but he thought there must be some kangaroo sickness where the animal could still eat, and yet be far from well.

"The keeper became so worried over the kangaroo's strange sickness that at night he would get up to see if the kangaroo was asleep. Every time he went to look, the kangaroo was sound, sound asleep, breathing very quietly. The keeper thought to himself that this must be a good sign, for if he happened to be suffering from indigestion he would certainly be moaning and having bad dreams. Finally the keeper decided the kangaroo must have heart failure.

"The next day the keeper sent for the doctor and the doctor examined the kangaroo's heart. He said that it was one of the strongest hearts that he had ever examined. And the keeper was still more puzzled.

"The kangaroo used to sit for hours and hours just playing with his tail. Sometimes he would think it was time to show how badly he felt by crying. So he would first look as if he just were able to keep back the tears, and then he would act as if he could keep it up no longer and would shake with sobs.

"Now this kangaroo had always been spoilt by his mother. When he was very, very young he could always have everything he wanted, so nothing was ever really a big treat.

"He always got sick at parties because he ate too much, and his mother would never stop him, and on holidays he always was allowed to turn things topsy-turvy. But one day when the animals were all to be given a special treat, little Fairy Silver Wings, who had heard of the kangaroo's sickness, whispered to the other animals to leave him behind to twist his tail and moan while they had their game of ball.

"Then the kangaroo set up a howling such as never had been heard in animal land, for he didn't want to miss a party—just as Fairy Silver Wings had said; so when they all thought he had learned a good lesson they went back for him. How ashamed he was when the animals at first snubbed him, but he never made a fuss again, for he had had a great fright that he was going to miss a party through his foolishness."

MAY 4: The Maple Tree Talks

I'VE heard people talking about their family trees," said the first maple tree. "And I simply don't understand it. They've said that so and so came from that branch of the family and I've never seen a few aunts who made up a branch or a few uncles who made up a branch or who looked anything like a branch. I never have."

"I can explain that," said the second maple tree. "When people speak of their family tree they mean their family and their family's ancestors or grandmothers and grandfathers. You see a family is like a big tree. There is the root of it all—the first family from which all the different relatives or branches sprung which are related to the family just as branches are all related to and connected with the tree."

"Oh, now I see, thank you," said the first maple tree.

MAY 5: The Daisies' Name

WE know what our name means," said the Daisies. "We come from the old family of Day's eye—the eyes of the day—because we're so bright and wide-awake and strong."

MAY 6: The Two Rabbits

THERE were two rabbits," said daddy, "which I want to tell you about. Their names were Clover and Pinky. Clover loved to hear her name. She loved to be called by it very often and she liked it best of all when her name was made very real by getting a lot of clover to eat.

"The other rabbit's name was Pinky. Pinky was so named because of his very bright pink eyes. They were really beautiful pink eyes. Clover had pink eyes, too, but they were not so bright; they were a little bit paler in shade than Pinky's eyes.

"Pinky thought they were very fairly named, for, of course, Clover should have the better name of the two, because Clover was Mrs. Rabbit and it was polite and nice to give the lady the nicer name.

"Both the rabbits were white without a touch of black. They were very fond of each other, they were very tame and fond of children and they were extremely fond of all the nice green things they were given to eat.

"Now the children who owned these rabbits didn't know that daddy rabbits were all right when their children were big but that when their children were small they weren't so nice because they were apt to kill them.

"The daddies didn't care for their babies when they were only little bits of fluff. They didn't see that they would grow up into nice rabbits later on.

"So these two rabbits, Pinky and Clover, were not separated, and Clover, somehow, wasn't as afraid of Pinky as sometimes a mother rabbit is.

"That is, a mother rabbit is never afraid of a daddy rabbit for herself, for she knows he will never hurt her, but she is afraid for her little ones.

"So when she knows that the little ones are soon to come she hides away from the daddy rabbit.

"Clover wasn't at all nervous. She saw that the children didn't know that they should be separated. And she somehow thought Pinky would act very nicely about the little ones.

"She made a little hole in the ground and gave birth to seven of the sweetest, most cunning little bits of white fluff you ever did see!

"She had quite a hard time naming so many little babies but at last she named them and these were the names she decided upon.

"Her eldest son was named Bun. Her eldest daughter was named Bunny. Her second son was named Pink after his dad, and the second daughter was named Cloverine after herself. The third son was named Spot, because of a little black spot which he had on his nose, and the third daughter was named Rabbity, while the fourth son was named Baby Bun.

"And do you know that Pinky never touched one of those children so as to hurt them? He didn't kill them, he didn't bite them.

"But instead he watched Mother Rabbit taking care of them, he saw her giving them their meals. He watched her as she taught them the lessons all rabbits must know.

"And he saw the children pick them up and handle them very gently and kiss them and say how precious they were.

"After they grew up into bigger rabbits some of them were given away and became the pets of other children and Clover and Pinky were together again once more without the young ones.

"'I miss them,' said Clover, 'but I know that children will be good to their rabbit pets, for I have always been treated so kindly and nicely by children.'

"'So have I,' said Pinky.

"And the rabbits sniffed and their little noses wiggled and trembled as they told each other what a nice world it was with children and clover both in it!

MAY 7: Evelyn Decides Something

THE other day Mrs. Heron was talking to Mrs. Bird of Paradise," said daddy.

"'Ah,' Mrs. Heron was saying. 'It does seem too bad that just when our little ones are born, just then, they shoot us, and leave our little ones to starve.

"'And all for fashions, too, friend! Think of mothers—wearing mothers on their hats whose little ones have been left behind to die. It's something I cannot, cannot understand.'

"'All we can hope for,' said Mrs. Bird of Paradise, 'is that lots and lots of children will come to the Zoo and that they will hear from the keeper about us and will go home and tell their mothers.'

"'Yes,' said Mrs. Heron, 'for sometimes I do believe people don't know or understand or they wouldn't do such cruel things.'

"'I am sure a great many must be ignorant, for I don't believe so many would be cruel, especially just for fashion and style,' said Mrs. Bird of Paradise.

"'I hope,' said Mrs. Heron, 'that children will remember when they grow up themselves not to wear aigrette feathers which destroy the lives of birds who want to live and care for their little ones.'

"'They strike us down when we're dancing and happy and have chosen our little mates,' Mrs. Bird of Paradise said sadly.

"'And mothers wear us on their hats,' said Mrs. Heron. 'They wear other mothers whose babies have died of starvation because of a cruel, cruel fashion.'

"'Let's hope for better times ahead for our families,' Mrs. Bird of Paradise ended.

"'Let's hope so,' said Mrs. Heron."

"Oh, daddy," said Evelyn, "I've made up my mind, of course, never, never, never in the world to wear feathers of birds where we're doing cruel, cruel harm. I know and I could never forget. But I've made up my mind to start a club of little girls who'll all promise never to wear the feathers of birds such as the herons or the birds of paradise or any other feathers where the birds have to be killed. We'll wear ostrich feathers and plumes which come out naturally.

"And I'm going to get any number of my friends together and we'll have meetings and at each meeting every member will tell an interesting story of some bird she has seen. Once a month we'll have refreshments.

"But most of all," said Evelyn, for she could see Jack smiling over the refreshments, "we'll never be cruel to birds."

"That's right," said Jack, "the idea of big creatures such as we are being cruel to little creatures like birds, and I'm going to start a boys' club where we'll study birds and take their pictures, but we'll never steal their eggs."

MAY 8: Bossy White's Escape

A LITTLE girl named Betty," said daddy, "once had a pet cow. Now, that may seem a very strange pet to have; but, after all, the cow was a very nice pet, for every morning and every evening she gave Betty delicious warm milk. Betty always milked her own bossy herself and would carry into the house twice a day a bucket of milk. But before she did that she always had to drink a little first, so the cow would be pleased and would look at her softly out of her great big eyes. Betty called her cow Bossy White, for the cow had a round white spot above her right eye.

"During the daytime Bossy White stayed in the pasture, and at night-time she came in to a warm, comfortable stall in the barn.

"Betty's home was very near a swamp, where a great many black racer snakes lived. But as the pasture had a wire fence all around it nobody was afraid the snakes could get inside. The black racer snakes adore chasing cows and try their hardest to catch them. Often they succeed.

"Nobody had noticed it, but a piece of wire had really broken in a part of the fence, and one of the black racer snakes got in.

"'Now,' said the snake to himself, 'I shall have lots of fun chasing this cow.' So he began to hurry through the grass, and poor Bossy White ran for all she was worth, almost frightened out of her wits.

"A little boy passing by saw the cow running and the grass moving, so he knew that a black racer snake was chasing the cow. He jumped over the fence and called: 'Bossy White!' (for he had often heard Betty call her). 'Come, Bossy White; follow me!' And he led a wild chase, running first to one side and then to the other until they reached the barn in safety. You see, with the cow following the little boy's crooked route, the snake could not keep up, but got way behind, for the black racer snakes lose so much time in going from side to side that that is the way to escape them.

"When the little boy and the cow reached the barn there was Betty waiting to milk Bossy White. She couldn't understand why Bossy White rushed into the barn nor why the little boy was so breathless.

"As soon as the little boy got his breath, though, he told Betty what had happened. You can imagine how happy Betty was to feel that her beloved Bossy White had been saved, and she told the little boy how grateful she was to him. She also said, 'Now I know how grateful Bossy White feels, and I'm sure she'd like to give you a bucketful of her delicious milk.' So the little boy, who was very poor and who had an invalid mother, took home his reward of a bucketful of delicious milk.

"A doubly strong wire fence was put around the pasture, so that Bossy White never again was chased by a black racer snake."

MAY 9: The Spring Snow-storm

W ELL," said the great big stone, "this is fine." The big stone was big enough so that quite a number of children could get on it at one time. It was away off in the woods, quite far from the nearest village, and it was a fine place to have a picnic.

Some children had decided to give a picnic there and they had asked their daddy to let them have two of the horses and the wagon to take them all to the big stone.

The stone was in some woods which belonged to a family in a neighboring farmhouse. They were not very well off, so they made a little money by charging people who wanted to go through their land a small amount to see the stone and have a picnic there.

And the most important thing about the stone has not yet been told. It was a rocky stone. Yes, that great big stone actually rocked when one touched it, just as a rocking-chair will rock.

All the children who were going to the picnic, went in the wagon and there were five children in all.

They reached the road which was a private one, and they stopped to pay to be allowed to go through to the part where the rocking stone was.

"How much is it?" they asked of the neighboring farmer's little boy.

"It's five cents apiece for children," he said. "And that lets you look at the stone and stay there as long as you want."

"How much will it cost to let the team go through?" the children asked, for they thought it would cost more with the wagon and horses.

The little boy thought for a moment and then he said: "There won't be any charge for them, because I don't suppose they will look at the stone much!"

They all laughed, and the children went through to the rocking stone. And it was then the stone said to itself: "This is fine." How wonderful it seemed! The stone was so big that they had to climb up a ladder in order to reach the top where they were going to have their picnic, and yet they could stand by it and move it so it actually rocked, not using more than one hand.

"Let's eat right away," some one suggested.

And it was such a good suggestion that they started in to eat at once. And such good things as they had! They had cocoa which was piping hot, because it had been heated in a kettle on a bonfire which they had made as soon as they had arrived.

They had sandwiches of all kinds, and cakes and bananas and oranges and all sorts of other goodies. And they had a box with hard candies in it which they all had decided was the best kind.

They had not been eating long when one of the children said: "I do believe I feel a drop of rain—no—it is a flake of snow. Yes, it is snowing!"

"It can't be," the other children said, "for the spring has come."

"But look, there are really snowflakes falling now. And such great big flakes, too!"

And, true enough, even though it was rather far north and though the spring had come, huge snowflakes fell upon the children as they ate their picnic lunch on top of the big rocking stone.

And they laughed and said: "Well, this is a real picnic and everything is very wonderful."

"Yes," said another child, "and it is so interesting as everything is a little different from usual. It is not usual to have a picnic on top of a huge stone upon which we have to climb by a ladder if we want to reach the top, and yet which will rock when we touch it, just as though it were a rocking chair. And now the snow is falling though it is spring."

The jolly old King Snow laughed as he heard this and said: "I like to give them a surprise in the spring when they think I've left them for good. And I'm glad I've given the children a good surprise, for it makes their picnic party all the more fun, for they like me, they do." And old King Snow chuckled and went to bed for the summer months feeling very happy indeed.

MAY 10: A Reward for Mr. Walrus

"THIS Winter," said daddy, "a Walrus was the Iceman in a Zoo.

"It was this way. The Keeper had noticed that whenever the Walrus' pond became frozen over on cold, cold nights he was just as happy as happy could be. He would chop up the ice with his sharp tusks—for the Walrus has his ice pick always with him! Then he would leave a clear, open space and down he would dive into his pond and have a lovely icy swim.

"The Walrus loved it nice and cold—and how he did love the cold water.

"Of course, at first, he simply chopped up the ice because he loved the feeling of working with such a cold substance as ice. But his main object was to get under the water and have a good cold bath.

"When the Keeper noticed that that was what the Walrus seemed to want more than anything, he had the regular Iceman of the Zoo pick up the pieces of ice as fast as the Walrus would break them up. These would go into the Zoo ice-house all ready for the hot days of the Summer.

"When the Walrus saw that he was doing some real work, and that as soon as he chopped up the ice it was taken away, he was delighted. For, you see, he was very fond of his good, kind Keeper, and he thought it a fine thing to be a regular business Man—or a business Walrus—and work hard each day. He enjoyed his swims more and more because he felt he was doing some daily work.

"And the Keeper was delighted and said many very kind and flattering things to the Walrus, which pleased him more than I can tell you.

"But alas! All too soon for Mr. Walrus came the warm spring days. The Keeper could not think of anything else for Mr. Walrus to do, and Mr. Walrus felt very sad that all the ice had gone away and that he couldn't chop any more.

"The Keeper really felt very badly that he had let Mr. Walrus do so much work and had nothing now for him to do. But the Queen of the Fairies came along and whispered to the Keeper a fine scheme as a reward for Mr. Walrus—she whispered this when the Keeper was thinking very hard one day about the Walrus.

"This is what she whispered to him.

" 'Mr. Keeper, go to the ice-house every day and pick out a nice big piece of ice for Mr. Walrus. Then have it carried over to his pond, and when you give it to him tell him it is his reward for working so hard all Winter, and it is to cool his water—not to chop up.'

"Well, the Keeper did as the Fairy Queen had suggested. At first the Walrus did chop up the ice—although it was such a small piece to chop up he did seem a little surprised when it was put in his pond. Then he waited for it to be taken away, but instead, the Keeper came and told him to play with it himself.

"After a few days the Walrus understood it was all for him because it was some of the ice he had chopped in the Winter.

"So every day when the ice would come he would be so joyful. He would take a rest on the piece of ice first—for he thought it a lovely, cool sort of chair—and then he would dive down into the cold water. And the Fairy Queen was so pleased that the Walrus was getting a good reward for his Winter's work."

MAY 11: Kay and the Trunk

KATHLEEN, or Kay, as she was always called for short, lived by the ocean in a little fishing village," said daddy. "She used to watch the men fishing all day and hauling their nets in at night. And she would watch her mother cook the fish for their meals, for they practically lived on it. One day a big trunk was washed ashore which without a doubt had fallen off one of the big boats passing by.

"In the trunk were lots and lots of lovely dresses—a pink dress, a yellow satin dress, a green velvet coat, a hat with soft, big plumes on it, and, oh, so many lovely things! Kay was breathless for a moment, she was so excited—all those gorgeous things for a little girl who had seen little else beside fishing-nets and such things.

" 'Is it for me?' cried Kay.

" 'Yes; all for you,' said her daddy. 'Nobody else wants these things here in our fishing village, and you can have them to play with.'

" 'Oh, how marvelous!' said Kay. 'I'll never be lonely now. I can play I'm a queen when I wear that yellow satin dress and the velvet coat, and I'll pretend that the fishes are my subjects, and I can play I'm a beautiful lady going to a ball when I wear the pink dress.'

"She jumped around and around with joy, crying: 'Oh, what a fine time I'll have dressing up! Oh, such fun!' "

MAY 12: The Sun Talks to Harry

THERE was a little boy," said daddy, "whose name was Harry, and he loved sunsets and everything that had bright colors. But as he had spent all his life in the city, he had not seen half the wild flowers and lovely wood flowers you children can always see.

"One day he had been playing very hard as it was his birthday and his mother had given him a party. So he was tired before it was time to go to bed, and he was sitting by the open window looking at the sun just beginning to think about going to bed too.

"But the Fairy Queen was whispering to the sun to tell Harry a story as a special birthday treat, and at the same time Harry was saying 'Oh, please go to bed, Mr. Sun, for I want to see all your bright colors.'

"But the sun had no intention of being hurried. He wanted to go to bed when he was tired and not before. Besides, in the warm weather he liked to stay up longer, and it was only in the cold winter that he cared about going to bed before the afternoon really was over.

"In a moment or two Harry was sound asleep in his chair by the window. And the sun had listened to the Fairy Queen's whisper, for soon Harry was having the most wonderful talk with Mr. Sun.

"He came right in the window, and sat on the sill, just as friendly as friendly could be. He told Harry the history of his life, and oh, how very, very old he was. It made Harry feel quite old too, to hear the sun talking, and he said to him, 'Mr. Sun, don't you feel very blue when you think how old you are?'

" 'Sometimes to be sure I do. That is only natural. And it is then that you see many blue clouds and pale lavender colors around me as I'm going to bed. But you will agree that isn't very often. For when I am sensible I say to myself that there is nothing disgraceful about being old. And it is then that I look bright and rosy. For it is very foolish to mind being old when you are as strong and well as I am and have such a wonderful long record.' "

MAY 13: Old Mr. Owl Writes a Book

OLD Mr. Owl wanted to write a book and he asked the fairies how to set about doing it," commenced daddy.

" 'Well,' said the fairy queen, 'it makes a good deal of difference, old Mr. Owl, what you want to write about.'

" 'What nonsense!' he said. 'It's just that I want to know how to start off with my book. Just think what a marvelous book it will be—for as long as folks can remember I've been called the Wise Bird—the bird who's awake at night and whose eyes are so very bright!'

" 'Before I started saying what a fine book it would be, if I were you, I'd write it and give other people the chance to say so,' said the fairy queen.

"Mr. Owl began to write with his pen, made out of one of Mr. Turkey Gobbler's best feathers, on a large, flat stone, which he put in the hollow of his tree. Very late in the night, he awakened his fairies who had been sleeping, and told them to listen to his book. Then he called all the owls from the neighborhood with a loud hoot-hoot. But before he began to read, he said:

"'I've not enough light. I will hurt my eyes—my beautiful, wise, big eyes.'

"You see he had made a special arrangement to have his own lights, and when he said that he hadn't enough, from all over came countless little fireflies. They sparkled and gave the most beautiful light all over the woods, and Mr. Owl put his spectacles on his nose, and said:

"'Now I see to perfection—which means quite all right.' And Mr. Owl commenced reading his book.

"It told about the parties, balls and picnics in fairyland, and of the wild adventures and happenings in the woods. The fairies were absolutely delighted that a book had been written with so much about them in it.

"And the fairy queen was more than happy, for the last chapter was all about her.

"'Well,' said Mr. Owl, 'you made me ashamed of myself for boasting about my book before I had written it, and so the only thing I could do was to write a wise chapter all about you.'

"And the fairy queen smiled with pleasure and also with amusement —for Mr. Owl had certainly thought he could write a wise book— though the next time, perhaps, he wouldn't say so before he had written it.

"The fireflies had been sparkling and flashing lights all this time, and finally they whispered:

"'Have a dance, all of you; we'll give you the light and dance too. It is not well to read books all the time—you must dance.'

"So they all ended off with a fine dance, and old Mr. Owl, with his book under his wing, danced with the rest of the owls and fairies. But before the evening was over he presented to the fairy queen a copy of his book, which said on the cover, 'A BOOK, by Wise Mr. Owl.'"

MAY 14: Two Verses from *Mother Goose*

Jack and Jill.

JACK and Jill went up the hill,
    To fetch a pail of water;
Jack fell down and broke his crown,
    And Jill came tumbling after.

TOM, Tom, the piper's son,
    Stole a pig, and away he run;
The pig was eat and Tom was beat,
And Tom ran crying down the street.

MAY 15: Billy's Trip in the Coach

"A LITTLE Boy named Billy was sitting in front of a fire," began daddy. "It was in his own bedroom and he was in a great big armchair toasting his feet before he got into bed.

"He began thinking of the picture over the fireplace. It was a most wonderful picture. There was a stage coach and a driver all dressed in red. There were eight white horses with big red plumes standing up from their harnesses, which made them look very fine indeed. And then there were two footmen just climbing upon the coach. They never seemed to reach the top; they always seemed to be in just the same place trying to get there!

"Now Billy wondered if they didn't get tired of being over the fireplace all the time, hanging up on a silly hook. To him the eight beautiful horses looked as if they needed a good gallop and run, and the little fat coachman in red looked as if he would like to be off for a trip too.

"As Billy was wondering about it, suddenly he saw the coachman wave his arms, flourish his whip and the two footmen jump—actually jump right upon the top of the coach.

"And then the coach began to fill with passengers. The Fairy Queen was there with all the little Fairies trailing along too. Billy didn't see how the coach could possibly hold so many passengers, but to his great surprise it began to grow larger and larger. And soon he heard a gruff voice.

" 'Well, Billy, do you want to see where we go when we take our trips? You musn't think we stay over this fireplace all the time. We have many friends, and we go upon wonderful trips when you're fast asleep. But this time we will take you with us.'

"Just then a little Gnome came down from the coach and began to help Billy up.

"Off they went, with the most dashing and daring speed. Around cliffs they tore, and over the narrowest and most dangerous roads.

"Finally they came to the very steepest cliff you can possibly imagine.

" 'Well,' said the fat little coachman, 'here we all get dashed to pieces unless the Tipping Bird comes along.'

" 'Dear me,' said Billy, 'I do hope he comes. I would hate to be dashed to pieces.'

The Bedtime Story
Page xv

"Hurry, Dream Fairies, tie up the dreams for me to take around."
Page 29

"We've been on this chair so long," said the fourth eagle.

Page 44

A lovely gray felt bunny and a brown felt monkey always were
with Lucy.

Page 50

"This is the season for us to tap the syrup from the maple trees, and you
are spending your time swinging in a hammock."

Page 73

Mr. Owl awakened the fairies and told them to listen to his book."
Page 111

"The Fairy Queen brings all the little fairies to admire us."
Page 142

The Fairy Queen was dressed in glittering gold.
Page 155

" 'Oh, that's just to make it more exciting,' said one of the Fairies; 'we won't really be dashed to pieces. The Tipping Bird is a Bird known only in Fairyland, and he always comes just as the Fairy Queen waves her wand.'

"And soon what should Billy see come flying along but a great big black Bird—the biggest Bird Billy had ever seen in all his life. They left the coach on the side of the cliff, and then the horses, coachman, footmen, Fairies, Gnomes, Billy and all, found nice little parts of the Tipping Bird's wings to rest in. Soon they were flying over the side of the cliff, and then landed in a beautiful valley of soft feathers.

" 'Oh dear,' said Billy, 'where are we going now?'

" 'You must sleep in your good soft bed instead of the chair,' said Billy's mother, who had carried him asleep to his bed while he had been dreaming of the trip in the coach."

MAY 16: Mother Maple Tree

I AM going to tell you," said the old maple tree, "a little family history. We belong to the Sugar Maple family. Our trees are often used in making furniture, and our sap gives wondrous maple sugar which boys and girls and ladies and gentlemen love so much!

"And when autumn comes we all dress up in the most wonderful costumes of red and orange and flaming gold. But we will not talk about autumn quite yet.

"The work for us to do now is to see that each leaf grows to be as big and beautiful as possible. For we have been known as one of the nicest of shade trees. We keep the sun from shining down too hard on people during the hot summer months. We make shady avenues and streets and driveways.

"Mr. Sun is a perfectly splendid old chap, but in the summer he gets so excited that he is very warm, indeed, and the people love the shade we can give. So you see, leaves, you must not be lazy!"

The leaves rustled and shook their heads. "No, Mother Maple, we will not be lazy."

"We have many cousins," continued Mother Maple. "There is Cousin Sycamore Maple whose family comes from far away. Cousin Sycamore is not very strong and its flowers are late in coming out. Now Cousin Norway Maple is quite different. A fine strong tree Cousin Norway is, and a tree that doesn't mind soot and dust and smoke or insects. Many of Cousin Norway's children are planted in city streets where there is a great deal of smoke.

"There is Cousin Box Elder which is a relation because it has clusters of 'keys' or seeds, which hang on all winter.

"Cousin Striped Maple is very beautiful with its streaked white lines. In the winter oftentimes its bark is used by boys for whistles and in the autumn Cousin Striped Maple is yellow and very handsome.

"As for Mr. Mountain Maple—well, Cousin Mountain is so named because upon all mountains the Mountain Maple loves to grow and Cousin Vine Maple is so named because it hasn't the strength to stand up by itself and its stems are like vines.

"Cousin Silver Maple is very beautiful but is not strong enough to stand the city. Cousin Silver likes parks which are given over to trees and greens and plants.

"And then there are the red maple and the black maple. Cousin Black Maple is almost exactly like us, but its branches are orange colored and its 'keys' spread more widely than ours do.

"Cousin Red Maple loves the swamps and is a beautiful tree, as are all his children, but I'm glad we belong to the Sugar Maple family."

"So are we, Mother Maple," said the leaves, as they all promised to be good and beautiful and strong.

MAY 17: The Sport Fish

AT the seashore the other day when it was so warm," said daddy, "I saw some great things which were made to look like big fish. They were made of rubber, I was told, and pumped up like automobile tires, and then they were covered with canvas.

"Their eyes were painted on the canvas, so were their fins and their tails. They looked like very funny fishes but still they did not look quite right. And people were riding on top of them in the water, and what games they did have with the breakers. The fishes would rush in to the shore when a great wave would come and the people would have a most glorious ride. And children rode them, too. They're not in the least dangerous, for if any one falls off in the water when he is riding a fish which lies right on top, he has no distance to fall at all, and simply gets a nice, jolly ducking.

"But by holding on fast no one need fall off—just lie or sit on the fish and the breakers and the fish do the rest.

"Well, such fun as every one was having at the beach. The children were laughing and crying out, 'Let's ride the sport fish.'

"Big men and grown-up ladies were saying, 'Let's ride the breakers on the sport fish. My, how they go! Aren't they fun.'

"And I am quite sure that farther out in the ocean real fishes were saying, 'Well, isn't it a shame! Here there are make-believe fishes that are thought more of than we are. And we're real, not just imitations!'

"But I also felt sure that old Grandfather Ocean Fish said, 'Now, look here, we have no right to get mad. We never offered our backs for folks to ride on. And we never rushed in to the shore on the great breakers. So we can't grumble. For the sport fishes—not real like us, to be sure—will help the grown-ups and children have the kind of fun they like.'"

MAY 18: Mother Sheep

MY beautiful baby, Laura Lamb," said Mother Sheep, "we always follow the leader. We're gentle and we're quiet. We're rather timid, too. We don't think a great deal for ourselves.

"They say," Mother Sheep continued, "that when people cannot sleep they make believe they are seeing sheep, and that they are counting them going through a gate. That is because sheep follow each other, and if one were going through a gate the others would be going through, too.

"Oh, they get tired, you see, of counting the sheep they make believe that they see! And so they go to sleep!

"And you see what a help we are to people when we do such things, so that they can see us in their minds going through a gate—one after the other.

"You see, my Laura Lamb, if sheep should go different ways then people couldn't be helped toward sleep by us, and it is nice to think of helping people to sleep, for we're gentle, kind souls, and it is nice to help.

"So, Laura Lamb, you, too, always follow the leader. Don't go through one gate yourself and have your cousins going through another and some other cousins through the opening in the fence and the others perhaps going under the fence.

"We must all go together, we sheep."

And Laura Lamb bleated and said: "Ba-aaa-baa-aaa, Mother Sheep! I will do as you say."

MAY 19: The Monkeys' Victory

T HE Animals in the Zoo were boasting one day," said daddy. " 'I am the most wonderful of you all,' said the Black-Footed Penguin. 'I live in water and on the rocks. My ways are interesting. I have strange habits, and what is more my voice is like a donkey's. I can bray most beautifully.'

" 'Well,' laughed the Donkey who was passing along the road. 'The idea of comparing yourself to me.' And the Donkey stopped quite still, even though he was pulling a cart in which was a little Girl.

" 'Go on,' said the little Girl. But the Donkey stood quite still.

" 'You can't bray as well as I can,' said the Donkey.

" 'I bray just the same way,' said the Black-Footed Penguin.

" 'Well,' laughed the Hyena, 'most People and Animals don't think a Donkey's voice is anything very fine.' And the Hyena went on laughing and laughing, almost until his sides burst!

" 'If you're going to be rude,' said the Donkey, 'I shall leave.'

" 'At last,' said the little Girl in the cart, 'the Donkey has decided to move. I thought I might have to sit here all day.'

" 'Ah,' said the Sea Lion, 'none of you are as fine as I am. I jump into the air to get my food. I don't get it in any commonplace, ordinary way. No indeed, I jump for it. Each time I do a trick. And they stop and look at me. For I am very interesting.'

" 'It's much nicer,' said the bushy-tailed Wood-Rat, 'to be what I am. My tail is the wonder of the world.'

" 'I never heard that before,' said the Flying Squirrels. 'Now with us, it is different. We can fly! We are like Birds. That's very superior.'

" 'But you're not Birds,' said a Sparrow, who was flying by the cages, and over the yards of the Animals. 'At the rate you are talking, I am about as interesting as any of you. I can fly for that matter, and I can pick up food. I fly down for it instead of flying up for it like Mr. Sea Lion.'

" 'I don't fly up for it,' said Mr. Sea Lion. 'I jump for it.'

" 'Oh, all right,' said the Sparrow. 'I'm sure I don't care whether you jump or fly. You're very fussy about words, it seems to me.'

" 'Look at me,' said the Seal. 'I come from a wonderful land, and I am a thing of great beauty. My skin is beautiful. And I swim so nicely, and I like the water so much.'

" 'You're no better than I am,' said the Alligator crossly.

" 'Nonsense,' said the Seal, 'but I won't quarrel with you about it, for I know I'm right.'

" 'I have the finest coat,' said the Zebra. 'Now, in truth, I am something worth looking at.'

" 'You're queer, that's all,' said the Rocky Mountain Sheep from his yard.

"The Australian Dog who looked like a Fox also got into the argument, but back in the Zoo house, the Monkeys were saying:

" 'Now, to-morrow let us see who gets the most admiration and attention. Then we will see who is the most interesting Animal in the Zoo.'

" 'All right,' agreed the other Animals, for each was quite sure he'd win. The word was whispered about the Zoo that the visitors should decide the question.

"The next day the Children began to arrive—and all day long they kept coming. Each Animal had fussed to look his best, and when the Children would pause and stop to admire any Animal the others would look angry.

"They stopped before every Animal for a few moments, and would say to each other:

" 'Oh, look at this queer Animal! See what he does!' But then they would pass on and in front of the Monkey cages they stood. The Monkeys performed tricks, they made faces and they ate peanuts which were given to them, and at the end of the day, alas and alack, every Animal had to admit that the one who received the most attention from the Children was the old Monkey and his family."

MAY 20: The Mosquitoes

WELL, friends," said the little mosquito, "how about a banquet to-night? It's the first warm evening of the season, and without a doubt the people will sit out on their porches and enjoy the beautiful air."

"They won't enjoy us," said the second mosquito.

"Well, I'm sure we wouldn't be flattered if they did," said the first mosquito. "If they enjoyed us it would mean that we didn't bite them, and that would never do."

"It would never do," agreed the second mosquito.

"Well, let's be off, for the sun has gone down and the people will have finished their suppers before long."

"All right," said the first mosquito, "I'm ready, and I'll give a call to the children and to the cousins and to all of the family and relatives."

"Buzz-buzz-buzz," came back the answers, and soon all the mosquito relatives had joined the first two mosquitoes.

"Is every one ready for a banquet?" asked the first mosquito.

"Every one, without a doubt," said the mosquitoes.

So they all started forth and buzzed along, talking of people who felt them most.

"We don't want to go to those who're not properly bitten by mosquitoes," said the first mosquito.

"I heard some one say, the other day," said the second mosquito, "that the two creatures she hated most were the flies and the mosquitoes. She said she didn't like yellow-jackets and hornets, but practically every other creature she liked.

"Now, wasn't that a nice compliment?"

"A large one," said they all.

"What do you mean by a large compliment?" asked the second mosquito. "You should say a big compliment. But still what do we care about words except a few choice ones such as bite and bitten and will bite?" So the mosquitoes hurried, and some of them went on one piazza where people were sitting and some on another, and were happy over their mean banquet.

MAY 21: The Potato Bugs

"WELL, it is time we should get started," said Mrs. Potato Bug.

"And we must work hard," said Mr. Potato Bug.

"We have such fun working," said the little potato bugs.

The potato bugs had six legs apiece. They had little black feelers and tiny eyes. They were yellow and black on the back, and blue and brown underneath.

They spit a little yellow juice on any one who took hold of them, for they said:

"It's all right for us to treat the potatoes badly, but it is a different thing for people to have the bad manners to pick us up as if we were little creatures of no importance."

There were also brick-red bugs with black dots on either side. These were the little potato bugs, while the others were the daddies and the mothers. They got on the leaves of the first potato crop and fed off them, eating away at the leaves as hard and as fast as such tiny creatures could do.

These little bugs were very anxious to kill the plants and they would have done so if they had made a good headway. That is, they would have done a great deal of harm if they hadn't been driven away in time.

But these bugs went to other potatoes and they saw some of the potato grubs, so they said to them:

"Potato grubs, what are you doing?"

"We're eating holes in the potatoes," said the grubs. "What are you doing?"

"We were eating leaves of potato plants," said the potato bugs. "We were driven away from some other plants, but here we are, and the dear little children have come, too."

"Are you going to eat the leaves here?" asked the grubs.

"We think they look good," said the potato bugs.

"They do," said the grubs, "but of course we pay all our compliments to the potatoes themselves. We don't bother about the leaves."

"Perhaps," said the potato bugs, "the potatoes wouldn't mind it if you didn't pay them such compliments."

"Perhaps not," said the grubs, "but we do, just the same. We say to the potatoes:

" 'Dear potatoes, we love you. Let us show you how fond we are of you by eating you.' "

"Ha, ha, ha," laughed the potato bugs, "that is a good joke."

"The farmers don't like the jokes, though," said the grubs. "They think they and their wives and their children and their neighbors and their friends are the ones who should pay such compliments to the potatoes."

"Absurd," said the potato bugs.

"Of course," admitted the grubs, "it is not so absurd if we put ourselves in their places, but who in the world ever imagined that a grub would put itself in the place of a person? No one would, so why should we do it? And we don't."

"That's so," said the potato bugs, "and neither do we. If we cared for people we wouldn't eat the leaves and we wouldn't try to destroy the plants."

"We're not friendly with farmers even if we do like potato hills," said the grubs.

"That's so," said the potato bugs, "and why should we be friendly with the farmers? They don't like us. They ask us to leave. They try to get rid of us.

"They never invite us to have some of the leaves of the potatoes, any more than they ask you to bite holes and eat of the potatoes.

"We have to invite ourselves and look after ourselves. It's too bad the farmers don't like us when we like the potatoes they plant."

And so the potato bugs and the grubs tried to do all they could to hurt the farmer's crop of potatoes. And they didn't even feel badly, they were so naughty!

MAY 22: Meadow Mouse and Mole

"THE Meadow Mouse and the Mole," said daddy, "had become very good friends. They both lived near each other in the field, and they used to visit each other in their holes under the ground.

" 'What do you think of the food this year?' asked Mr. Meadow Mouse, just as if he were staying at a hotel and wanted things the way he asked for them.

" 'Well, I think it's pretty good,' said Mr. Mole. 'The farmer planted all the things I like best this year, and so I've had a very good time.' Just then they heard a voice say:

" 'I advise you not to stay,
You had better move away.
For, some day when the farmer passes,
He may chop your heads off with the grasses.'

" 'Oh, who could that have been?' asked Mr. Meadow Mouse. And the voice went on:

" 'I cannot be seen,
I'm the Fairy Queen.'

"Pretty soon Mr. Meadow Mouse and Mr. Mole were off for the next meadow, where the Fairy Queen told them they'd be safe, and all their children with them. Mrs. Meadow Mouse and Mrs. Mole didn't care about moving, but when they were told that their heads would be chopped off if they didn't, they hurried along!

"And when they got to the next meadow, they began to burrow in the ground and dig it up with their little noses. Especially good for such work was Mr. Mole, and his children all copied him, and were a great help.

MAY 23: Wishes

"HELLO, aprons, gloves, toys, books, games, gold fish, party dresses, gingham dresses," called Fairy Grant-Your-Wishes to the toys and clothes in the children's big store.

They all called back "Hello." That is, all those did who were awake this evening and who weren't so tired that they went to sleep at once.

"What is this I hear that you want?" she asked.

"We all wish we were something else," said the gingham dress. "I'd like to be a party dress, and the party dress is tired of its ribbons and laces. The gold fish down the aisle wants to be—what is it you want to be, gold fish?"

"I want to be a toy," said the gold fish.

"And oh," said a pair of brown jumpers, "I want to be myself. But I want a playmate. I'd like to have a doll, please, Fairy!"

"The doll you shall have," said the fairy. "I'll wave my wand."

As she did so the whole store began to grow and grow, it seemed. Each counter was now like a store in itself and none of the counters were near each other. There were great, enormous roadways between the counters and the things themselves were all different. The gingham dress was now a party dress. It was wonderful how a party dress had been made out of the gingham one, for the gingham dress saw that there was some of the old dress left.

"Oh," said the gingham dress, now a party dress, "I do want to go to a party now."

"You shall," said Fairy-Grant-Your-Wishes, suddenly appearing again. "Every one is to have a complete, whole wish granted this evening. And all of the others will go where they please and be what they please."

Such a change as there was. The gingham dress, now a party dress, found herself at a great party. There were many boys and girls and they looked at her as she came in the doorway. Oh, how strange and uncomfortable she felt. It was really a most miserable feeling.

"Do we make mud pies later on?" she asked of another party dress.

"Ha, Ha," said the other party dress, "where did you come from that you didn't know that at parties such as this we don't do such things. We couldn't soil our clothes. I do believe your grandmother must have been a gingham. My grandmother," the other party dress said very proudly, as she walked off tittering and giggling, "was a Lady Lace and she went to court affairs where my grandfather, Lord Velvet, met her."

"What horrid, snobbish creatures," said the gingham dress. "Oh, dear, what shall I do? No one will be friendly with me. I wish I were going to a good outdoor garden-playground party where children and clothes did things so I wouldn't feel so strange."

"All right," said Fairy-Grant-Your-Wishes. "I will make you happy and change you back to what you were."

MAY 24: The Tree's Complaint

THE house near-by is receiving a coat of paint," began the tree, "and it is trying to pretend it's the only thing that was ever painted. It is very proud and disagreeable about it.

"If the house were receiving any other kind of a coat I wouldn't be angry with it. I would never expect to have a coat of cloth or rubber for the rain or fur perhaps for the winter, but then I'm not a boy, a girl, a lady or a big man. I'm a tree, and the house is a house."

"Perfectly true," said the song sparrow, "I don't wish to correct a thing you have said."

"But a coat of paint is entirely different."

"Entirely, chirp, chirp," agreed the song sparrow. "I don't suppose a girl or a boy, a lady or a big man would care for a coat of paint."

"Whiz, whiz, I should say not," whistled the wind.

"But the house," continued the tree, "pretends it is very wonderful. It is trying to look so fresh and stuck-up."

"You must forgive those things," said the song sparrow, "as the paint makes the house behave like that."

"That's so," said the tree. "I suppose I was a bit harsh. But you know my trunk was painted this spring, painted white, to protect me and to look after me. So, I didn't like seeing the house act in such a proud fashion."

MAY 25: Saving a Tail

EVELYN rushed up to Jack as soon as he came out of school one day.

"Oh, Jack," she said, "something is the matter with Marian. She behaves so queerly. She said she wanted to have me play with the other girls; she had something special to do at home. She really wouldn't let me go home with her. I would have been mad only she was just too queer for anything. I don't understand."

"Jock was the same way; let's go back, anyway, and see what is up." Jock and Marian were cousins who had recently come to town.

They hurried down a street, running most of the way, and then turned down another and ran almost all of five more blocks to reach their cousins' home.

Jack went half-way down the hall when he bumped straight into Jock coming up from the cellar. He was holding in his arms the little fox terrier Marian had bought just a week before with her birthday money. The dog was only a tiny puppy still, a lovely little soft white puppy with one brown ear and one black one and two black spots on his soft white back.

"Oh, did Buster get hurt?" Jack shouted. Buster, of course, was the small, gay, naughty, happy puppy.

"No, he didn't," said Jock. "And it's none of your business, anyway, even if you are our cousins."

"That's so," said Marian, who came up behind Jock. "If we want to have Buster's tail cut, it's no one's business but our own. It was just like you to find out somehow."

"Going to have his tail cut?" gasped Evelyn and burst into tears.

"Yes, fox terriers look absurd with long tails," said Jock; "every one says so. And, besides, he'll be all well in a week, quite well."

"And for the sake of a little style," said Jack, his teeth clenched tightly together, "you'd let that dog suffer for a whole week. I just wish I could cut off a part of your arm, that's what I do."

"The bones are soft," murmured Marian. "He'd look foolish with a tail, so every one says."

"What do you care what every one says?" screamed Jack; "you are two horrid, cruel children, and if you don't let that poor puppy, who has never done you any harm, and who is at your mercy, alone, you'll never be friends of ours, and we'll tell others of your cruelty. We mean it, too."

And they did mean it, for they didn't care what any one thought of them so long as they saved the puppy from being hurt.

But after Jack and Evelyn had told Jock and Marian of the suffering it would mean for Buster, of course they didn't do such a cruel thing. They weren't really cruel, only they didn't know that such a thing hurt dreadfully. They had never been told the real truth, and they were glad they had heard it in time!

MAY 26: Life in the Fireplace

JAMIE and Jackie had both fallen asleep in front of the fire," commenced daddy, "and now instead of the fire they saw huge castles and towers and turrets and bridges and royal people. Far over in a corner, too, they saw a dark gray stone cave in which was sitting an old, old Witch dressed in a scarlet robe, with a tall black hat on her head.

"Soon they heard the Kings and Queens and the Princes and Princesses talking. They had low voices, but every little while a sudden gun would go off and for a moment they would all keep very quiet.

" 'What do those guns mean?' asked Jackie and Jamie together.

" 'It's the Fireplace clock,' the Sparks answered.

" 'But it doesn't seem to keep very good time—I heard the gun go off three times in a hurry and then not for ages,' said Jamie.

" 'It keeps as good time as we care about,' said the Sparks. 'We're not so awfully particular. Anyway, our bright colors and our gorgeous castles should be fine enough without hearing from you that our clock doesn't keep good time.'

" 'Indeed, we do think you're all beautiful, and we love a cool evening when we can have a fire. We don't mind if your clock doesn't keep good time,' said Jamie.

" 'What are you saying about the time?' said the Mother of Jackie and Jamie. 'Bedtime, eh?' for both Jamie and Jack were being shaken gently and told to trot off to their real bed. But as they both crawled into their nice soft sheets, they found that they'd each had the very same dream—and both had seen the Fireplace castles and heard the Fireplace clock which kept such bad time!"

MAY 27: The Jewelweed's Visitor

I AM the Jewelweed flower, though I am sometimes known as the Touch-Me-Not flower, too.

"I have little seed pods and boys and girls love to pop open these pods, for then my seeds jump forth quite wildly and excitedly. I mean by my name of Touch-Me-Not, that no one must touch me unless he wants to be very much surprised!

"I am orange yellow in color and I have reddish spots upon me. I have also sometimes been called the Wild Lady's Slipper because I am shaped something like that. And sometimes I've been called Lady's Eardrops because my shape is something like a lady's eardrop, too.

"I'm hoping I will have a caller to-day. I'm expecting one, I know. And I hope I won't have to wait long. I haven't seen this caller for some time.

"It is most exciting to expect a caller. Very, very exciting!

"They call me Jewelweed because in the early morning when I've taken my morning bath, as all good flowers do, in the Magic Dew Water which the Dewdrop Brothers bring around to us, I sparkle like jewelry.

"Oh, indeed! I always take a morning bath. Sometimes when it showers I take an extra bath.

"And always, when my bath is over, I look for Mr. Sun and I ask him to make my jewelry look pretty.

124

"Then my pretty leaves look so bright and sparkling. Yes, that is one of the reasons for my name.

"I do hope my visitor will be along soon. I asked him to come as soon as he came up this way.

"I sent word by the Breeze Brothers to be sure to let him know that I was waiting for him and that I hoped he would come to see me as soon as he arrived.

"Ah, I believe I hear my visitor coming. I believe I do."

"May I come in, buzz-z-z-z-z-z-z, may I come in?"

"Oh, do," said the Jewelweed. "I am expecting you."

Then appeared Mr. Ruby-Throated Humming Bird who had just arrived from the South.

"Well," he said, "how glad I am to see you."

"And I am so glad to see you," said the Jewelweed. "You must have a cooling sweet drink. I didn't let any other visitors take any of it. No indeed! There was the Bee who tried to get me to give him a sweet drink, but I keep it deep down in my very center dining room where even the Bee with his long, thirsty tongue can't get at it.

"I kept it for you, and you, with your tongue which can stretch out farther than your long bill, will be able to get it.

"Dear Mr. Humming Bird, I am so glad you have come. And you will have some refreshment, will you not?"

"Indeed I will, thank you, Jewelweed," said the Humming Bird, "and it is indeed good of you to save your sweetness for me."

"Ah, our families have been friends for so many years," said the Jewelweed, "and I like to do as my family have always done."

"I must be off now," said the Humming Bird, "for as I have only just arrived I have a good many calls to make. There are a number of my flower friends who are expecting me to call as soon as I arrive. But may I come and see you again?"

"Oh, indeed yes," said the Jewelweed, "and you will always be welcome. Make your other calls, but come back again soon."

"I'll be back soon," said Mr. Humming Bird. "I have had such a charming call and it has been such a pleasure to feel that my visit has been so welcome."

"Your visits are always welcome and always will be," said the Jewelweed, "just so long as there are Jewelweeds and Humming Birds!"

MAY 28: Peter's Birthday Party

A LITTLE dog named Peter Murray," said daddy, "was just one year old. His Mistress was a little girl named Inez and she was almost fonder of Peter Murray than of anything else in the world. Inez sent out invitations several days in advance to a number of the little boys and girls she knew who owned pet dogs. The invitations read:

'Mr. Dog Peter Murray,
At Home,
In Honor of his First Birthday.'

"All of the little dogs who were invited accepted and the day of the party came at last. The first thing that Inez did that morning was to rush over to Peter Murray's basket and say 'Many happy returns.' Now, of course, Peter Murray woke right up and was out of his basket with a bound.

"He jumped up and down for Inez, which was his way of saying, 'Thank you, Missy,' and he wagged his tail for all he was worth.

" 'We have lots to do to-day, Peter Murray,' said Inez, and Peter Murray knew just what she meant. He put his head first on one side and then on the other. And when he saw Inez take a little purse out of her pocket and jingle some pennies he put his ears up in the air as if to say:

" 'What do those funny things mean?'

" 'They mean,' said Inez, 'that we must get goodies for the party, bones and such things.'

"Now, when Peter heard the word 'bones' he wagged his tail, for he knew perfectly well what bones meant.

"At last the time for the party came. And such a time as they did have. Every little dog brought Peter Murray a present. He got wonderful things, too. He was given a great pink bow and a new collar by his Mistress, which, of course, he wore to the party. Then he receive a fine hard ball, a stick to play with, a second-best collar and a box of chocolates, for Peter Murray loved candy, too.

" 'Supper time,' shouted Inez, and all the little dogs wagged their tails and jumped for the bones that Inez threw up in the air, until every little dog had one.

"You see they were not fussy like people, and didn't sit down to eat their bones, for they had much fun throwing them up in the air and playing with them. And then came the ice-cream, which they ate out of little bowls, and for a surprise they had wonderful sugary cake, with a little dog made in sugar on the top of it! Inez cut the cake, for in each piece she had to take out a little bell which were the presents Peter Murray gave to his guests on his birthday!"

MAY 29: The Spring Flowers' Talk

"GOOD-BY, good-by," called the trailing arbutus family. "It's getting a bit too late for us. We will be around next spring, though."

"Good-by, good-by," said the hepatica family. "We will miss you, but we're going ourselves soon. We're glad to have seen you. How lovely and pink you were this year."

"And how lovely and blue you were!" said the trailing arbutus flowers. "Some of you were the most wonderful shades of lavender and purple and even pink and white!"

"We like to have different colored frocks," they said. But then fearing that they might hurt the feelings of the trailing arbutus family they added:

"We wouldn't care about it, though, if we had the lovely pink dresses you have!"

"Thank you, thank you," said the trailing arbutus family. "We're very grateful to you."

"Well, good-by," said the hepatica family.

"Good-by," said the arbutus family.

"Next spring, next spring," added the hepatica family.

"Yes, next spring, next spring," said the arbutus family.

"And we'll come again, too," said the little wild violets. "We're early spring flowers, you know."

"Of course you are, dear little violets," said the arbutus and hepatica families together. "Next spring, then, little wild violets."

"Next spring," the violets whispered very softly.

MAY 30: Memorial Day

"THE soldiers who have fought for their country should indeed be remembered by placing on their graves the flag for which they fought—the flag for which they gave up everything," said daddy, on Memorial Day.

"Not only is Memorial Day a memorial to the brave men who have lived and died for their country, but it should help to make us worthy of these men who gave their all," he ended.

MAY 31 : What the Flag Said to Fred

"THERE was once a little boy named Fred," said daddy. "He was very fond of soldiers and bands. He had a great many little toy soldiers, and he would have the most wonderful drills with them. Last Memorial day his grandfather, who had since died, had given him a little, old, ragged flag. But it was the stars and stripes, and Fred cherished it. His grandfather had fought in the Civil War and all through that war had carried the little flag. Now his grandfather was gone, and yesterday they had put a fresh flag on his grave. But Fred had the little flag that had been through the war.

"That night he was very tired, and he went to bed early. The cool white sheets and soft pillow were delightful to a very sleepy little boy, but soon he seemed to be sitting up on the pillow, and before him was the flag.

" 'I have come,' said the little flag, 'because I thought you would like me to talk to you. Your grandfather went to the Civil War, as you know.

" 'He was so brave in the war, and, oh, I was so proud while I was with him all the time that it was for my sake he was fighting! It's the most wonderful thing in the world to be a flag even if you're in rags.' "

JUNE 1 : The Robin Parents

"OVER a little balcony," said daddy, "where a lady used to sit and sew, there were several roofs adjoining and going off from different sides of the balcony, and there were eaves running along the balcony. "In the spring a Mr. and Mrs. Robin looked about them for their home. 'How about this?' asked Mr. Robin. He was pointing to the eaves right over the little balcony.

" 'There is some one there,' said Mrs. Robin, 'but she looks very nice and as though she wouldn't hurt a little bird for anything. I think it is perfectly safe. See, she is looking at us and her voice is low, and she is not frightening us. She is speaking to us; listen to what she says.' And they listened and heard the lady say: 'Dear little robins, have you come to call on me?'

" 'Ah, her voice is so sweet and so nice, and she really seems to be glad to see us. Let us build our nest here.'

" 'I think it will be a good idea,' said Mr. Robin.

"So they built their nest under the eaves, right over the balcony where all day the lady sat, most of the time sewing, some of the time reading.

"She would have visitors there, too, and sometimes she would tell them of the robins who were so near-by, but she always saw that no one frightened the robins, and that they were well looked after.

"She used to put bread-crumbs on the roof near the eaves. And a little pan of water was always there, too, for bathing or for drinking!

"Mr. and Mrs. Robin built a lovely big nest, and there Mrs. Robin laid the eggs. After a little while the baby robins came, poor little timid creatures, with scarcely any feathers at all.

"But Mr. and Mrs. Robin loved them and thought they were beautiful, just as boys and girls think their little baby brothers and sisters are beautiful, even if they have no hair on their heads—in fact, they like them that way, for then they look so appealing and so cunning and so helpless and yet so glad to be in the world. Usually Mother Robin guarded the nest, while Father Robin went off for food, for he was a very fine robin to go to market and pick out all the best things. He just knew so much about it all and was such a good business robin that he was a very fine provider.

"And, too, he knew that by helping Mrs. Robin he was sharing in everything, and he shared in doing what was to be done, it was not only fair to Mrs. Robin who would get all tired out alone, but it was also much more fun to help one's mate.

"So the little robins grew up happily and safely in their nest by the little balcony."

JUNE 2: The Robins Come to the Rescue

I AM going to tell you," said daddy, "about the mother humming-bird whose little ones were about to be attacked by a snake when they were rescued by some brave robins.

"The snake had come over from the vacant field and had crawled up the honeysuckle vine as the mother humming-bird had gone off for some food. Some robins hovering near had seen the snake. They had cried out in terror and had flown over to the nest.

"The mother humming-bird heard the cries and hurried back, but the robins had frightened off the snake. The snake was not a very large one, and really he had been frightened by all the noise the robins had made, and when he saw so many birds flying toward him he got away very quickly.

"The mother humming-bird got back just as the snake was leaving the nest.

"She couldn't thank the robins enough for flying to the rescue and saving her beloved little ones, but the robins didn't want any thanks. They were thankful, too, that the dear little birds had been saved, for birds are very loyal to one another and will risk any danger to save each other."

JUNE 3: The Persian Lilacs

YOU know," said one of the flowering almonds, "I think a special vote of thanks should be given to the Persian lilacs. Every year they come out, and after they go their lovely bushes are still so pretty with their green leaves.

"But best of all is the visit they pay us every single spring. They are so small and dainty a lilac, their color is such a soft shade of lavender, they are so beautiful and so flowery and so soft and sweet, and they are so very, very fragrant that we should tell them how much we love them and how glad we are each year to see them.

"It is only right to tell nice creatures and things that we like them. It would be quite unfair any other way at all, and so we should tell the Persian lilacs that we love them and that we welcome them and that we are looking forward to seeing them next year.

"We know how the people love them; we know that for years they have looked forward to seeing the Persian lilacs in the spring and enjoying them right through the spring, too. We know how, after the other lilacs have come out, the Persian lilacs bloom and then they last longer than the others, because they have come later."

"Ah," the Persian lilacs said, "it is good of you all to be so kind to us. Our bushes are all very grateful. But you know we couldn't help but come out each spring. Beneath our bushes are beds of lilies of the valley, the sweet, fragrant lilies of the valley, that nestle in among their green leaves, and they always talk softly to us and send us their sweet greetings.

"Then the people are so fond of us; they love their Persian lilacs so, and all the flowers are so kind to us and help us add to the fragrance of the spring garden. There is no jealousy, and every one is trying to add his sweetness to the whole. We will always come out, never fear!" they ended.

JUNE 4: How a Wish Saved the Raccoons

"ONE day Mother Raccoon was just about to start telling one of her stories," said daddy, "when Daddy Raccoon saw all the children around her.

" 'Now this afternoon,' said Daddy Raccoon, 'I want to take all those silly little 'Coons and show them how they can become brave big 'Coons such as I am.' And he thrust his tail this way and that with an air which said, 'I'm certainly one of the finest, bravest Animals any one could hope to be like.'

"All the little 'Coons looked very mournful when they heard that they were to be taken off to learn how to hunt in the swamp near-by. They were always very much frightened when they went near the swamp, for they had often heard the sound of a big gun, or had seen a dangerous Man with a gun over his shoulder getting in behind the bushes.

"They began to wail and yell, but Daddy Raccoon was firm and as he was the head of the house—or rather the big tree without any leaves—Mother Raccoon had to let them all go.

"But as they were following Daddy Raccoon, she called out to them, 'If anything happens to you wish very hard that you will be all right and the Fairy Queen may possibly be near-by and will grant you the wish.'

"Daddy Raccoon sniffed with scorn at such a remark, but he said that Mother Raccoon was such a sweet old dear she even thought well of the Rabbit family—and so she was apt to think so much of the Fairies in the same way.

"And off they all started. Some of the little 'Coons were rather proud at going off to hunt in the swamp and really pretended they were tired of Fairy Stories and were glad that Daddy Raccoon had thought it was time for them to grow up.

"Soon they reached the swamp and in they went to hunt for food to last them many days, as Daddy Raccoon had said.

"They did just as they were told and were beginning to be very good hunters and were learning just how to pick out the best parts of the swamp—when suddenly—an awful bang was heard near-by.

" 'Oh, dear; oh, dear,' shouted the little 'Coons.

" 'Do be quiet, or they'll know where we are,' said Daddy Raccoon.

"The second bang sounded very much nearer and they all trembled, when one little 'Coon said, 'Oh, if any little Fairy is hovering near—please tell the horrid man with the gun to go away.' And, would you believe it, that man was heard to say:

131

" 'Well, I guess they're all away for the day and I won't try to catch Raccoons until to-morrow.' Then Daddy Raccoon took all the little ones back to the old tree where Mother Raccoon was sitting curled up, shaking with fear while waiting.

" 'Tell them all the stories you want to,' said Daddy Raccoon, 'for one of your Fairy friends saved all our lives and whispered to the man with the gun to go home!' "

JUNE 5: The New Mole Home

M R. Mole was going to get married," said daddy, "and he wanted to build a fine, fine home for the new Mrs. Mole. So he went forth into the nicest meadow he could find, and there, just at the end of it, near an old fence, Mr. Mole started to bur-row into the ground.

"You know the Moles live underground almost all of the time, and there make their homes. Just near the fence Mr. Mole began to dig and dig. First of all he made a long, long tunnel, a funny underground passage which he called the Drive-Way of his Home!

"Of course the callers of Mr. and Mrs. Mole could hardly drive along this tunnel, but they could run and scamper along, and they liked to call it by a big name like Drive-Way.

"And after the long, long tunnel Mr. Mole started in to make a fine house out of the earth. He made lovely rooms, one for Mrs. Mole, one for himself, one for the little Mole who was to do the cooking and housekeeping and several guest rooms. For, as you can imagine, Mr. Mole was very fond of company. In addition to all this Mr. Mole built a very fine picture gallery—made in tiers of earth and mud—long rows and rows of it. On these he put pictures of his family which he made out of earth, too. Of course, Mr. Mole made every member of his family look just alike, but that didn't make any difference. The Moles are not very fussy if their pictures aren't very well taken, for they can't bother to look at pictures much of the time.

"You see their eyes are very small and they like to look at things more worth while—such as food and corn starting to grow in the ground and all the things the farmers plant. They love farms, you know, where wonderful vegetables are planted deep down in the earth. They are very apt to burrow along and make paths so they can walk to a farmland and have a feast.

"But I must tell you more about Mr. Mole's new home. The very last thing he did was to build a beautiful throne in the picture-gallery for Mrs. Mole.

"At last it was time for her to come to her new home and Mr. Mole had invited their friends and cousins, the Mole-Crickets, to come, too. These cousins have very strangely shaped front legs with which they burrow homes just like the regular Moles, and so they are considered relations.

" 'Here we all are,' said Mrs. Mole, and she blinked her very small eyes, while all the other Moles blinked their tiny eyes, too, and looked about them. Through the Drive-Way they ran until they came to the house with all the beautiful rooms.

"The room Mr. Mole took them to last was the picture-gallery, where Mrs. Mole sat on the throne in honor of her wedding day, and the little Mole, who cooked, brought out some of the delicious stewed vegetables she had made for the wedding feast.

"You should have heard the Moles as they looked at the pictures. They thought every picture was one of their own relatives.

"One Mole would say:

" 'Why, there's Mama,' and another would say:

" 'Why, no, that's not your Mama, that's my Papa.' However, they didn't get in the least angry about the pictures—in fact, they thought it very clever of Mr. Mole to make pictures which looked like all their relations at the same time.

" 'But you haven't noticed my wedding dress,' said Mrs. Mole. 'I think my new Home is S-C-R-U-M-P-T-I-O-U-S, which means beautiful in case any of you little Moles don't understand the word I've said in honor of the day. And now that you've all admired my home, please admire my dress.'

"For the first time the Moles noticed that Mrs. Mole had attached to her tiny ears little earrings made of mud with a red berry in each, and she wore a necklace to match. Her dress was of dull oak leaves which Mrs. Mole had saved for a whole year to wear on her wedding day.

" 'You're a handsome Mole,' said Mr. Mole, 'and I'm so proud you're to share this home I've made,' and all the other Moles grinned and ate more and more of the vegetable wedding feast to show what a good time they were having."

JUNE 6: The Green Canoe

I THINK I will tell you about a very lucky little girl who once received a canoe from her big brother," said daddy.

"This little girl loved the water. She had always lived near a lake, and she could swim and row.

"Now, this little girl had a great big brother who worked in an office in the big city. He had only a short holiday every year—just two weeks—but during those two weeks he would come home and teach her new strokes in swimming and new ways of diving, for he was very anxious that no one should be able to excel his sister as a swimmer.

"And secretly he longed to give his sister a canoe so she could go on the water just as much as she wanted to, and, as she was such a good swimmer, he felt it would be perfectly safe for her to own one.

"But, of course, a canoe is quite expensive, and the heads of offices in the big city do not consider that the big brothers may want to buy their little sisters canoes with the money they earn. Perhaps they think it is very silly to even dream of such things as canoes. But slowly during the winter the big brother had saved just as much money as a canoe would cost, and in June he wrote his sister a little note.

"In the note he said that he had a 'little present' for her which he had had put in the cellar and that she would find it there if she went and looked.

"Now, the little girl could not for a moment imagine what kind of a present would be put in the cellar. But she hurried down to see.

"And there—right before her eyes— was a lovely big green canoe— just the very nicest shade of green—and there beside it were the two paddles. Well, she could hardly speak. She had never dreamed that she would own a canoe, or, anyway, not for years and years and years.

"On the canoe was printed 'Indian Girl,' but she at once named it Papoose, which means, you know, a little Indian baby.

"You see, her big brother had arranged that the canoe should be taken down into the cellar when the little girl was asleep, so the surprise would be perfect. And it certainly was!

"In another week the big brother came up from the city, and they spent all their time in the green canoe on the lake."

JUNE 7: The Bunnie and the Fox

IN the woods," said daddy, "there lived a mother Rabbit and all her little children. They had a beautiful home—as nice as could be, in one of the finest brier patches ever known. Mother Rabbit was really extremely proud of her home and used to give many fine receptions there for the animals. Especially wonderful were her carrot receptions. The thing that worried Mother Rabbit most of all was that little Bunnie Bonnie, her youngest son, was very, very curious. Of course, Rabbits are always inclined to be curious, but Bunnie

Bonnie was even more so than most of his family. And he was so-ciable. Entirely too sociable his mother thought.

"He liked to go to every party that was given in the woods—even if the parties were not given by his friends.

"Now, one day a black fox moved to the woods to live. None of the animals were pleased to hear that he'd come to stay, for that meant they would have to think of getting out of his way, and doing as he said. Many of the animals left food at the entrance to his home so he wouldn't eat them up instead!

"Mr. Black Fox looked all about the neighborhood and he noticed Bunnie Bonnie scampering around more than any of the others. So one day he spoke to him and this is what he said:

" 'I'm glad to see you're a brave Rabbit, and that you're not afraid of me. Some of these other silly Rabbits tremble when they see me and leave me good things to eat—but I know why they do that. They want me to get all through my meals at home, and not go looking near their homes for extra delicacies—such as their small children.

" 'But it's so absurd. They're abusing me. Just because I have a gruff voice doesn't mean that I'm cruel and bad. In fact, I'm very kind and very good.'

"Of course, Bunnie Bonnie should have known that if Mr. Black Fox was so good he wouldn't have found it necessary to talk about it. But Bunnie Bonnie never thought of that—and he forgot—completely for-got—that the Fox family is known to be very sly.

" 'And,' continued Mr. Black Fox, 'I'd be greatly honored if you'd come to supper with me this evening.'

" 'I'd be pleased to,' said Bunnie Bonnie.

"Now, Bunnie Bonnie's mother was giving one of her receptions that afternoon so she told the children to play in the little garden she had back of her home in the brier patch. And Bunnie Bonnie left his little sisters and brothers to have supper with Mr. Black Fox.

"Mr. Black Fox was sitting outside his front door waiting for Bunnie Bonnie. He was chuckling to himself, and his eyes looked very wicked and cruel. But when he saw Bunnie Bonnie running up his path-way, he began to smile and called out in the pleasantest tone he could use:

" 'Hello, Bunnie Bonnie.'

" 'Hello, Mr. Black Fox. Here I am, and, oh, I'm so hungry, too. I didn't stop to get any of my Mother's carrots as they were being fixed for her party, but came right along!'

" 'I'm going to have something better than carrots for my supper.'

" 'What?' said Bunnie Bonnie in a cheery tone, for little did he suspect the old Fox.

" 'I'm going to have you, you little stupid,' roared Mr. Black Fox, but Bunnie gave one bound and ran for the brier patch. He just reached there ahead of Mr. Black Fox, and never again did he leave his family for new friends."

JUNE 8: The Homebody Bee

"AH," said Queen Bee, "I do not work, but I lay the eggs, and so I am called the Queen Bee, for all the little eggs are my subjects and all around me do everything they can to help me and to wait on me.

"When I tell you how many eggs a day I lay during the time when I feel in the mood for laying, you will be surprised. The number amounts to from two to three thousand eggs.

"You see, buzz buzz, I don't like to do anything that is small. I don't care about doing little bits of work. I like to do a lot. That is why I'm a queen; I am an important creature, and not just like all the rest!

"And I am waited on by my helpers who digest the food, the pollen which I eat.

"I am fed royal jelly, a most deliciously sweet food made only and served only to a Queen Bee who has been brought up in the Queen's royal chambers, or in the Queen Bee cell, as it is usually known.

"My workers have better eyesight than I have, and so they go in search of the honey. During the summer I go from one cell to another laying my eggs.

"But I never leave the hive, though I may live to be several years old. Sometimes it is true I go off upon a flight with my mate or with a swarm of bees, but Queen Bee is a homebody."

JUNE 9: Ladybug's Lecture

"DEAR little Ladybugs, gather around me," said Ladybug, "for I am going to give a lecture.

"It will be a free lecture, and pray, Ladybugs, do not think that on that account it will be poor. Too many folks have the idea that nothing is good that is free.

"They don't bother to find out how many nice things are free, and they don't stop to think about them. Take birds and their concerts—quite free.

136

"And lovely wild flowers—quite free. And the woods and lakes and rivers and ponds—practically all of them free. And many free concerts and oh, so many things that if I go on talking about them I will never have time for my lecture.

"So I shall begin my lecture if all the Ladybugs are ready, and if the Ladybug who has charge of this hall (for I must call this place where I am lecturing a hall) will kindly bring me an acorn filled with water I shall be much obliged. Lecturers should always have such things by them, and oh yes, a light and a pointer to point to my maps and my pictures. But on second thought they won't be necessary for I have no maps and no pictures. Well, then, are we all ready?"

A little Ladybug came hurrying up with the acorn filled with water and said in a low tone, "If you want any more I'll bring it in to you."

"Thanks," said the Ladybug, who was about to lecture.

"Now, friends," she began, "Mrs. President, Lady Chairman, I greet you."

There was no Mrs. President and no Lady Chairman, but that didn't make any difference.

"I have something very fine to tell you. Something very fine upon a subject which strikes close to the heart of all of us."

Ladybug, the lecturer, placed one of her legs in the direction of her heart and looked very fine indeed doing so.

In a moment or two she went on: "I have heard, and it is quite true, that we have all been paid a very great compliment. We have been paid one of the greatest of compliments.

"It has been both expensive and a bit difficult to get to Europe of late—especially has it been too expensive, and I don't believe any of the Ladybugs have enough money in the Ladybugs' bank to use that to go to Europe.

"It's a fine bank and it is nice to go to a bank where ladies are especially looked after and all of that.

"But we haven't enough money in the bank. Dear me no, not nearly enough.

"However, those of our family who were chosen to go weren't asked how much money they had at all. They weren't even asked if they had any money.

"They weren't even asked if they would pay for their laundry and their own food.

"They were just invited to go and were told the work they would do would be enough thanks for the opportunity they were having to travel.

"Yes," said Ladybug, "many, many, many Ladybugs have been shipped to France to destroy bad insects.

"Of course, I'm not sure whether the Ladybugs can talk French or not, but they can work anyway and make the whole Ladybug world proud of them.

"But I think it would be interesting if we all studied a little French so that we would be able to say how-do-you-do and good-by and pleased-to-meet-you in French, in case we're called upon next. And my lecture is not only free. It is quite, quite true."

"Ah," said all the Ladybugs when they had finished cheering the speaker, "we will all study a little French and be ready. Ah, what an honor for the Ladybugs of this land!"

"Gorgeous," said Ladybug, the lecturer.

JUNE 10: The Waves' Wishes

WE are mad, Mother Ocean," said some of the waves. "We've never been given a fair chance. We've always been here—your children; we've had to do just as you said. We've been allowed to play when you've been perfectly willing we should play and when you've been willing to ask the Wind to play with us. But we've had to do as you and the Wind said.

"And we've had to sleep when you've told us to. It's not fair. Just because we're only some of the drops of water which belong to you we haven't any say of our own."

"What is it you would like to do?" asked Mother Ocean in her deep, great voice.

"We'd like to see more of the world," they said.

"We'd like to go traveling. We'd like to see what the cities and forests are like; we'd like to see some other creatures beside fishes and people swimming in us. We're tired of an ocean life.

"We want to live on the land. We want to do great things—what do we do here that ever amounts to anything?"

"So you'd like to see the world?" asked Mother Ocean. "Well, Waves, go forth; I won't stop you. And may you come back to me with stories of adventures!"

JUNE 11: The Waves' Adventures

WHEN the waves were told they could leave Mother Ocean they weren't so happy as they had expected to be. They had really expected Mother Ocean to forbid them to go—then they could continue grumbling, which they were quite en-

138

joying. Now they felt they must start at once to show that they were really anxious to see the world. They didn't want to let Mother Ocean see that they would rather stay where they were quite comfortable and where they could grumble! Mother Ocean was sighing a little.

"I'm sorry to see you go," she said. "It's the first time any of my children or grandchildren have wanted to leave me."

The Waves didn't look at Mother Ocean. Instead, they pulled their beautiful white caps down over their heads and shed a salt water tear or two. Then they picked up their shell suit-cases from Mother Ocean's ground floor, packed in their sea-weed nighties and their best sea-green suits and sea-blue party dresses and were off.

They ran over the beach and rudely went right over the feet of some people who were sitting down on the beach reading books. Then they scrambled on, stumbled and scrambled on a little farther.

"Oh dear," said one of the waves; "oh dear, the sun makes me feel so dizzy."

"And I feel so hot and dry," said another. "Oh dear, oh dear! I must weep." But not even any salt tears would come to the wave's dry eyes.

"Are you ready to have adventures?" asked a little creature who suddenly came up to the waves. He looked like a little brownie and he seemed quite amused at meeting the waves. "I've heard you wanted to see the world and to do great things," he continued. They wanted to tell him he would look far better in a cool green suit than in his warm-looking brown one, but suddenly they realized that they could only speak the language of the ocean and that he couldn't understand them, though they could understand him, for they had so often heard people speak.

"I don't know what you're trying to say," he grinned, "but I suppose you mean to say 'Yes,' as I've been told you've come to see the world."

"Well, first we shall take a trip through some forests."

They tried to follow the brownie, and found it was very hard work. He led them along so fast, and they couldn't make him understand that they'd like a drink of water and a cooling bath.

Pretty soon they found themselves in some very dark forests. All around them were strange birds calling to each other and singing songs about juicy worms. The waves trembled, for they thought the birds might sing soon about juicy waves, and then might swallow them down!

And they saw strange animals, rabbits and woodchucks and squirrels, all quite small but very terrifying to the waves.

They saw some little red lizards and small snakes which wriggled along and which didn't seem in the least friendly like fishes.

After they had passed through the forests and had been frightened almost out of their wits the brownie hurried them along to the edge of a city and then right into the city.

JUNE 12: The Waves' Story

THE Waves begged the brownie to take them back to the ocean for they said they had had adventures enough. And the night they got back Mother Ocean gave a great ball. The wind came and danced and sang, the waves all danced, the sea-shells laughed and sang and through it all Mother Ocean kept smiling and singing to herself:

"Away from home.
They wanted to roam,
    Away from the ocean deep.
And I did not say 'No,'
But I let them go,
    Though many salt tears did I weep.
But now they are home,
They no longer will roam,
    Away from the ocean deep.
And they will say 'No,'
If I suggest that they go,
    So now I can sing and not weep."

And ever since that day none of the Waves have ever wanted to leave their Mother Ocean to adventure over the earth.

JUNE 13: A Poor Weed

SOMEHOW," said the yarrow weed, "I have been left here and only a little of the hay is left. It has all been cut down to feed to the animals. The animals don't like to eat me. They say I am so bitter. Ah, poor me, I cannot help it if I am bitter."

"Do not be so sad," said Old Hay. "It isn't so wonderful to be eaten. Aren't you happier above the earth, having the sun look down upon you and the wind rustle by you, than to be inside a cow or a horse or a sheep?

"The farmer does not like you because you take up the room which might be used by some grass which would be good for his animals."

"Yes, I'm like an unwelcome visitor, a guest who isn't welcome."

"My dear Yarrow," said Old Hay, "you mustn't mind it if some creatures don't like you. There will always be some creatures who don't like something or some one. It is a waste of time worrying about it."

"I won't worry about it any more," said the yarrow weed, "but I do wish that I didn't look so ragged and shabby all the time. I am such an ugly gray color. My leaves look old as though I were very poor."

"Oh dear," sighed Old Hay, "I no sooner get rid of one worry for you than you think up another. It's all right to wear old things if you want to. I have heard of people who wear their last year's clothes so they can do fine things with their money."

"But I haven't money," said the yarrow weed.

"Dear me," said Old Hay, "please cheer up. Of course you haven't money. You're a weed, and as you say, you are a poor and rather unpopular weed.

"But you mustn't be discouraged, for I've heard you were often used as a charm. You are supposed to bring good luck and a long, happy and prosperous life. So some people save a bit of you to keep for luck."

"Ah, yes," said the yarrow weed, "even though I am a poor weed I have something to make me very proud and glad."

JUNE 14: The Bicycle's Joy

I REMEMBER a story of my grandfather," said the bicycle. "He was given as a surprise to a little girl by her brother. She didn't know what she was going to have, only her brother told her she was going to have a great and enormous surprise. I think my grandfather has often told the story.

"The brother made up puzzles to help the sister guess what her surprise was going to be but she simply couldn't guess anything so wonderful as a bicycle.

"The brother had saved up for ages and ages to give it to her—all paid for out of money he had earned himself.

"Well, when my grandfather was given to her, he said that the little girl just said, 'Oh, brother,' and put her arms around her brother's neck and the tears came to her eyes for very joy of the great, great surprise.

"I was afraid such days had gone. But at last I was sold and I find there are lots of bicycles around and that children still do enjoy them."

"Oh yes, indeed they do," said the second bicycle.

"Oh," said the first bicycle, "I am so joyous. My tires are full of joy and air. My bell rings merrily. Oh, I'm a happy, happy bicycle.

"Now I don't care if children do love airplanes and automobiles and all sorts of modern toys and if they like kites because they fly so high in the air and are so lovely, for they still have room in their hearts for the loyal old bicycle friend.

"It's a great joy to be a bicycle after all."

JUNE 15: The Best Apple Tree of All

O F all the trees in the orchard," began daddy, "every spring this old apple tree I am going to tell you about had the most beautiful of blossoms. And when midsummer came the apples that came out on that tree had, somehow, a better taste than the apples from any other tree. And one day I found out the reason.

"I thought the hammock, which hung under the apple tree, looked very comfortable, and so I made myself most cozy and happy. It was not long before I dozed off into a nice little nap, and then I heard what the apple tree was saying to the little unripe apples on the boughs.

"'You must grow to be fine and ripe, and you must keep all the little apple-seeds good and warm so they can be just as brown as brown can be. That will mean that little boys and little girls can eat all they want, for so long as the seeds are brown they can never do any harm. And, you apples, you must be very sure that you turn around and have the sun warm you and make you bright and red.'

"As the old apple tree was talking, I noticed that the apples just grew a little bit bigger, and redder and fatter, and looked as they were— oh, so juicy and wonderful inside. I was certain, too, that the little seeds were growing browner every minute.

"'You see,' he continued, 'it's such an honor for us. You know that on the day we're ripe the fairy queen brings all the little fairies to admire us, and they sit on the boughs and wave about with us. And more than that—you know the apple that is ripe first goes to the fairy queen and then some more go to the little fairies.'

"The fairies are too kind to take away the apples that real people like to eat—and so the old apple tree has arranged to have a great many more that we can't see—they're called the apples of fairyland.

"And the tree still went on talking:

"'I, too, am working hard. I am practising my best bow to make to the fairy queen when she arrives the first day all the apples are ripe. So she is to come very, very early in the morning while every one else is sleeping. And when the children get up and find the apples are ripe so quickly, won't they be delighted!

" 'Now, get around so Mr. Sun will help you along. He's the greatest help in the world to us—such a dear old soul.'

"Of course that flattered Mr. Sun so he helped still more, and just as I could feel him shining down with all his might—I woke up.

"I moved away from the apple tree then, for it was no longer shady; the sun had come around and told me to get up! But as I walked away and saw the apple tree waving around I knew it was practising for its bow and making the little apples hurry up and ripen."

JUNE 16: An Elephant's Wanderings

THERE was once an elephant who got tired of the circus and wandered off one night when nobody was noticing," commenced daddy.

"You see the circus was getting ready to go on to another village to give a performance and it was late at night. They never thought of an elephant getting away, but they hadn't heard Jumbo telling the elephants of late how exceedingly tired he was of circus life and circus food and circus parades. He was not only tired of it all but he said he wanted to be a gentleman.

"The other elephants had asked him what a gentleman was, and this is what he told them:

" 'I heard two little boys talking of what they were going to be when they grew up,' said Jumbo, 'and one of them said he was going to be an engineer and build bridges. The other little boy had said he was going to be a gentleman and do nothing. The first boy thought he was quite wrong and very silly, but then and there I decided that it would be beautiful to do nothing.'

"The other elephants had asked Jumbo how an elephant could be a gentleman, any more than a gentleman could be an elephant, but Jumbo was determined to lead a lazy life. And you see neither Jumbo nor the little boy knew what being a gentleman really meant.

"So Jumbo escaped and the next morning Jumbo was in a barnyard, and as you will never be able to guess the friends he had chosen I'll have to tell you. He was playing with a big brown dog, a mother hen and a whole lot of little chickens.

"Of course, he had to be very careful not to move so as to step on his new friends, for he knew it would be most impolite and not at all gentlemanly to step on a friend and crush him! But as he had wanted to stay quiet and do nothing he was very happy.

"The hen sat proudly on one of his ears, while the little chickens all sat on his head, and ran races up and down his marvelous trunk. The dog got up on his back and jumped off and on again and again. Meantime the elephant was sitting down in the barnyard looking very enormous and very much out of place.

"Soon the little girl, whose name was Betty, and who lived in the house beyond the barnyard came running out to give her pets their breakfast.

"At first Betty was somewhat frightened at seeing the big elephant, but then she felt that if the little chickens were so friendly with him, he must certainly be friendly.

"The elephant stayed some time with the animals of the barnyard and with Betty. But one morning bright and early she found Jumbo with an old ball and bat in his great trunk. He was practising baseball so he would not be put off the team when he got back to the circus for he had been planning for some time to return to his first friends.

"Well, this morning he had decided to leave. For late the night before he had heard the circus he belonged to arriving in the village where Betty lived.

" 'I've had a powerful good time,' said Jumbo to Betty, 'but I must be off. I haven't done a thing for weeks and if this is what it means to be a gentleman I'd rather be an elephant—which, of course, is very easy for me to be—as I am one, don't you see?'

"Now Betty didn't understand what the elephant was really saying, but that afternoon when she went to the circus there she saw Jumbo in the baseball game, and doing all the tricks better than any other elephant. He was so delighted at having something to do again that though Betty missed him, still she was glad he was back where he was happiest."

JUNE 17: The Story the Oak Tree Told

A SOFT breeze of early summer had been blowing all day. The leaves were looking so fresh and green and having a beautiful time in the warm sunshine.

"Well," began daddy, "I must tell you the story the oak told to the other trees to-day.

"The other trees would sometimes sigh, 'How nice!' or something like that, but for the most part they let the oak tree do all the talking.

"It was a very young tree, but it looked as if some day it would be a fine big oak with spreading branches and great strong roots which nothing could shake.

" 'I was one day picked up as a little acorn by a small boy,' said the tree.

" 'He carried me around in his pocket for days and days. I spent all my time sleeping, for his pocket was very dark and I could not stay awake in it.

" 'One day he happened to notice me especially. He wondered why he had been carrying me around for so long, for he himself couldn't think of any reason why he should want me.

" 'And then he thought he would plant me. So he put me in the ground and covered me over carefully. He watched to see when I would come up. When first he saw me sprouting above the ground I thought he would go mad with delight, for he had really been very much worried about me. After having planted me he was very anxious that I should grow up right away. So he was a very happy little boy when he saw that I was really going to become a tree.

" 'Now he comes every day to look at me and has done so ever since I was born.

" 'You see it will make me a fine tree to have the pride of that little boy centered in me.

" 'And what is more, it will make him, I think, grow up to be a fine man, brave and strong like his tree, for that is what he calls me.

" 'So I feel that we will both help one another, and perhaps some day when he is an old man he will lead some little boy by the hand and will tell him of how he planted me and how he tried to grow up to be strong like his tree, and that will help the little boy, too.

" 'We trees can do a lot of good if we want to. Just think how nice it will sound to be called a fine old oak, and when we feel proud of ourselves we can think it is even better that we have helped little boys to be stronger too.' "

JUNE 18: The Weeds and the Flowers

THE Elves," commenced daddy, "were playing in a garden one morning just at the break of day when all the flowers were opening their sleepy heads, and the ones which had not been sleeping were looking about them more brightly than ever.

" 'Good morning, Flowers,' said the Elves. The flowers nodded their heads and smiled and waved about in the warm breeze. But the Elves heard some very strange sounds—not quite like the talk of the flowers—for to the Elves and Fairies, you know, there is a Flower language, and a Flower's way of talking.

" 'What could these other sounds mean?" they asked each other.

" 'We'll tell you,' said these voices. 'We're the Weeds. And some of us are beautiful, but all of us are strong. Yes, we're so strong that no matter how they try to dig us up and throw us away we're up again in no time. We're little fighters—yes, we are. We have our Army headquarters. Indeed we do! And our Generals are very fine. They're the great, tall Weeds you often see, and my, but it's hard to get them out of the earth. If they are beaten more Generals take their places, for the motto of the Weeds is, "We'll always be strong— there will always be Weeds." '

"And so they chatted on. The Elves were very much interested, but still they couldn't quite see, when the Weeds were doing so much talking and bragging, how the flowers could smile so happily.

"So they whispered to the Flowers very gently:

" 'Tell us, Flowers, why are you so happy?'

"Then in lovely, soft rustling voices the Flowers said:

" 'We are going to have a Book written about us to-day. Yes, a real Book, and our pictures are going to be painted. We're very proud and happy. We have a Mistress who comes out every morning and most of the day she is with us. She bends over us and digs up the earth around us so it is nice and soft and comfortable. And every evening after Mr. Sun has gone to bed she gives us cool drinks of water.

" 'It was only yesterday she told us that some Noble Grownup was going to write a Book about us and call it "The Ideal Garden." We think that ideal means something like perfect—anyway it's something extremely nice. And she has been making us ready for the Book. Oh, we're very proud indeed.' And then the queer sounds came again, and the Weeds spoke up:

" 'Yes, and we're going to have a Chapter about us. We don't quite understand yet what a Chapter is—but it's a great deal—we're sure of that. The Grownup told our Mistress that she was going to say something about pretty Weeds in a garden.'

" 'Well, we like you all—Flowers and Weeds,' said the Elves."

JUNE 19: The Insulted Flowers

I DO feel insulted," said Mr. Orchid.
"It's too absurd," said Miss Lily of the Valley. For a lady was wearing a bunch of orchids and lilies of the valley and one of the orchids and one of the lilies of the valley were talking to each other. They felt very much hurt that they had been crushed and forced into such a great big bouquet to be worn, when a smaller one would have been so much prettier and nicer.

"Yes, we are being insulted," said Mr. Orchid. "She doesn't care one scrap for flowers. She just wants to look rich and so she bought us—and plenty of us, and that is what we call insulting."

"It most certainly is," said Miss Lily of the Valley. "No one who cared for flowers would wear as many as she is crushing together; no, indeed."

JUNE 20: The Colored Bags

SINCE Melly had been a little girl her Auntie had been very fond of her," said daddy.

"One day Melly's aunt was looking over a great box she had with pieces in it when Melly saw all the odd pieces of silk. 'I wonder,' said Melly's Auntie, 'if you would like to have me make you little bags, so you can carry your purse and your handkerchief in one when you go shopping, and your handkerchief and other odds and ends you carry around at other times in other bags? I could make you so many bags of so many different colors. Some, you see, could be yellow, some blue, some pink, some gray, some orange, some purple, some tan, some rose, some green, some white.'

"So that was the way Melly's bags came about, and her Auntie on her birthday and Christmas always gave her a few new bags made from the old silk.

"How gay and pretty they were and how Melly loved them.

"Now one evening Melly had gone to sleep and the bags were talking.

" 'Ah,' said the bag of pale blue, 'I'm but a baby. I am only a few years old.'

" 'And I'm very old,' said a little plaid bag. 'I belonged to her grandmother!'

" 'Well,' said a purple bag, 'it does seem funny to see the world again. It's nice to be young once more. Why, I was getting so used to the darkness of the piece box that I blinked, actually blinked—at least as much as a bag can blink—when I first got out again.'

" 'And isn't it fun,' said the green bag, 'to see so many things? I went on a picnic yesterday, and a piece of bacon got into me in some way or other, a nice little crumby piece. Well, I did feel funny. I felt like a person having breakfast. I must say I didn't eat it up—I'm not fond of eating—mostly because I'm without a mouth and a stomach, but it is fun to go to so many different places and to see what is going on in different places.'

" 'I'm so glad I was made,' said the rose bag. 'I'm going to a dancing party this afternoon. They'll have ice-cream there and I'll hear all the children play and laugh and I'll hear them say, "Oh, Melly, which bag have you got with you to-day?" And then I will be shown.'

" 'We're the lucky little pieces of silk who are seeing the world for a second time,' ended the yellow bag."

JUNE 21: A Spider's Curiosity

"THEY may not think the spider is a curious creature, though again they may think so," said Mr. Spider, "for I am sure I cannot keep track of what they think.

"But last summer I was attracted to a house which looked rather cool and comfortable and as though the people who lived in it had gone away and left the blinds down.

"Now when I say I was attracted to the house I mean that the house looked attractive to me and so I went there. I went in first through a crack under the door. I looked about me when I got inside and I thought to myself: 'Dear me, I have the whole place to myself.' But I found that a number of spider friends and cousins had come to the house too.

" 'Well,' they said, upon seeing me, 'have you come to this hotel to board? It's really quite good. Meals are fine. We've found a number of delicious little creatures to nibble at.'

" 'Yes,' I said, 'I've come to this hotel to board, but I won't pay my board.'

" 'Oh, won't you?' said they.

" 'I will not,' I answered. 'I do not pay board. It's a foolish thing to do, a waste of time, and besides I haven't the money. I wouldn't pay board for anything, for it spoils people.'

"Yes, they think they can do anything when they charge board. They can be rude and only give you so much of this and so much of that, and they have to watch over you to see that you don't eat more than you are allowed. At least that is my idea of boarding, though I suppose for those who have plenty of money it is all right.

"But I have no money, none at all."

"Neither have I," said the spider who was listening.

"Therefore I cannot board," said Mr. Spider.

"Well, as I was saying, my relatives and friends talked to me and when I said that I wouldn't pay my board they said: 'Oh, that is quite all right, Mr. Spider. None of us do. Besides, we feel sure the people who have gone away will be glad if they hear that some of the Spider family are watching over their house in their absence.'

"So I settled down, but after a time I began to feel as though I would like to be busy. Every one around me was working.

148

"And one day one of the other spiders said to me: 'Mr. Spider, did you bring your work?'

" 'Yes indeed,' I answered, 'I have it here with me.'

"Then, of course, I thought I would choose a good spinning table or spinning chair, or some place where I would be comfortable and cozy a-spinning.

"Just as I was thinking about it I happened to take a look at a telephone upon a table.

" 'There will I go,' I said to the others.

" 'But,' they told me, 'the telephone is a modern thing and spinning is an old, old thing to do.'

" 'Well,' I answered, 'I will mix the old and the new, I will work around the modern telephone. I will spin a web so when the people come back they will have to talk through Spiderland in order to talk to their friends.' "

JUNE 22: The Sun-Dial

I FOLLOW you so that people can tell the time by me," said the sun-dial. "And how am I able to tell time for them? All owing to you. I depend upon you to help me tell the time, for you cast your shadow over me, and people know just the hour of the day it is. There is the sun-flower which is named after you," continued the sun-dial. "It is so called because it is so bright and golden and it is big too!"

"That is so," said the sun. "I am very fond of the sun-flower."

"And think of all the flowers, like the marigold and the morning-glories, which open when you arise, and go to sleep, closing their eyes, when you go to bed.

"Then there is the sunfish, so named because he is round and fat and supposed to be slightly like the sun in shape."

"I had never heard the reason for his name before," said Mr. Sun. "Thanks for telling me."

The sun-dial moved a little and so did Mr. Sun, for the time was going on.

"Then there is the sun-gem," continued the sun-dial. "He is the humming-bird, you know, and he has such glorious bright colors that they have named him after you."

"I never knew that before," said Mr. Sun. "How very interesting. Pray go on."

"There are the sun opals—beautiful stones—and sun perch—like the sunfish family. There are sun plants and sun ferns,"

"Indeed," beamed the sun.

"And there are sun shades," continued the sun-dial.

"Oh dear," said the sun, "people use those to keep me out of their eyes, don't they?"

"Yes, that is so," said the sun-dial. "Dear me, I didn't mean to say anything about sun-shades. And there is sun fever and sun stroke."

"Oh dear, dear, dear," said the sun, growing very red and angry. "They are horrible things people get when their heads ache and they feel quite miserable."

The sun was very red and very mad now, and the sun-dial knew it had said too much. "I am so sorry," said the sun-dial. "I grew a little careless in what I was saying."

"Yes, you did," agreed the sun. "But no matter; I shall sleep and forget about it now."

And the big red sun went to bed behind the hill and the sun-dial said to itself it would never make such mistakes again!

JUNE 23: Shoes and Stockings

IT seems so funny," said Mrs. Cow. "Really, the fuss that children make about going around without any shoes or stockings.

"I don't mean they make a fuss about going without. Gracious, no, they love not to wear shoes and stockings.

"It's very funny, though, the way they think it is such a treat to go without.

"Now, we never wear shoes and stockings. We think that would be ridiculous.

"We would never say to our mothers, 'Oh, mother, can't I please go without any shoes or stockings all afternoon?'

"No young cow or calf would say such a thing. But children are always asking if they can't go without as a great treat. How funny they really are!"

JUNE 24: Mosquitoes and Snails

WELL, are you here again?" said the Snails to the Mosquitoes.

"We are indeed," buzzed the Mosquitoes. "But you don't say that as if you were pleased. In fact, we don't like your manner at all. We think a little nip and a wee bite might help you. It might make you more polite."

"Ah, there you are wrong," said the Snails. "To be sure, our manner was not so very polite. But we don't feel so polite toward your family. And as for teaching us manners with the aid of a little nip and a wee bite—well, that is absurd, as we have shells and we can go right back into them. We may be slow, but we can get into our shells quickly enough."

"Yes, cowards," hissed the Mosquitoes.

"Not at all," said the Snails. "It's not cowardly to avoid being bitten. It wouldn't help any one if we were bitten. There would be no good done because of it. We simply do not wish to be bitten and give you a chance to say:

" 'We bit the Snails to-day. That was part of our pleasure.' For it is a pleasure to you to bite, and we don't intend to help along such selfish, mean, cross creatures."

"Then why are you talking to us?" asked the Mosquitoes.

"Because," said the Snails, "you have just missed a picnic party that went by here a little time ago. A nice picnic party of children. We won't tell you where they went—no, indeed. And you've lost them now. We only talked to you because we wanted you to miss one horrid adventure. We wouldn't have wasted our time otherwise. And we talked slowly to give the children more time." The Snails wiggled and squirmed a little. They were very much pleased with themselves.

But, oh, how mad the mosquitoes were! They buzzed and sang their ugly little songs. They tried to bite the snails, but they had gone inside their shells.

They were so furious that they had wasted all that time. But the snails were happy! They knew that the children were far away by this time, and they had been saved from having the horrid, uninvited mosquitoes go along, too.

As the mosquitoes flew away they said: "Never again will we talk to those slow snails. They make us lose time."

And the Snails were delighted that their slowness had helped.

JUNE 25: The Rose-Breasted Grosbeak

T HE rose-breasted grosbeak," said daddy, "is a very useful bird, and at the same time an extremely beautiful bird.

"Mr. Rose-Breasted Grosbeak wears black and white, with a handsome vest of rose color and under his wings he has the same decoration. Mrs. Grosbeak is not so handsome. She wears a brown frock, and looks not unlike her cousin, Mrs. Sparrow.

"They have some fine relations, too—there are Mr. and Mrs. Blue Grosbeak, and there again Mr. Grosbeak is very beautiful. He wears a deep blue suit and his shoulders are trimmed with chestnut-colored feathers. Mrs. Grosbeak is of grayish brown and grayish white, having the top side of the first color, and the bottom side of the second color.

"Then there are the Evening Grosbeak family. Mrs. Evening Grosbeak is paler than her husband but their coloring is not so different from each other as in the other members of the Grosbeak family. The Evening Grosbeaks are of brown and yellow with touches of very dark brown and white-tipped wings.

"And we mustn't forget the Pine Grosbeak family. Mr. Pine Grosbeak is of a wonderful shade of red, while Mrs. Grosbeak is yellow and gray in her coloring.

"The Pine Grosbeaks are fond of the winter; they are not afraid of the cold. In fact, they are not afraid of anything and they trust people and let them come close to them. They have low, warbling voices and whistle in a beautiful, clear fashion.

"The Evening Grosbeaks have very large bills and eat many seeds, berries and insects, as you may imagine. But they can sing and whistle, too.

"The Blue Grosbeak family sing, too, in a nice warbling fashion of their own, which is a little like the song Mr. Indigo Bunting sings, but Mr. Grosbeak's is a little stronger and louder—a little more of a song. They probably like to sing songs that are somewhat the same, as they are both blue birds and so have the same taste in color and in music.

"But it is of Mr. Rose-Breasted Grosbeak that I want to tell you, for he is not only beautiful, but, as I said, he is very useful.

"And he can sing, too! Oh, how Mr. Rose-Breasted Grosbeak can sing! He chirps in low, deep and lovely tones and he sings from morning to night in the most glorious manner.

"But he does a great deal else beside singing. He helps the farmer and the owner of the orchard.

" 'Yes,' said a Mr. Rose-Breasted Grosbeak to his mate, many, many years ago, 'I am not going to be satisfied just to be beautiful and to have a nice voice.'

" 'What is it you want to do?' asked Mrs. Rose-Breasted Grosbeak.

" 'I will have to think about it a little,' he answered. And then after he had thought a time he said,

" 'I have it.'

" 'Tell me,' chirped Mrs. Rose-Breasted Grosbeak.

" 'We will help the farmer and the owner of the orchard. We will destroy bad bugs and insects which would hurt the crop. We can easily change our diet so that these things will taste delicious to us. And we will be doing some good work, too. It's horrible to be lazy and beauti-ful and rich and superior. It's much more interesting to be busy and see things finished that we've done ourselves.'

"Mrs. Rose-Breasted Grosbeak agreed, and thought they would enjoy life a great deal more by being busy.

" 'It would be so tiresome,' Mrs. Grosbeak told her mate some time after this, 'if we did nothing all day but sing. Why, we'd have nothing to sing about after a time, no joyous news to tell the world!'

"And so from that day to this, the Rose-Breasted Grosbeak family have been a great help. They eat caterpillars which would destroy trees, many moths, bugs, worms, and insects which would hurt growing vegetables and trees bearing fruits.

"They eat cucumber beetles, too, but mostly they eat potato-bugs. And so they are a great, great help, and are often called 'Those dear little Grosbeak birds!' "

JUNE 26: The Goldfishes

I AM pretty mad," said one of the goldfishes in the bowl, whose name was Mr. Tokio Jones.

"I'm mad, too," said Mr. Pekin Baxter, the other goldfish.

"That little girl said, you remember," continued Mr. Pekin Baxter, 'Oh, look at the wings on the fishes.' Such ignorance! Of course, she meant fins, but it made me pretty mad to think there was a person who knew so little about fishes."

"And what made me mad was when her playmate said to her: 'Why, Marion, those aren't wings, those are fins,' and Marion said: 'Well, what is the difference which I say, wings or fins?'

"That certainly made me mad."

"It did me," said Mr. Tokio Jones, "but let's not excite ourselves any more; let's be like the lazy snails, who are really sensible not to get angry, for it does no good at all."

JUNE 27: The Pigeons' Bath

N OW the four pigeons I want to tell you about were a daddy and mother pigeon, and their little pigeon children whose names were Peter Pigeon and Polly Pigeon," said daddy. "And I saw them to-day.

153

" 'Polly,' said her mother, 'be sure you wet your feathers. Now a good shake! There, that's the way!' And then the mother pigeon would give herself a good shaking in the water to explain.

"And Daddy Pigeon was saying to Peter, 'There, Peter! That's the way. Don't be afraid of the water. A bath will do you good. And the day is warm, the sun is shining, and we'll get good and warm after this. Our feathers will be warm in no time!'

Now, Peter and Polly Pigeon were being told just how to bathe in the best way by their fond parents. But it was not hard for them to learn. They had lots of fun spattering each other, and they played all sorts of games. And after they were really through bathing and had shaken their feathers they began to get dry in the hot sun.

"Polly and Peter Pigeon were quite sleepy, after their playing, bathing, splashing and spattering, and they began to coo very softly before going to sleep. But as they were just dozing off Mother Pigeon said:

" 'If we're all good pigeons, the Fairy Queen, who looks after pigeons, too, will come and whisper in the ears of children to give us bread crumbs. She will tell them that in the hot days of summer we like little cooling drinks which they can put in pans and saucers around their yards and on their porches. Yes, the Fairy Queen will tell them all that, if we're good pigeons.'

"Of course Polly and Peter made up their minds they would be very good indeed so as to receive the rewards about which the Fairy Queen would whisper to the children. And in case she hasn't already told you I want to let you know that it will make her happy to think of children all over the world, when the warm weather comes, thinking of the little creatures who can't turn on the faucet and get a good cool drink of water, but who must wait for the rain or kind people."

JUNE 28: The Man in the Moon's Party

IT had been the first hot day. Even the sun felt tired. That may sound very strange, to think of the sun feeling tired," said daddy. "But still can't you imagine that on the first hot day that comes, when the sun has been shining with all his might and main he gets a little bit tired and is glad when it is time to go to bed? Many strong people may get tired at night.

"As the sun went to bed, the moon began to peep up and laugh. He grinned from ear to ear, for he said to himself:

" 'To-night I really will be appreciated, for the sun has overworked to-day and no one ever gets any thanks for overworking. It is as bad as not working enough.'

"Of course, the moon was the very sort to talk that way. For, can you imagine that jolly old man whom you see grinning at you so often as ever really working very hard?

"Just then the moon began sending out his invitations for a party.

"He sent them in this way: he whispered to the tall pines that he wanted to have a party and to invite all the little fairies. Also he added that they must wear their very best clothes, for when he gave a party he liked to see folks in their party clothes.

"'The fairy queen was dressed in glittering gold. She wore a gold crown on her head and carried a gold wand with gold stars glittering from it.

"All the other fairies were dressed in silvery costumes, for the man in the moon is very fond of silver. You will sometimes notice that he puts on a silver robe himself, and he is very friendly with the silver clouds that float in the sky at night.

"They did have the very best time, and they all enjoyed the party so, so much. The man in the moon laughed his head off—at least the fairies were afraid he would—as he said he had never before seen the pine trees behave so like silly little trees, instead of like big, dignified trees they had always prided themselves on being.

"But the pine trees didn't care, for they were having a beautiful time waving and singing. They sang for lots of the lovely dances the fairies did. As for the fairies, they felt it was a very great honor for them to be given a party by the wonderful old man in the moon, who had such splendid guests as the pine trees!"

JUNE 29: Billy and the Dragon

BILLY was very, very fat, and, oh, so lazy! The reason he was so fat was because he ate everything he wanted. He used to spend every penny he ever got all on himself, and he always bought candy.

"When supper time came he really made himself very sick over jam, for he always persisted in eating loads and loads of jam and would not even spread it on his toast, but would eat it plain out of a spoon.

"One afternoon he went to a party. He was very disagreeable and wouldn't play any games at all. He simply sat in a corner and waited until supper time came. Then he ate all the ice-cream, all the candy and all the cake that he could get hold of. None of the other children went near him, for they didn't care about a little boy who only cared about eating all the time.

"That night Billy felt very sick when he went to bed. But he soon

155

fell asleep. In his sleep, though, a great horned dragon appeared and said to him:

" 'Billy, it's for your sake I'm coming here tonight. We dragons aren't nearly so dreadful as we're made out to be. We take a great interest in children, and I am going to take a great interest in you.

" 'Before you made such a little—yes, I must say it—a little piggie-wig of yourself you were a very nice little boy. But now you're fat and lazy. So every night I shall chase you around in your dreams until you give up eating so much jam and candy and until you once more enjoy playing around with the other little boys and girls.'

" 'Oh, please don't!' said Billy, who was terrified.

" 'Yes,' said the dragon; 'I'm a good friend of yours, and I shall help you be a happy boy. In a few weeks you really won't know yourself.'

"With that he was gone, but he kept his word, and every night chased Billy around in his dreams until he gave up eating so many sweets and played games and enjoyed other children."

JUNE 30: Cozy Balsam Flowers

I AM sure," said daddy, "that the scarlet flowers known as the Balsam flowers love the very coziness of a fireplace. For they always thrive better in a room where there is an open fire than they do with Mr. Sun's rays shining down upon them.

"And perhaps they can read stories in the fireplace. Perhaps they can see fairy-tales being acted in the blue and red and orange flames.

"Anyway, they love the open fires, and so I think we ought to call them the cozy Balsam Flowers!"

JULY 1: A Brother's Plan

THERE was once," said daddy, "a boy whose name was Worthington, and for short they called him Worthy.

"He had a sister whom he called Mimmie, and it is a story of these two I want to tell you this evening."

Jack and Evelyn looked very much pleased. They loved to hear about other children, especially of boys and girls about their own ages.

"Worthington was unlike some brothers, but he was like you in this way, Jack; he liked to play with his sister. His sister liked, too, to play with him. He never frightened her, but he showed her how to do things, and she was never afraid when she was with him. In the fall he took her for rides in her express-cart, and he made a high seat in the cart for her when he took her for slower and more stylish rides.

"He taught her to climb trees and to swim and to do tricks on the trapeze. And she, too, used to play in the snowball fights, back in the forts which he and the other boys would make.

"Well, it was summer, and Worthington was not going to school. He thought and he thought and he thought, and finally he said:

" 'I wonder if it couldn't be done. I will try anyway.' He worked out the whole scheme in his head, and the next day he went to his aunt who owned a garden, and he said:

" 'Auntie, I have been thinking about something.'

" 'This summer,' he began, 'I could hoe the beans in your garden, and I could weed the garden paths. I could water the flowers every night, and do all the weeding, in fact. You wouldn't need to have a man do the work, except one day a week to do the heavy things. And then I thought I could give Mimmie a present of skates and boots out of my own money in the fall.' And Auntie engaged him as an assistant gardener then and there."

JULY 2: The Best Dream

SOME children," said daddy, "were playing.
" 'Let's pretend we're awfully rich,' said two of the children. 'We shall have motor-cars and we shall have airplanes to fly in. We shall have quantities of people to give orders to. We'll never have to tidy our rooms, and we'll never have to run errands.' So they began to play.

" 'Three other children said, 'Let's be very famous. We shall have all the people in the world swarm around us as the bees do around the flowers for the honey. They shall say how fine we are, how brave we are, and how noble. They'll put up monuments to us.'

"And still three other children wanted to play. 'We want to play that we have a few animals. They are such fun! More fun than anything. And if we treat them right we'll be loved so much. Yes, we shall play we have two dogs and a little pony.'

"Now the Dream-King was sitting on a throne made of silver threads so beautifully woven that they held together and gave him the most wonderful of thrones. Over his head were little boys and girls flying about, and there were Fairies, Gnomes, Elves, Brownies. And that night the Dream-King sent dreams to these children. They all had their play-games made real in their dreams. The two children who wanted to play they were very rich, dreamed they were rich, but oh, how they hated it! All around them were butlers and servants in wonderful liveries. And they had great motor-cars which were driven by quiet, stiff persons who wouldn't answer questions. They felt as if they owned absolutely nothing at all, for everything was taken care of by some one else. They weren't allowed to play and get the least little scrap dirty, for they had to wear such wonderful clothes! Oh, it was a very miserable dream.

"The children who wanted to be very famous dreamed they were surrounded by people who never let them move so they could play. They saw a monument put up in a park with their names written in stone. But the monument was too big to play with.

"The children with the dogs and the pony were having the most gorgeous dream. They were taking such care of their pets and the animals loved them so.

"But at last the Dream-King left them, and they awoke suddenly.

"And one and all agreed that animals and games were fun, but that riches and fame were very, very dull."

JULY 3: The Hash and the Watermelon

THE hash was talking to the watermelon. "I must tell you what the lady of the house said. 'Well, we'll have to have some hash, I fear. I know every one will be furious, but still one can't waste food. And I'll have watermelon as a great treat for dessert to make up for having hash first.

"Oh, dear," said the watermelon, "that was too bad. I should think you would hate me as a result."

"Well, I don't," said the hash, "for I haven't a jealous disposition. I know that I've got to be made and so have the members of my family all over the country, right down through history, I believe, for things must not be wasted. But it doesn't seem as if I were so dreadful as they make me out to be. I think that if cooks bothered a little bit more about me and put in some nice seasoning people might get so they'd say, 'Oh, we're going to have hash to-night; goodie, goodie!' That would certainly rejoice the family of hash if such a thing ever happened."

"I do believe some day people will come to see your true worth," said the watermelon.

"Ah, that's it," said the hash. "I have so much true worth and no

158

charm! I wish I had a little charm, so people would relish me and enjoy me. But I do send out an entreaty to cooks to please season us and make us as nice as possible, for hash is getting tired of insults and would like to be liked just for a change."

JULY 4: Independence Day

THE bird," said daddy, "which has been chosen as the emblem of this country—the bald eagle—has very wonderful and amazing vision or eye-sight, which seems so particularly splendid.

"And doesn't it seem fine to think that our national bird is not only so powerful and free and so much a part of the whole country—for his range is not limited to one part—but that he can see so far?

"For when our national bird can see so far surely it must make us try to see far ahead too and to see clearly and to see truly so that we can all do our best to march on along the paths set for us that July 4th, 1776, in Independence Hall, Philadelphia."

JULY 5: The Sun and the Thunder

NOW Mr. Sun was feeling lazy," said daddy, "and besides this was his day for playing tag with the King of the Clouds and old King Thunder. For (would you believe it?) Mr. Sun is very fond of a good old-fashioned game of tag once in a while, and he began now trying to catch King Thunder.

"As he did so he got back of one of the clouds and it became quite dark on the earth. 'Here,' he said, 'old King Thunder, come here! Those people down on the earth said they were glad you had stopped making such a noise! I wouldn't stand it if I were you. Go back and tell them what you think of them! Roar your hardest!'

"And sure enough the Thunder and Rain began again, and the Earth People said: 'We're having one of those days when one moment the sun is shining and the next it is thundering and raining.'"

JULY 6: The True Story of a Dog

THE Fourth of July had passed and Jack and Evelyn were still very tired, but daddy had a story to tell them, a really true story, and, of course, they were very eager to hear it.

"There was a dog once named Dash. He was an Irish setter, and he belonged to an army family. His master was a young lieutenant in the army, and his master's father was a general.

"Now, this dog was quite old, but he had led an active life which had agreed with him splendidly, and he didn't behave as if he were old at all. There were several young children in the family, and he was made a great pet. What he liked above everything was the sound of guns.

"He had been to numerous army posts, and each one seemed to him to be quite perfect, especially on the days of target practise or when the salutes were fired.

"But, alas, one summer the family went to live in a stupid, quiet little village, where there was absolutely no life at all.

"Dash seemed to be pining away in the village. Quiet country life didn't agree with this dog of the army. The family thought that maybe Dash was going to die of old age until one day came—the day of joy to so many thousands of people! And it was the day for Dash. 'Could it be true?' he thought to himself when he first heard the sound of a huge dynamite cracker. Then came another. With a bound Dash was out of his corner, wide awake and barking furiously. There was no more sleep for that household that night, but little did they care, for all wished to enter into the celebration.

"Late in the day the young lieutenant said to a friend of his: 'Let's go off to the river. I have several cannon fire-crackers to send off. I didn't dare to fire them to-day, as I was afraid they might break the windows. But we can throw them over the bridge. Dash has gone to have his supper and is somewhat calmed down.'

"So off they started for the river, and over the bridge they threw a lighted cannon cracker. Just before it landed in the water off it went with a terrific report.

"They had lighted the other and thrown it into the water when Dash went bounding into the river, swimming toward the awful firecracker. These crackers had been recommended as 'sure to go off,' and there was the beloved Dash going for it.

"But the firecracker did not go off! Dash sniffed at it disgustedly, while his master breathed the biggest sigh of relief and thanks of his life."

JULY 7: The Rabbit Named Pigeon

WHY, what is the trouble, Mrs. Pouter Pigeon?" said Mother Rabbit.

"Oh," sobbed Mrs. Pouter Pigeon, "I have fallen and hurt myself terribly! I won't be able to get out of reach of bigger animals who may want to eat me up, and I don't want to be eaten up."

At that she burst into more sobs.

"Well, to tell you the truth," said Mother Rabbit, "I don't believe there is a creature living who wants to be eaten up. But you come and live with us, and I will see that you are protected."

So Mrs. Pouter Pigeon went to live with Mother Rabbit. They became very friendly and attached to one another.

And then when the next little bunny rabbit was born his mother said, "Now I shall name him Pigeon after you, Mrs. Pouter Pigeon."

And Mrs. Pouter Pigeon strutted about and said, "You have not only saved my life by having me come and live with you, but now you are paying me a fine compliment."

JULY 8: The Big Tent

THIS story," said daddy, "is to be about Peter Gnome's circus. " 'This way to the Big Tent! This way to the Big Tent!' he called. Over and over again he kept saying it until finally he had enough little creatures following him to fill as big a Tent as ever you've seen.

"At last he stopped, and there every one saw an enormous tent made out of birch bark and moss. Inside there were seats made of old trees, and there were also Reserved Seats of old pieces of trees covered with moss. Most of the Fairies took Reserved Seats.

"And there were poles to keep the tent up. Some of the Spiders and Caterpillars who had followed along climbed up the poles. For they said they might miss a great many sights if they stayed on the ground, but if they were high up they would see everything that was going on.

"Then the circus began. And such a circus as it was. The Gnomes had certainly practised some very fine tricks, and the way they dashed about the ring in the center of the tent, and the way they turned somersaults and did tricks, made the Brownies and Elves and Fairies delighted beyond words that they had been invited.

"But when all the tricks were over, and all the little creatures thought it was time to leave, out came Peter Gnome and stood on the platform made of a toadstool in the center of the ring.

" 'Ladies and Gentlemen,' said Peter Gnome—for he had heard that was what they were called in the real circus tents—'I want to take up a few minutes of your time.'

" 'It's not our time any more than any one else's,' interrupted one of the Snails who had come in late.

" 'Well,' continued Peter Gnome, 'for a little while I wish to talk to you. And this is what I want to say. After this circus there will be a concert—one of the finest concerts ever heard. And in addition to that there will be a Side Show where will be seen the Bearded Lady and the Tallest Man living. All keep your seats and one of the Gnomes will be around to collect from you the extra payment of two stems of grass.'

"All of the Fairies and the rest of the audience laughed when Peter Gnome said that. For well they knew he didn't want any payment for the concert and Side Show, but that he thought it would be so much more fun to have a Gnome go around and make believe to collect it."

"Who was the tallest man?" asked Jack.

"Old Mr. Giant," said daddy. "He had been made to come just this once, and he did enjoy being made such a fuss of. The only thing he didn't like so much was when some of the Spiders crawled up his great long legs and tickled him a little. But soon they stopped when they saw he didn't like it and began weaving webs instead.

" 'All right,' said Mr. Giant. 'Make all the homes you like. I'll carry you to my Cave when I go, and you can have your homes there.' The Spiders, of course, were delighted.

"And the Bearded Lady turned out to be none other than Peter Gnome himself—dressed in a fine gown of oak leaves and wearing over his face a mask made out of the roots of trees!"

JULY 9: Mrs. Hippopotamus

L ADIES," said Mrs. Hippopotamus, "are often very vain. They care about their figures and about their looks and about their hats and about their shoes. They care about their dresses and they care about the styles, while I, the fine Mrs. Hippopotamus, am above such things.

"I do not care if my legs are short and my body enormous and all out of proportion to my legs.

"I do not care if my mouth is like a cavern—it is so large. I do not mind it that my skin is so queer, of a funny dark brown color with all sorts of little holes and marks and such all over me.

"I have horribly oily stuff over me too, but I do not mind. What is more, there is great sense to that. That keeps me from getting ill when I go about rivers in Africa where there are all kinds of fevers and much sickness.

"I have great teeth, teeth such as no lady would like, I'm sure. They like little white even teeth, silly little things.

"I'm above such things. I'm not ashamed of my teeth. I like them. They're good sensible, strong teeth. And I'm not going to worry because they're irregular. I'm not so vain as to long for regular teeth.

"My teeth and tusks can act like scissors for they're shaped so as to act that way. That's better than having white even teeth.

"I live in the water and there I go and look for my food. I don't go into silly shops and to market as ladies do.

"But there is just one thing I feel in sympathy with ladies about—at least all ladies who are loving mothers—I can understand what it means to have a baby look at its mother out of its lovely baby eyes which are as beautiful as anything in the world. And I can see its love for its mother, and oh, my whole heart goes out with love for it.

"Yes, sometimes when you see the great old ugly hippopotamus you must not only think of the ugliness but you must say, 'Back of that thick hide, behind that awful jaw and those hideous features, deep down in the heart of a mother hippopotamus there is love and devotion and the beautiful joy of giving of that love to one's own baby.'

"For a baby hippopotamus is a baby to be loved by a mother hippopotamus."

JULY 10: The Papoose

I N a quaint old city," said daddy, "Indians come into town every Saturday morning with bright-colored baskets and beaded moccasins. They make these things and they make beaded bags and purses and little ornaments.

"They drive oxen instead of horses and the oxen move as slowly as if they did not care in the least if they ever got anywhere at all!

"The Indian women, or squaws as they are called, carry large baskets upon their heads in which are the things they have to sell, smaller baskets, purses and moccasins.

"Sometimes, too, they bring into the town flowers in the summer and in the autumn red berries—for they have a little village of their own out in the country.

"One day a little girl named Olive was sitting in her room reading when she heard the front door bell ring. She went downstairs and there was a little Indian girl, not any older than herself.

" 'Will the beautiful lady buy a pretty basket?' asked the little Indian girl.

"Olive was so pleased! She was not nearly big enough to be called 'lady,' for she was still very young, and she was quite sure that she was not beautiful at all.   She had freckles and a very big mouth, and she had only a little hair which was quite straight.   And she was tall for her age and much too thin.   But she had never been called beautiful before and though she felt the little Indian girl was quite wrong, still she was delighted.

" 'You are beautiful yourself,' said Olive.   For the Indian girl had long black hair and enormous dark eyes, wonderful dark skin with quite a good deal of color.

" 'Me beautiful?' she asked.   'Oh no, I'm not beautiful at all.'

"They each thought the other beautiful because each was so different.

"Olive bought some baskets for her mother and a little beaded purse for herself and then she said to the little Indian girl:

" 'Won't you have some cocoa with me?' The little Indian girl nodded her head and said: 'I like goodies!'

"So Olive and the little Indian girl went into Olive's room and had a fine feast, using blue cups and saucers and eating bread and butter from little blue plates.

" 'Can I tell you a story?' asked the little Indian girl.   Olive was delighted.

" 'Please,' she said.   And the little Indian girl began:

" 'My brother is a very big man.   He is tall and strong and has plenty of muscle.' She bent her arms to show what she meant by muscle and she stood up with her arms above her to show how tall he was.   'He built a boat,' she went on, 'a red boat—a canoe—and he took it along the water so it never made a sound.   He knows how to paddle so!   Never a sound!

" 'We have a river by our hut and he keeps the boat by the bank, tied to an old tree.   He takes us all out in it, but what do you suppose he calls that boat?'

"Olive couldn't guess.   She tried many names she thought the boat might be called, but they were all wrong.   'Tell me,' she begged.

" 'My brother doesn't call his boat after a great strong man, or after a warrior; no, he calls the boat after our little baby brother—who mother calls the little wee one.   He call his boat the Papoose which means an Indian baby—and he means our baby.   His boat which can go out into the big waves and not upset—which is so strong, like my brother—it is named the Papoose after the baby!' Her eyes were dancing with joy but it was time for her to be off.

"She put her basket on top of her head and started off.   'Will your father bring you to see the big Papoose and the little Papoose?' she asked as she left, and to Olive's great delight her mother called out:

" 'We will take you some time.' And both little girls left each other smiling and happy."

JULY 11: A Feast for the Mice

I AM going to tell you about Mr. Gray Mouse's feast," said daddy. "There were biscuits of all sorts and soft cream cheese—such cheese as mice had never had before. Their mouths and paws were covered with it, and one of the little children mice said:

" 'Let's not wipe off our whiskers. We can do that later on when we may be getting hungry again—perhaps after we're in bed.' So all the children mice had very sticky mouths and whiskers. But the big mice said:

" 'Let the children have a good time, for this is a real party.' And Mr. Gray Mouse was very much pleased that all his guests were having such a good time.

"When the party was over and it was time to go home, Mr. Long-Tail Mouse said: 'I'm getting tired of our present home. Let's all have a change. I have been looking at new homes for a little time to be ready in case we ever wanted to move, and I know of a fine one.'

" 'Let's go,' said Grandpa Gray Mouse. 'I never believe in living in one home too long. That's why I'm such an old mouse, and have lived so much longer than most. I keep changing homes—and I fool the cats!'

"So all the mice went to a new home—for they knew in a short time after the feast they had just had that a cat would be invited to the house to live!"

JULY 12: As I Was Going to St. Ives

A S I was going to St. Ives
I met a man with seven wives;
Each wife had seven sacks,
In each sack were seven cats,
And each cat had seven kits.
Kits, cats, sacks, and wives,
How many were going to St. Ives?

JULY 13: Flower Dreams

T HE Fairy Queen," said daddy, "gives sweet dreams to all the flowers. It is part of her work. That is why the flowers are happy and rested and beautiful everywhere. Even out on country roads where there is dust, hard ground and rough places, lovely flowers grow up and are proud and happy as they hear people going by in their automobiles or carriages or walking, exclaiming how wonderful they are.

"Now and again, some little flower turns to one side in the wrong way and it has a bad dream, and then when it wakes up it is not lovely like its brothers or sisters. But that seldom happens. And so, you see, flowers know about sweet dreams—all owing to the Fairy Queen."

JULY 14: The Naughty Breezes

ONE day old Mr. North Wind had been very busy," commenced daddy. "He had told the Breeze Children that they must be very good because he had so much work to do.

" 'What have you to do?' they asked him.

" 'I have to go to the woods and knock down all the old branches so they won't fall on people's heads! I must attend to many things.'

"Now the Breeze Children were very apt to be naughty. 'Let's do some work too,' they said.

" 'What shall we do?' one of them asked.

" 'Well, let's blow about a little and find something.'

"Pretty soon they passed by a window of an office. There were a great many papers lying about on the desks and as one of the little Breeze Children said:

" 'There doesn't seem to be much to do here,' the papers began to blow this way and that.

" 'Oh, let's blow papers,' they shouted as they saw what had happened. And all that day they went about from window to window blowing all the papers they could find. Such a time they had!

"That is why there are paper weights—all because of the Breeze Children who are almost too fond of fun."

JULY 15: The Coral Families

WHY aren't we called coral insects any more, mother?" asked the small coral polyp. Coral is a hard substance used for jewelry and ornaments, you know.

"Because, my dear," said the mother, "you are a kind of animal, and not insect. It is incorrect to call you an insect, just as it would be wrong to call me one."

"But somehow," said the coral polyp, "I would rather be called an insect than a polyp. A polyp doesn't seem to mean much."

"It means what you are," said his mother. "But perhaps that doesn't mean much. We aren't big enough to think of what we are called. We just belong to a big group and you and I have grown friendly. That is why you call me mother polyp. But maybe I am your mother polyp after all. It really is too much trouble to think about. We have beautiful homes and so have all the members of our family. Just think, we have an island named after our homes. It is called Coral Island.

"Oh, I do feel so sorry for those who live in wooden houses and in brick houses. How ugly their homes are. Think of wood and brick compared to coral. Now we live and get all our support from our coral homes. And think how wonderful they are? Some are of red coral and some of pink, but all are beautiful.

"Yes, the more I think of it, the more I'm sorry for the creatures who live in houses of wood or brick, ground holes or rough nests.

"Besides, it is so much finer to have a home on the water—a coast home is far nicer than an inland home."

"Well, I suppose," said the young polyp, "that it all depends on how one looks at it."

"I look at it from the standpoint of a polyp," said the mother polyp proudly.

"To be sure we are wonderful to have such homes," said the young polyp. "And still finer than that is the fact that we have a shoemaker in the family."

"What?" asked mother polyp.

"To be sure," said the young polyp. "There is the coral shoemaker, and he is a relation."

"That's so, that's so," said the mother polyp. "But of course we don't wear shoes, and so he isn't of much use."

"That's true," said the young polyp, "but it is always useful to have one in the family. And it sounds so businesslike to speak of Cousin Coral Shoemaker."

For there is a little creature with just that name and he is a cousin of our friends who live in the coral reefs.

And no wonder the coral families boast and brag of the homes they live in, for very few of us could even dream of living in a jeweled home. But after all, for people and animals a coral reef would be very uncomfortable, and besides people and animals have so very much more sense!

JULY 16: The Garden Tools

"IT'S great fun to be a rake," said the rake, "and to make everything look nice and tidy. And in the autumn it is such fun raking up all the leaves and getting ready for the big bonfires.

"It is fun, too, to rake the freshly mown grass and to make everything smooth and nice."

"Ah, but it is such fun to be a trowel," said the trowel, "and to dig around the garden flowers and to make them grow. They like to be made all nice and comfy, to have the dirt loosened about them to give them a little breathing space.

"They don't like too much! They want to be held in the earth firmly but with soft, nicely pressed earth about them. And our family attends to that."

"Ah, but it is nice to be a hoe," said the hoe, "for I can do such a great deal of work. Just take the work I do with string-beans alone.

"I don't suppose there could be any string-beans if it weren't for me. I do such a great deal with the string-beans. I keep them cheerful. I pay them some attention. I make them feel like growing up into nice vegetables. I hoe all about them."

"But think of all the help I am when any one wants to transplant anything," said the trowel. "I can dig up the root so that plenty of its dirt comes up with it. Plants don't like to leave all their soil behind; they like to take a little of it along with them, just as people do when they're going away for the summer—they like to take along with them some of their photographs and little odds and ends, some of the things near and dear to them."

"It is the same way with the plants and I help to make that possible."

"Well," said the lawn-mower, "I like to make the lawn and the terraces look nice and I do make them look so neat. I'm the lawn's barber, I am!"

All the other garden tools moved about and laughed in their funny tool way at the joke the lawn-mower had tried to crack.

"Pretty good, pretty good," they said.

"And a garden fork like me," said the garden fork, "can do a good deal of work too. I like to do my share."

"We can do a good deal," said several balls of string. "We keep things from falling down and we give them a little help and encouragement."

"So do we," said some little sticks up which some plants were climbing."

"We try to do our part," said a little two-pronged fork and a shovel together.

168

A two-pronged fork is a fork with two prongs instead of three or four as a fork usually has, you will notice.

"But I feel as if I were a great deal of help these days," said the hoe, "just when those string-beans need so much attention."

"And I must thin out some of the flowers," said the trowel. "Some of them are growing so closely together that they won't live that way and so I am going to separate them and put them in other beds."

"And you will need my help, too," said the watering pot, "not to mention the water!"

"That is so," said the trowel. "But I have a great deal of important weeding to do."

"And I will have to rake up the weeds that you have dug up in the garden path," said the rake, "or things won't look tidy and neat."

"And I must water all the flowers for there hasn't been any rain in some time and it's up to me to do a great deal of work," said the watering pot.

"I really think," said the rake, "that we are all useful. We all help the one who owns the garden. Yes, every one of us helps.

"We must all work, each do his part, for each one is needed for something or other."

"You're right," said the hoe; "none of us should boast alone. We should all work together for the good of the garden and for the good of the flowers. Then we will each be doing more, for when creatures and things work together and don't waste time boasting and arguing then a lot gets finished."

JULY 17: The Jolly Dust Brothers

ALL the dust in the world belongs to the Family of the Dust Brothers—just as every little Toad or Frog belongs to the Toad or Frog family," said daddy. "One day not long ago, a group of the Dust Brothers had moved to all the window sills in a little house they thought was very nice. Some of them had chosen to hide behind pictures, and under chairs, and on the glass mirrors. The ones who hid on the glass mirrors thought they would have lots of fun because folks could not see themselves so plainly—and then they would see the new-comers to the mirrors. Not, of course, that it was the first time any of them had ever made mirrors their homes—but they hadn't been back since the last dusting day.

"The best friend of the Dust Brothers when they are wide awake is old Mr. Sun. Then they can all be seen by the lady of the house and what fun it is for them to be scolded at and to dash off again—only to come back whenever they feel like it.

"When they have moved to a new home and are tired and sleepy the dark clouds are their friends, and Mr. Rain; for then it is so dark they can't be seen and they have a good old sleep.

"But yesterday when the Dust Brothers were having such a frolic it was a beautiful day. Mr. Sun had just decided it was getting up time—and he had dressed slowly and with great care so he would look very fine and stylish.

"As he was ready to peep in the windows to see what was going on he saw a lot of little Gnomes perched all around talking to the Dust Brothers.

" 'Why is it,' asked Peter Gnome, 'that you are so anxious to live where you know you'll be sent away again? Why don't you choose some home where you can stay?'

" 'Oh, Peter,' they cried in shocked whispers, 'you don't understand us. You truly don't.' And if they could have cried without drowning themselves I am sure they would have—for they sounded very sad for a minute. But then they became happy again for they explained it all to Peter Gnome.

" 'You see,' they continued, 'if we live somewhere and are not driven away too many of the Family come to join us—and it's more fun to have lots and lots of homes than a few big ones for all of us. It would make us have a life like a hotel—ah no, we must have a home life—just a few of us living together at a time. Of course, we don't take up much room, so more of us can live together than most folks.

" 'And as for wanting to have our adventures any different—dear me—we wouldn't change for all the world. We can tease and tease and tease those big grown-ups with their brooms and dusters. Hurrah, hurrah, what merry lives we lead.

" 'And now, Mr. Sun,' they said, 'shine for all you're worth—so the grown-ups will see us. Then we'll be off for a scamper.'

"Sure enough, Mr. Sun did just as the Dust Brothers had asked him to, and as the Gnomes were rushing off to call on their old friend Mr. Giant, they heard the Dust Brothers laughing and saying,

" 'They drive us away, but we always come back,
We say Hurrah, but they say Alack!' "

JULY 18: The Bad Poison Ivy

THE little white berries of Poison Ivy," said daddy, "are clustered quite near together on the stem, that is, they are all near each other, and then from the little part of the stem which is the fattest goes up a longer, slimmer stem from which branch out three leaves, all of them pointed somewhat and very clearly and evenly marked with veins.

"Now, sometimes Poison Ivy is to be found in swamps and in ponds and along the sides of the brooks and in the woods, too.

"Keep away from it and from what you think is Poison Ivy.

"A very good way to do each summer is to go to a library and get hold of a big nature book or ask the librarian what book one shall look at in order to see a picture of Poison Ivy. And then remember what it looks like. For the Poison Ivy family is a mean one."

JULY 19: The Sun Fairies

M R. Sun slowly went behind a hill—but what should remain in the sky after he had left but wonderful spots and dots of red—bright, bright red—just the color Mr. Sun had been before he went behind his hill for his night's sleep," said daddy.

" 'They must be the Fairies of the Sun,' said the Fairy Queen. And that is what they were!"

JULY 20: The Meadow Fritillary Family

I MUST tell you this evening," commenced daddy, "a story about the meadow fritillary family."

"Oh, gracious, daddy!" exclaimed Jack. "Now really!"

"Well," said Evelyn, "at least I understand it has something to do with a meadow, but it may be a flower, fruit, animal or bird for all I know."

"None of those," said daddy laughing. "Guess again."

"Well, it might be the name of a big rock," said Jack.

"Wrong," said daddy. Both the children laughed and started to think of some other creatures and objects which might be in a meadow.

"Of course," said Evelyn, "there are the meadow larks, but they are birds, and daddy said these fritillaries aren't birds." Evelyn had a very hard time calling them by their name and Jack said admiringly: "Well, Evelyn, I wouldn't dare try that!"

"There are meadow crickets," said Evelyn.

"Now, we're coming a little bit closer," said daddy.

"Oh, do tell us," urged Jack.

"The meadow fritillaries," said daddy, "are butterflies!"

"Gracious," said Evelyn, "that's a pretty hard name for a little butterfly to carry."

"They have cousins named the Silver-Spot Fritillary family and the Gulf Fritillary family, but it is of the meadow ones I am going to tell you, and I think it would be easier for us to speak of them as the Meadow family and leave out their long last name.

"Mother Meadow had become a butterfly in June and after four weeks had gone by she laid her little eggs, and in another week there were little caterpillars. After that Mother Meadow knew there would be butterflies; and it would take a month for them to become chrysalides and another week for them to become full-fledged butterflies. So Mother Meadow was much excited.

"And after a time there would be more butterflies and she would be a grandmother, and still more and she would be a great-grandmother. All that would happen in a summer. And there would be still others but they wouldn't become full-grown until another spring came around. They would stop feeding and sleep throughout the winter as many butterflies will do.

"The latest children of the Meadow Fritillary family in September feed upon the leaves of violets which they think are particularly delicious.

"When it gets cold ahead of time in the autumn the little half-grown butterflies go right to sleep and don't bother about food, but when the next spring comes they make up for it and eat twice as much.

"Mother Meadow lives in the lowland meadows and near swamps. She loves a home near the spots where blue and white and purple violets grow, for she knows her children love the sweet leaves.

"The Meadow family also takes honey from mint and other plants that grow near the swamps.

" 'Our cousins,' said Mother Meadow to her brood one day, 'are very much like us except for the row of silver spots which line their wings. That is why they are called the Silver-Bordered Fritillary family. But we are nice brown speckled butterflies and are as happy as our handsome cousins.'

" 'Have we any more cousins?' asked the Meadow children butterflies.

" 'Oh, yes,' said Mother Meadow, 'there are the Silver-Spot Fritillaries, the Great Spangled Fritillaries and the Regal Fritillaries as well as different kinds of the silver variety. But we are just as happy and contented as any of them, even if we are rather plain and dull and brown for butterflies.

" 'And, my children, you rested on violet leaves when you were little eggs. Some of you rested on the stems of the violet plants, but most of you were right on the beautiful green leaves.

" 'So though we're rather simple little butterflies, we mothers gave you beds fit for princesses.'

" 'Ah, we're happy,' said the little butterflies, as they flew about in the warm summer sunshine."

JULY 21: George and the Goblin

A LITTLE boy named George," said daddy, "was very ill. He had not told his mother he felt sick and wretched because he was afraid she might give him some horrid medicine, so he went to bed without saying a word.

"He felt as though he had been in bed for hours and as if he would never go to sleep when suddenly a little Goblin hopped on his window sill, peeped around the curtain, and said:

" 'Good evening. May I come in?'

" 'Who are you?' asked George.

" 'I am the Goblin who looks after little sick boys—when they have your kind of sickness. The only trouble is that I can't see half the little boys I want to—for I can only go at night-time when they're sleeping, and there isn't time for my rounds. I do believe I shall have to get some Assistant Workers,' and the Goblin looked puzzled.

" 'You're a Goblin?' gasped George.

" 'To be sure,' said the Goblin.

" 'Why,' continued George, 'I thought they were terrible looking creatures.'

" 'Ha, ha,' laughed the Goblin. 'You make just the same mistake that so many boys and girls do. You see I am not terrible at all. In fact, I am very nice and I cure little boys and girls of their pains.'

" 'Are you a Doctor Goblin, then?' laughed George.

" 'No,' smiled the Goblin. 'Doctors and I really need have nothing to do with each other. Doctors should only be called in when little girls and boys are really, really sick and not when they're only pretending.'

" 'I'm not pretending,' said George, almost in tears. 'I feel just as sick as can be.'

" 'Nothing to brag about, is it?' asked the Goblin.

" 'No-o,' said George.

" 'And why are you sick?' asked the Goblin.

" 'I don't know,' said George. For surely, he thought to himself, the Goblin couldn't know what he had been doing in the daytime—and George did know, perfectly well, why he was sick.

" 'Did you enjoy those candies?' asked the Goblin, and George looked quite uneasy.

" 'I don't know,' said George.

" 'I suppose it is hard to make up your mind now whether you liked them or not—since they have made you sick.'

" 'Oh dear, oh dear,' cried George, who had thought he was going to have fun with the Goblin, and he hid his head under the bedclothes in shame.

" 'You see,' continued the Goblin, 'you were getting into the habit of really making a little piggie of yourself! You were getting too fat and lazy. You didn't like to play ball with the boys nearly so much as you once did. Isn't that true?' And George, who had stuck his head out of the bedclothes again, nodded.

" 'And some of the boys were beginning to call you "Roly-poly George," weren't they? And they were telling you that soon you'd be able to join the circus as the fat boy? It wasn't very kind of them perhaps, but it was true, eh?' And the Goblin grinned.

" 'Yes,' was all George could say.

" 'And last of all, you ate that whole layer of chocolates in the box that was hidden in the party; you thought you were having a great feast. Until—until—until—'

" 'Oh I know,' said George. 'I felt dreadfully sick—but I'm better now. Don't scold me any more, please.'

" 'I won't,' said the Goblin. 'I visit little boys and girls like you because I know you don't want to get sick—and half the time you don't know that so many sweeties are very, very bad for you—and that you'll grow fat and lazy and no one will care for you when it comes play time.'

" 'I'll be good—and not a piggie any more!' said George. 'I did feel so sick—and I don't want to be the fat boy in the circus. I want to stay at home and play with my friends!'

" 'And you will!' said the Goblin. 'To-morrow morning you'll be all right—but first of all—to-night we're going to take you for a sail in our airboat just to show you that Goblins are really nice creatures after all!'

"And several weeks later, George was so well and so strong and quick in the games that he was made Captain of his Baseball Team!"

JULY 22: Jack-in-the-Pulpit

I AM Jack-in-the-pulpit," announced a wild flower one day.

"Are you?" asked the gnats and flies walking and flying about.

"I am indeed," said Jack. "If you don't believe me, you can have a look."

"We are invited to have a look," said the gnats to each other and the flies said: "We can call upon him, and he looks very fine, too."

"In the spring," said Jack, for he thought it was the correct thing to preach a little sermon as he was in a pulpit, "in the spring," he continued, "I have many bright red berries. Years and years ago the Indians used to boil these berries and found them very good to eat.

"But at this time of the year, I am simply at my best. Oh, yes, I feel so jolly and well, so happy and gay."

And Jack smiled at the little creatures around him.

"You would be surprised, no doubt," he went on, "if I should tell you a few things about my family history. Some I will leave unsaid, however," he added with a roguish look.

Now, over Jack's head was a part of the flower which looked like the sounding-board of a pulpit. He stood very straight in his pulpit, which was very handsome, striped in greenish-yellow, white and orange-yellow colored decorations.

"I have a fine cousin," he said, "and this is the part of my family history I want to tell you. My cousin is the Calla-lily and she has a beautiful white gown which she wears. But she is striped as I am, and she is a cousin, though she cares more for dress than I do, and looks very stately and fine.

"I am more natural," said Jack. "I'm a good sort of a chap. I like to talk to my little friends and give them advice because I am very fond of preaching."

"He must be very fine," the gnats said.

"How beautiful to give us advice," the flies added.

And to himself Jack was saying: "The poor little insects, little do they know me. I am not as fine as I make myself out to be. I should just say I'm not.

"For I do not practice what I preach. I don't believe in doing such a foolish thing. That is, I preach to the little creatures and then I let them come and see my pulpit—and then, it's very, very seldom that I ever let them out again." Then Jack began to preach once more and gathered about him more stupid and innocent little gnats and flies! But, of course, as he is only a flower we can't blame him too much.

JULY 23: The Tide

BILLIE BROWNIE was talking to the High Tide as it came up over the beach," said daddy. "'Don't you ever work any faster or any slower?' asked Billie Brownie.

"'Certainly not,' said the Tide. 'Why should we?'

" 'It would be nice, I should think, to change some day and rush in very suddenly, and then some other day stay way out on the beach and not come in for hours and hours—long after you are due.'

" 'That would be very wrong,' said the Tide. 'We are helped in what we do by two very noble creatures.' And all the time the Tide was talking its voice would get louder and louder, for all the waves were roaring and making such a racket.

" 'Who are they?' asked Billie Brownie.

" 'The Sun and the Moon,' roared the Tide. 'The Moon is three times more important than the Sun—but the Sun is mighty helpful too. We do as they say, you see. Twice every twenty-four hours of your time we come in and go out. And we do this at such hours as the Sun and Moon wish. So if people ask the Sun and Moon, or watch them for a time, they will be able to tell just what we are going to do. And we never change the time they've given us—never—NEVER!' And the Tide bellowed this for all it was worth.

" 'I wouldn't keep such good time,' said Billie Brownie, 'no, not for any creature—not even Mr. Sun or Mr. Moon. And yet I'm a great friend of both.'

" 'Ah, you're not such a friend as we are,' said the Tide 'We have always done as Mr. Moon said for years and years and years—too many for me to remember.'

" 'But you might just as well be a clock and get wound up if you're going to keep such good time and do things just exactly when you're supposed to. It seems very foolish to me,' and Billie Brownie put his head to one side as he thought about it.

" 'Ah,' said the Tide, 'that's just where you're so wrong. A clock has to be looked after. Some one has to wind it up. No one has to wind us up. And a clock often gets out of order and goes to the clock-maker to be mended. You never heard of the Tide going to a Tide Mender to be mended, did you?'

" 'I never knew there was such a thing as a Tide Mender,' said Billie Brownie.

" 'There isn't!' said the Tide. 'That's just it. We don't need one—for we never get out of order. And no one has to worry about us or fuss about us. We just do as Mr. Sun and Mr. Moon say—especially Mr. Moon, as I've told you, for somehow,' and the voice of the Tide grew lower, 'Mr. Moon has better judgment. I can whisper this to you now, for Mr. Sun has gone to bed and won't feel hurt! And now I must go out to the ocean again—for I've been talking to you for hours.' "

JULY 24: Little Edith's Garden

W HATEVER shall I do?' said little Edith to herself," commenced daddy, " 'I do want to have a garden so much and yet the snails eat it up!'

"While she was wondering like this a little voice whispered in her ear:

" 'Edith, Edith,' it said.

" 'Yes,' answered Edith looking about her. And then, seeing no one, said:

" 'Who are you? Where are you?'

" 'I'm the Fairy Queen,' said the voice, 'and you can't see me because I've put on my invisible robe—which no one can see but a Fairy. I've come to talk to you. I know how you love your garden and that you've not been able to make anything grow this summer. Listen!' And a queer swishing sound passed through the air.

" 'There!' continued the Fairy Queen, 'I have waved my invisible wand and it will bring you luck. Do not plant any seeds for a week —then the snails will think you have decided not to have any garden at all! It will be a joke on them—but they have had enough feasts and now it is time for you to have a garden!'

"In a short time Edith had real flowers, and her garden was more beautiful than ever it had been, and often when she was working among the flowers, she said half aloud:

" 'If the Fairy Queen is around me in her invisible robe, I want to thank her, oh, so much, for my lovely garden.' "

JULY 25: The Earth Visits the Moon

W HEN Mr. Moon is 'eclipsed,' as they say, it means the earth gets in the way, and when Mr. Sun is 'eclipsed' it means that Mr. Moon is in the way. And that makes it dark—for an Eclipse is a shadow," explained daddy.

"Mr. Moon was shining hard. He was very bright and the sky seemed to be lighted up by him. All the stars were out and were twinkling with joy and fun, for well they knew what was going to happen.

"Mr. Moon was also looking very fat and well! Goodness! but he was round and big and jolly! He blinked one eye and then he winked with the other, and he said to himself:

" 'The Earth is going to pay me a visit to-night. I am highly honored. It's not often that the earth comes my way—and that's why I am all dressed up in my best.'

"Pretty soon the grown-ups on the Earth saw a shadow come over part of Mr. Moon's face. Very, very slowly he grew darker, and the Earth people all came out of doors to watch what was going to happen.

" 'I'm pretty important, I am,' said Mr. Moon to two very tall pine trees. And the pine trees whispered back in the slight, rustling breeze:

" 'Yes, Mr. Moon, you're very important. And you show us off too. We look handsome, and dark, and tall, when you throw your light over us.'

" 'Hush—' said Mr. Moon. 'The Earth is on its way.'

"And only half of Mr. Moon could be seen now. The other half was covered up by a dark shadow.

" 'That's the earth throwing its shadow on the moon,' said the grown-ups to each other. But up in the sky the Moon was saying:

" 'Well, how do you do, Mr. Earth? It's a long time since I've seen you. And how have you been all this time?'

" 'Well,' said the Earth, as it cast its shadow over Mr. Moon still more, 'I've been in my usual good health. I still am a pretty good and solid soul, you know. I stand for so much too! I let folks walk all over me, and still I never murmur in the least. I let the King of the Clouds pour down on me—and Mr. Sun warms me up with his rays so that I begin to grow thirsty again.

" 'And,' the Earth continued, 'sometimes the children dig me up—and I don't mind in the very least. It's just my nature, I suppose!'

" 'Yes,' said Mr. Moon, 'you are a good-natured old soul.'

" 'Old?' asked the Earth. 'Why, every spring I am just as young and fresh again as if I were not a minute old. Whatever do you mean, Mr. Moon?'

" 'That's true,' said Mr. Moon. 'You certainly do come up younger every spring—but you have been around a great many years.'

" 'It's a good thing I have,' laughed the Earth; 'and now tell me how you have been?'

"Mr. Moon was almost entirely covered by the Earth's shadow as he began his talk:

" 'I am shining as brightly as ever, and I still change my suit several times a month. In fact, there's not much difference in me—or in my life. I do much the same things always. I'm what you might call a very sensible old fellow. I do everything right on time, and enjoy myself hugely.'

" 'There, there,' said the Earth. 'I must be going again.'

" 'What short visits you pay,' said Mr. Moon as he began to show his brightness again.

" 'Do you know why I do that?' whispered the Earth.

" 'No,' said Mr. Moon, and he took a little walk along the sky.

" 'Because,' said the Earth, 'grown-ups think it's a wonderful thing when I call on you. I don't let them get used to it—and so they think that it's very, very m-a-r-v-e-l-o-u-s! Look at all the Earth people, and then you'll agree with me.'

"And of course, true enough, down on the Earth, every one was looking at the Eclipse."

JULY 26: The Elephant's Toothache

THE Elephant's mouth was very much swollen," said daddy, "and the Zoo dentist said, 'He has a very bad tooth, but we'll fix this right away, so he won't have any more pain.'

"So they put something in the tooth and all around it so the elephant wouldn't feel any pain at all. It made it feel quite dull and the throbbing which he had felt for two weeks went away.

"In a very few minutes, with the help of an instrument which made the elephant shake a little nervously as he saw it (for he couldn't imagine what it might be), out came the tooth.

" 'There,' said the Zoo dentist, 'you will have no more pain.'

"In a few days the elephant was himself again. The soreness had all gone away and he was eating once more—and eating the most delicious of dishes, for the keeper said:

" 'I want to reward you all I can, as you're the bravest creature I've ever known, for you've had this toothache for some time and we never knew it until your mouth became so swollen. Yet you never complained. And that was why you haven't been eating well lately.' "

JULY 27: The Potato Skins

THE potato skin is receiving fair treatment and justice at last," said the second potato skin to the first potato skin. "What is justice?" asked the first potato skin.

"Justice," said the second potato skin, "is being just and to be just is to be fair. Now do you understand?"

"I do," said the first potato skin. "Please go on with your story, and forgive me for the interruption. I don't know much about manners I haven't been up in the world enough. The ground is no place for manners, you know; at least I didn't think so. And then our chief callers and friends were the potato bugs. They're not overly mannerly."

"I will forgive you," said the second potato skin. "For I don't know that I am mannerly myself." The second potato skin had been trying to tell a story.

"A great professor made a study of us and he decided we were not poisonous, as some people have tried to make out, but that we were healthful and good, and that for people who didn't care much for the taste of the skins, we could be ground very fine and cooked with cream," continued the second potato skin.

"Fine, fine," said the first potato skin. "To be cooked with cream sounds very nice indeed."

"That is the way we're going to be used," said the second potato skin. "And isn't it wonderful to think professors study us and our good points?"

"It does sound mighty fine," said the first potato skin. "Somehow one doesn't think of the two together—professors and potatoes—but it is nice to think that we are high enough up to be the companions of professors."

JULY 28: The Traveling Flowers

A GREAT, great, great many years ago, oh, so many, many, many years ago, there were not so many big cities as there are now," said Mother Nature one day to her children.

"There was more room everywhere and people almost all had gardens and flowers and could walk just a little distance and gather all the wild flowers they wanted.

"But the cities grew up and somehow, without meaning to, I'm sure, they pushed the flowers out of the way.

"Many of the people missed the flowers and the ferns and the shrubs and the Nature children. But they couldn't do the work they had to in the city and have gardens, too, for there wasn't any room in the city for the gardens.

"Well, when the spring-time came along one year, after so many cities had grown bigger and bigger and so many people had gone to live in the cities, the Nature children called and said:

"'Mother Nature, the Dream King has told us that many, many people from the cities will be out in the country places for holidays and for week-ends this spring.

"'So we have thought up a plan. You see, the Dream King tells us that every once in a while the people get very tired from all the business they must do and all the studying they must do, too.

" 'So we've decided we would look our very best all the time, so that when the people from the cities come out to see us they may pick some of us and take us home with them so we'll cheer them up.'

"I told them I thought their idea was wonderful. And ever since then the flowers have all looked their best and the shrubs have all looked their best and the ferns have all looked their best, so they could cheer up the city people when they were taken back after holidays.

"So when any of you are picked and carried to the cities, keep your prettiest and freshest smiles on your faces."

And they all promised Mother Nature they would.

JULY 29: The Visitors

A LITTLE girl named Lillian," said daddy, "had a very sore throat and could only swallow soft foods.

" 'I think I will call my desserts my visitors,' she said one day, 'for I will have to have some make-believe games now that I have to be in bed a little while longer.'

"So when lunch time came and there was cornstarch on her tray, she would say: 'Welcome, Lord Cornstarch! How is Your Highness to-day? Of course you can't talk to me. But I can talk to you, and I will do you the great honor due one of your rank and station—that is, I will eat you! Then she would eat her dessert of cornstarch until it was all gone.

"When supper time came and she had cornstarch again, she would say: 'Well, I am glad to see you, Lady Cornstarch. How is Your Highness this fine evening? I don't suppose Your Ladyship cares to have a little chat, but I am sure Your Ladyship wouldn't mind being eaten, eh?' And so Lady Cornstarch would disappear.

"On jelly day she would greet her lunch time jelly by saying: 'Glad to see you, Prince Jelly. It's nice that you are such a pleasant prince and will slip down so easily. I wouldn't like it at all if you were horrid and stiff, as I imagine some princes might be.'

"Her supper jelly she would greet in this fashion:

" 'Good evening, Princess Jelly, how are you this evening? I hope your taste is very fine and that I will enjoy you.' And then she would eat Princess Jelly.

"And it made the time she had to spend in bed pass much more quickly this way."

JULY 30: The Little Bumblebee's Mistake

T HE fairies had a fancy-dress ball last night," commenced daddy.

"They all went as different flowers. One little fairy was dressed so she looked like a bright red nasturtium, another was dressed as a pink rambler rose, another as a yellow golden-glow, another as a pansy, another as a little forget-me-not, and all of them, in short, in lovely costumes like flowers.

"The Fairy Queen wore the costume of the American Beauty Rose, and her wand was one tall, tall rose, very full and big and splendid.

"They had dancing and games and all the elves, the brownies and many of the wood creatures had been invited. But one of the funniest things happened you can imagine. Some of the fairies had dressed themselves as honey-suckles. They kept together and danced together so they would look like a vine. Others had dressed as a vine of morning-glories.

"Pretty soon a buzzing was heard. It was louder than the band of crickets they had engaged for the music; it was louder than the sounds that came from the laughter of the fairies.

"You see, nobody had thought of such a thing happening. The bumble-bees and the humming birds, who had all gone to sleep, had in their dreams imagined they saw lovely morning glories still awake and lovely honey-suckles all over the vines.

"One little bumble-bee went to his smaller brother and nudged him, saying,

" 'Oh, look over there; morning-glories!'

"The other little bumble-bee was about to turn over and go to sleep, for he had scarcely so much as peeped to see, when he, too, suddenly noticed all the morning-glories. They awoke all the bumble-bees far and near and made so much fuss and noise that they woke up the humming-birds, who always notice what the bumble-bees are up to.

"Of course the humming-birds immediately spied the honey-suckles, and you should have seen them scamper.

"When the fairies realized what had happened they almost lost their balance in the dances, for they shook all over with laughter.

"As the bumble-bees and the humming-birds got nearer they, too, saw that they had made a mistake, but the fairies at once called out,

" 'Come to the party and dance, too, and we will give you honey, for we are having it for supper. We couldn't give a ball and dress like flowers without having flower-honey for supper.'

"And this delighted them all."

JULY 31: Ripe Raspberries

"D ID you hear the great news?" asked one of the raspberry bushes of another bush.

"No, what is the great news?" asked the other raspberry bush.

"There is going to be a great raspberry hunt to-day," the first raspberry bush said.

"Well, if they see us they won't have to hunt very far," the second raspberry bush said.

"That is so," answered the first raspberry bush, "and they know we're here. We let some of our messengers tell them. The only thing is they are not sure whether or not we are ripe, and so they will be delighted when they find how easily we come off the bushes. For when we're ripe we come off easily and when we're not ripe we stick on and show we aren't ripe enough to come off."

AUGUST 1: The Brave Mocking Bird

"I HAVE a true story to tell you this evening, children," said daddy, "of a mocking bird.

"Mr. Mitchell Mocking Bird was his name and he was a pet in a large family of children. They all loved him and he could speak a good many words, and he could sing like ever so many birds. He was allowed out of his cage, too. One night Mitchell began to scream. How he did yell! Piercing yells went all through the house! And he hurried from one bedroom to another. He awoke the mother and daddy of the children first and then he woke up the children.

" 'Come!' he called. It was a word he could say, and he kept repeating it over and over again.

" 'Come! Come! Come!' And they all hurried, one after the other, and followed the mocking bird downstairs.

"What should they see but a tiny blaze, which every few minutes seemed to grow and splutter and burst into a bigger flame.

" 'Water! Every one get water!' shouted the children's daddy, and the mocking bird kept calling:

" 'Come!'

"They were all thoroughly frightened but they kept their wits about them and kept filling buckets and jugs with water which they poured over the flame.

"After a little while it was out. The Mocking Bird looked very tired.

His eyes blinked as if he could hardly keep awake, and it was just then that every one of them noticed him.

" 'Mitchell, you have saved the house and our lives. That fire would have spread and goodness knows what would have happened,' said their daddy. 'What a fine, brave bird you are.'

"And the children stroked Mitchell and said:

" 'Fine, brave bird. Daddy says so, too! Our lovely Mitchell Mocking Bird.'

"Mitchell was almost asleep. The fire was out. He had finished his work. He was ready to rest now. He didn't care about praise. But he was happy that they all loved him so. And how he cared for them. He had saved them and they knew it. He was very happy. And in his own bird way he had thought all this out.

"But to the great surprise of them all, Mitchell said a word they had never known he could say, but it was just the right one. 'Safe, all safe,' said Mitchell, as he went to sleep."

AUGUST 2: The Milkweed Plants

NOW the milkweed plant is rather thick with a hollow center and through this center the white milk goes which gives the plant its food. The milk doesn't care for the air and so that is why the milk stains our hands when we pick the plants.

The leaves are large and of a yellow, gray-green color, while the flowers which grow in clusters are of a pink-lavender shade.

But the little pods filled with seeds are the things the children like and if you see a milkweed plant just look at the little pods.

"I must have milk to drink and to make me strong," said Milly Milkweed.

"So must I," said Mamie Milkweed.

"And not only does it make us strong," said Milly, "but it gives strength to the butterflies which feast upon us, for if we are strong and delicious it makes them strong and beautiful.

"Ah," said Mamie, "it's fine to have butterflies and children for friends, and to have our very own milkman always with us. We're never forgotten in the early mornings by any possible accident. No, we always have our milkman and we have friends."

AUGUST 3: Telephone Peas

HELLO, Telephone Peas and String-Beans," said Lord Lettuce. "Lady Lettuce and the Lettuce youngsters are coming up, too, and there are going to be lots of crops of us. We make a fine salad, we're so young and tender and fresh. Seems to me,

Telephone Peas, you hurried me up.   You know this is our second crop. We've been here before.   But I do believe it was your very name that hurried me.

"I heard you say it and I acted as my relatives say people do when they hear the telephone.   I've even heard that they've left the salad on their plates and have answered the telephone before they ate their salad.   Yes, your very name and saying it must have hurried us."

"Well," said the Telephone Peas, "we feel up to date.   We don't know that there is any special reason for our name, but we have grown to like it mighty well.   We're supposed to be a large, good kind, too; in fact, one of the best there are."

"Dear me," said one of the String-Beans, "I wish some one would call our family the Airplane String-Beans or something like that.   Or perhaps we might be called the Submarine String-Beans."

"There wouldn't be much sense to that," said the Potato, almost ready to eat, "for you are up on vines.   Now we might have that name because we're in the ground, though it is true we are not under the water."

And the garden vegetables all agreed that that was true but that the Telephone Peas had a fine family name in reality.

AUGUST 4: The Harebell Umbrellas

"THE musk-ox," said daddy, "is prepared for the rain by the coarse hair which grows on top of his nice, soft hair.   This coarse hair, as you know, catches the rain and then he shakes it all off so that his body doesn't get wet.

"The umbrella bird can put up some of his feathers just as people put up their umbrellas and that protects him from the rain.

"Both the great big musk-ox and the little umbrella bird are very proud that they always have their rain protectors with them, and they have very little use for people who forget their umbrellas and borrow other people's and then forget to return them.

"Of course the musk-ox and the umbrella bird can't very well lend their umbrellas because they don't carry them around by the beak or front paw, but instead have their umbrellas attached to them.

"But they aren't the only creatures to be so careful about the rain, that is, there are some flowers who are just as careful, and the harebell, of which I am going to tell you, sees that none of its family will ever drown.

"Now, the harebell family of flowers are blue in color.   The flowers grow on thin, rather tall stems, and when the flowers are in bud they grow very straight and stand right up. When the tiny buds burst into flowers, if they stayed straight up, as they stand when they are buds, every time the rain came it would fill the little flowers and completely drown them, and make them droop forever.

"The little blue petals aren't strong enough to stand the rain, and the flowers are shaped so the rain would come right into them and fill them up—for the harebells are like little bells. So they drop their little heads just before they open and then the rain can't hurt them."

AUGUST 5: A Children's Circus

THIS way to the big show," some children were shouting. "Come right along," they said. "This is the way to see all the wonders of the age. Look at the Frog-Child, the Snake-Lady, the Toad-Man, the Turtle Babies."

All the children went in the direction from which the shouts and orders were given.

The children who were shouting were very much excited. "Admission to the show, ten cents," they kept saying. "It's the most wonderful show in the world."

There were a dozen children giving a play-circus which was supposed to be very much like a real one. They had asked all their friends and the money they received was to go to a children's ward in a hospital. Every one of their friends came and soon the circus began. First of all there was a long parade while some of the children beat drums, and others played tunes on combs covered with tissue paper.

Two little girls rode ponies and on the heads of the ponies sat two monkeys made of cloth! They had bead eyes!

A boy did a lot of fine tricks on a rocking horse, and there were all the usual circus tricks, although perhaps not some of the more difficult ones.

After a little while a boy came out on the platform and said,

"Ladies and Gentlemen, Boys and Girls, Cats and Dogs, we have now to offer a fine performance—a side show. We have shown you the regular acts of the circus and we trust that you are pleased." Here followed a great deal of clapping and shouting.

"And," the boy continued, "we are now to have the great privilege of seeing the Frog-Child, the Snake-Lady, the Toad-Man, the Turtle-Babies. Step this way, Ladies, Gentlemen, Boys, Girls, Cats and Dogs. Come right inside the tent at your left and there you will see these things. There is no extra charge for admission."

All the children at once began to troop to their left through the side tent.

"What could it mean?" they asked each other. What surprises they were getting!

When they were inside the tent how they did laugh! One of the children was in just such a green suit as Mr. Frog would wear and really looked quite a good deal like a grandson of Grandpa Frog. He was hopping about singing in a queer croaking voice,

"Galloo, Galloo, Goog-a-room, Goog-a-room."

Another child who looked like a snake, because she wore an imitation snakeskin, said, "Come and see the Snake-Lady. I eat things whole." And as she said this she swallowed a tiny crumb.

"I am the Toad-Man, come and see me," grunted the Toad—or rather the child who was dressed like one.

"We are the Turtle Babies. We snap, we play, we draw in our heads under our shells!" And sure enough they were doing all these tricks.

Their costumes were really quite wonderful, although they had been made mostly out of paper.

All the children who were looking on were quite delighted and said,

"We think you are marvelous!" And all the children dressed like animals made bows and said thank you in voices that sounded a great deal like the voices of snakes, toads, frogs and turtles.

AUGUST 6: The Bank Swallow

W ON'T you tell me what your name means?" asked Effie Elf of Mr. Bank Swallow. "Really, you have such a curious name and I've always been anxious to find out what it means."

"My name is Bank Swallow because I and my family build our nests in holes in banks. By banks I mean the banks out of doors and not the banks where one saves one's money.

"We are very friendly with one another, and we have big towns and villages and cities of nests of Bank Swallows.

"We're the very smallest of the Swallow family, I believe. And we can always be known by our neck bands which we wear on our gray throats. Our neck bands are much darker and show very clearly.

"We dress in simple brown and gray, though our throats are white.

"We have tunnels and long entrances to our homes, and at the end of our tunnels we build the nest. Yes, we're rather unusual, I believe."

"Very unusual," said Effie Elf. "Fancy nesting in a hole in a bank rather than in a tree. That is quite odd, quite different from most of the birds.

"So your name has nothing to do with banks where they have money?" she asked.

"Nothing at all," said the Bank Swallow. "We haven't any need of money. Of course if we needed it we'd probably save some for the bad days and spend the rest on good insects to eat and other delicacies. But we don't have to pay for what we eat, so we don't need any money.

"Besides, we'd be ashamed to open bank accounts for the banks are used to so much money that they'd laugh at us."

"Oh, nonsense!" said Effie Elf, "the good ones wouldn't do that, for no one who amounts to anything makes fun of any one else not having so much.

"People who don't amount to much put on airs."

"Then I'll always be able to tell," said the Bank Swallow.

AUGUST 7: The Cuckoo-Clock

JULIUS was very sleepy and he could hardly keep his eyes open. The whole trouble was that he hated to do things on time. He did not like to go to bed at the hour he was supposed to and he never, never wanted to get up in the morning when his mother said, "Time to get up, Julius."

And now he was sleepy, now in the middle of the afternoon. It was raining hard outside and in the big library where he was sitting a large open fire was burning merrily. Near the fireplace was a cuckoo-clock and Julius always loved to watch the little cuckoo come out and tell any one who happened to be listening just what time it was.

"It's almost time for the cuckoo to come out," said Julius. "But oh gracious, how sleepy I am. I know I was late in going to bed last night but I don't see why I should be so dreadfully sleepy. I do hope I will stay awake until the cuckoo says five o'clock. It is so much nicer to hear him on the hour than at other times, because he only says 'cuckoo' once when the hand is at the half hour."

"Cuckoo," said the cuckoo bird in the clock. And then he said it four times more. Each time he made a little bow as he spoke and when he had said "cuckoo" for the fifth time, Julius was waiting to watch the little door close.

The cuckoo in the clock always lives behind a little door over the face of the clock, and when he is not telling the time he is in there.

But this time the door did not close. And the cuckoo stayed out of his little home bobbing and saying "cuckoo" many times over, until at last it sounded like "Julius, Julius, Julius."

"Yes," said Julius, "you are calling me by my right name. How are you, Mr. Cuckoo Bird of the clock?"

The little bird was made of wood, to be sure, but he seemed so certain of himself and so well satisfied that Julius felt he must be alive.

"'I am well, I thank you kindly," said the cuckoo bird. "But I don't have to ask you."

"Why not?" asked Julius.

"Because I know," said the cuckoo bird. "You are sleepy, and it's not the time to sleep. Ha, ha, ha. Whatever would you do if you were a clock, or if your home was at the top of one?"

"Well, I am not a clock," said Julius, "and I am jolly glad of it."

"Tut, tut," said the cuckoo bird. "You are getting quite cross, Master Julius. Too little sleep. Well, well, I suppose I must forgive you. But it's a shame you couldn't live in a clock for a time."

"What do you mean?" asked Julius, who was quite frightened now. He felt the little cuckoo bird would hop down and pick him right up and put him in the clock.

"If you could live in a clock and take my place you would have to be on time. Six o'clock would mean six o'clock and not half-past! Seven-thirty in the morning would not mean a quarter past eight! Ah no, in the clock we keep good time We live on the moment and on the hour and half-hours we come out to tell people to remember that the time is going by and they mustn't waste it for it is so extremely precious."

"Don't you believe in people sleeping?" asked Julius.

"To be sure, to be sure," said the cuckoo, "but I believe they should sleep at the right time. They should not choose another time for it, such as the middle of the afternoon, because they sat up too late the night before."

Julius was very much ashamed. He felt the cuckoo bird knew that he had been doing all that and he wished the bird would go back in his little home and shut the door. He was getting more afraid every second that he would be taken back there. And oh dear, how he would hate to live in a clock.

"Just suppose," said the cuckoo bird "that I did things at the wrong time. Suppose I should come out at six o'clock and tell every one it was eight? You can't imagine it, can you? And why not? Because I have had the training of a clock. I have been an assistant in keeping the time and if I don't notice that you think more of the time I will put you back of the clock." The cuckoo bird banged his little door, and Julius, awaking with a start, rubbed his sleepy eyes, and said,

"I shall always do things on time from now on for how dreadful it must be to live back of a clock and have the hours depend so much on you."

AUGUST 8: Zuzeppa, the Monkey

"ZUZEPPA," said daddy, "was a monkey who had come from Africa and he was going to give a special performance of his acting. The special performance was to be given on a day set aside by the keeper. Of course it couldn't be advertised all around as a circus could, but the keeper told all his special children friends who came to the zoo very often and they told their friends, and it got around so that for the day of the performance the monkey house was filled with children.

" 'Let me shake hands with the performer,' the keeper said, and he shook hands with Zuzeppa. Then they each bowed, and the keeper said, 'Now Zuzeppa will show you his circus tricks.'

"So Zuzeppa hung by his tail and turned many somersaults; he swung back and forth and jumped and twisted and turned. He did the most marvelous of circus tricks and all the children clapped their hands and the other monkeys yelled and screamed, 'Well done, Zuzeppa.'

"No one else knew what the monkeys meant but every one knew they were excited. They weren't jealous of Zuzeppa, for they knew he wanted to learn tricks and be a trick-performing monkey. Besides he had worked hard enough to have a whole monkey house to himself for all afternoon.

" 'Now,' said the keeper, 'Zuzeppa will do his special trick. It has been done before by monkeys but Zuzeppa never did it before, and he has been practising it so he could do it beautifully for this performance.'

"The keeper took out a little wooden table and put a napkin upon it and a cloth. Then Zuzeppa spread the cloth over the table, reached down in a box the keeper had, and took out a knife and a fork and a spoon. He put all these on the table and then tied the napkin around his neck.

"Next he took a little broken chair which was in his cage and sat upon it.

"The keeper acted as the waiter, and passed things to Zuzeppa. And what do you suppose Zuzeppa did?"

"What?" asked the children.

"Zuzeppa behaved at the table just as though he were a real person. He ate with his fork and he cut with his knife. He peeled his banana which he had for dessert and then he ate it, wiping his mouth with his napkin.

"But when he was all through his meal and had put his hands in a finger bowl to make them nice and clean, he took a pipe, which the keeper handed to him, struck a match and lighted the pipe. He only smoked for a second or two, blowing the smoke out, as he didn't especially care

190

for it. But oh, how happy he was when the children laughed and clapped their hands! And this is a true story!"

AUGUST 9: Mr. Bullfrog

I AM the king of this pond," said Mr. Bullfrog. "If any one comes here I don't like, I swallow him! That is the way to get rid of creatures you don't like!

"Just swallow them!

"I've heard people talking who were rowing on the pond and who were gathering pond lilies, and I've heard them say how they were interrupted by other people when they had some important work to do.

"And that the people didn't care in the least if they were interrupting!

"Goog-a-room, goog-a-room, I can imagine nothing more annoying.

"But I cannot understand why people do not swallow these other people who come and annoy them and interrupt them.

"Just suppose an insect hops on my nose and says:

"'Sorry, Mr. Bullfrog, but I do hope I'm not annoying you. I don't pay any attention to that speech. I know it's not so. If he cared about not annoying me he wouldn't land on my nose.

"But I don't bother to answer him back, for that would be beneath my dignity. So I just swallow him!"

AUGUST 10: Allie Baa's Letter

ALLIE Baa," said daddy, "is a rag doll. Her real name is Alice Gustava Ariel Star Jewel Bright Carol Carmen Cucumber-Green.

"Mrs. Cucumber-Green is her mother's make-believe name, or I should say it was her mother's make-believe name.

"Her mother is a grown-up lady now, but still she has kept Allie Baa, and when little girls go to call on her she brings out Allie Baa and Allie at once makes friends.

"Now, this summer Allie's mother went to the seashore. She left Allie in charge of the city apartment. She told Allie to keep watch over the apartment and to see that all was safe. Allie was the name she was always called by for short, as you know.

"Now, when Allie's great-aunt's birthday came she wanted to send her a present as she had always done. So she sent some pillows for the porch where her great-aunt loved to sit.

"On the day of the birthday in the excitement Allie's great-aunt did not see the little card which said:

" 'To Dear Great-Aunt Mary, with love and many happy returns from Allie Baa.'

"But the next day when Allie's great-aunt was looking over her presents she found the little card and knew that it belonged with the present of the pillows which she had opened and which she had thought some one else had given to her.

"Well, she sat right down and she wrote Allie Baa this letter and sent it to be given to Allie Baa, care of Allie's mother, who was at the seashore, as I have told you.

"This was the letter Allie received, and because she thought it was such a nice letter she wanted to let Jack and Evelyn and their friends hear it, too.

" 'My dear Allie Baa,' the letter commenced.

" 'I find this morning on reading over my birthday cards that the pillows are from you, so will you please accept my thanks for your sensible, most useful, pretty gift. When I received my presents yesterday it was a distinct loss not to find a gift from you, and I thought perhaps you were too hot to shop or had some other good reason. But I am glad I thought wrongly and you did remember me as of old.

" 'I shall think of you as I lie, sit, or "back up" against these pillows.

" 'I suppose you are in the city this summer, as I have not heard of any "ocean dips" on your part.

" 'Perhaps salt water might not agree with you. It is well to be cautious, which means careful, and run no risks! You might feel a responsibility with guarding the apartment but you have a calm, brave, quiet nature which will keep you from becoming upset, I feel certain.

" 'With love and thanks,

" 'Affectionately,
" 'GREAT-AUNT MARY.'

"Wasn't that a nice letter. Well, Allie's mother, on a trip up to town took the letter to Allie, for she couldn't very well go to the door and get it from the postman if her mother had sent it on by mail. But oh, she was so pleased to have a letter from Great-Aunt Mary.

"And she smiled in her rag doll way, and the paint on her face cracked just a little with joy, for she loved Aunt Mary, who had often let her sit near her and draw up close as an affectionate, loving doll likes to do.

"And she told her mother to tell Great-Aunt Mary that she was so happy with her letter, and that she hoped Great-Aunt Mary would have many, many happy returns of her birthday, for she was the best Great-Aunt Mary that ever lived!"

AUGUST 11: Chickadee

I CAN'T understand," said Mrs. Chickadee, "how creatures can live together and quarrel all the time. It is such waste of perfectly good time in the first place.

"In the second place it isn't any fun. Now, singing and chirping and worm hunting and bread-crumb parties are all lots of fun.

"But quarreling isn't any fun at all. It makes creatures unhappy and it makes them very often quite sad. Even if they get the best of a quarrel they don't feel all happy and excited as they do after a fine party.

"Now, the Sparrows fight all the time. But no one would ever describe the Sparrow as a merry, happy little bird.

"There is the Starling. No one would describe him as a happy bird. And the Starling is a fighter, too.

"We scold in fun, nice chuckling, scolding notes we give, but we are famous for our good spirits. Chick-a-dee-dee-dee.

"I'm sure most people know what we look like with our little black-capped heads and the patch of black right under our beaks.

"We have pretty throats, we're told. The black patches are soft looking and rather smart, too.

"We wear simple gray suits and have white touches on our wings.

"In the winter time we like to be about, too. And nothing upsets us. We never grumble over the weather. We can't understand how people can grumble over the weather.

"To us it is so foolish. The weather is going to do just what it wants to, in the first place, and isn't going to pay attention to any one, nor is it going to pay any attention to what any one thinks. And yet how few seem to realize that!"

AUGUST 12: The Little Caterpillars

D ID our mother receive this leaf as a gift?" asked the first little brown caterpillar.

"Oh no," said the second little brown caterpillar. "She just liked the looks of it or thought the taste of it would be good for us and so she just took it and left it here."

"Gracious," said the third little brown caterpillar, "you know caterpillars can't wait until they're asked to have their meals."

"They can't wait to be given leaves," said the fourth little brown caterpillar.

"They'd never get them if they did," said the fifth little brown caterpillar.

"And we must have leaves in our lives," said the sixth little brown caterpillar.

"How handsome we will be when we become Blue Swallow-tail Butterflies," said the seventh little brown caterpillar.

"I greatly look forward to that day," said the eighth little brown caterpillar.

"And then we shall fly about and drink honey," said the ninth little brown caterpillar.

"And people will forget that we were caterpillars and will say,

"'Look at those beautiful butterflies with their blue markings,'" added the tenth little brown caterpillar.

"We will pretend not to hear them but it will please us," said the eleventh little brown caterpillar.

"Of course it will please us," said the twelfth little brown caterpillar.

"We will eat and grow strong so we will be very beautiful," said the thirteenth little brown caterpillar.

"And eat, too, because it is so pleasant to eat," said the fourteenth little brown caterpillar as he took an extra large nibble at their leaf dining-room.

So they ate until they were a little bigger and then they went off, each one alone, to look for more food and adventures.

AUGUST 13: The Catbird

TELL me what happened, Mr. Catbird," said Billie Brownie. "Well, I was sitting on the fence, this very same fence upon which I'm now sitting, and some children were playing in the yard near-by.

"While they were playing I made all sorts of queer sounds just like a cat.

"You know how I can take off the various sounds of a cat?"

"I most certainly do that," said Billie Brownie.

"They didn't know where the cat could be, and they began to look for the cat.

"I almost fell off the fence laughing when they started to look for the cat.

"Then when they were looking by the cellar stairs and under the old tree yonder I took great chances that they might see that I was not the cat, and I made the same sounds again.

"They kept saying to each other:

"'Well, I'm sure I heard a cat that time.'

"I really and truly almost fell off the fence laughing. Then they came back and went on with their games. They saw me sitting here and I had my beak tight and looked as though I hadn't made a sound."

"I know," said Billie Brownie.

"Then I sat very still, of course, and one of them said:

" 'Well, all I can see is that gray bird with the black cap.'

"Of course they meant they could see me, and I was the one making all the sounds like a cat.

"They finished playing after a time and began to dig in the garden, transplanting the lettuce and hoeing the beans and watering the vegetables.

"Then I began to make sounds like the different birds and they would turn to one another and say:

" 'What song is that? Whose voice was that? Do you know what bird that could have been?'

"And they'd look about and not see any of the other birds, for hardly any birds were around then, and I sat, looking so quiet and meek.

"And then I heard one of them say:

" 'I still don't see any other creature but that gray bird.'

"I thought surely then that they knew I was fooling them, but I found out they didn't know I could make sounds like a cat and sing like the other birds and sometimes like a mocking-bird, too.

"But they didn't know. And they've all gone off now. And still they're wondering where the cat could have been which they thought they heard, and where all the birds were they were unable to see.

"Ha, ha, ha, that is the greatest joke—to think I fooled them all."

"Well, you're a smart bird, there is no mistake about that," said Billie Brownie, "and I can tell you I admire your smartness."

"I fooled them, I fooled them," chirped Mr. Catbird. "They didn't know the catbird when they saw him, nor did they know him when they heard him at his little jokes!"

AUGUST 14: The Fairy Queen's Story

THIS was the story the Fairy Queen told before her banquet the other evening.

"An old lady had a little cabin home just off these woods. Her only companion was a cat. The cat was black but two paws were white, and the old lady thought they were very wonderful.

"Now and again the old lady had to go into the village to buy food. Sometimes the cat would follow, wearing a little jingling bell, for the old lady wanted to be sure that the cat had lots to eat, but that he would never get a bird.

"That was why she had him wear the collar with the little bell. The bell warned the birds he was coming, so they could get away. He could be heard coming along by the sound of the tingling bell.

"But this time, when the old lady went into the village the cat was sleepy and sat on the porch in the sunshine.

"'Will you come, pussy?' she asked. But the pussy blinked his eyes as though to say, 'I am sleepy.' So she went off.

"When she came back she found to her horror that the cottage had been burned down. Some one had left a match lighted in the woods, and a fire had started which had spread. But even though the house had burned down the cat sat in front of where the house should be trying to say, 'I am sorry, but at least I am here to welcome you.' And the old lady hugged her cat and said:

"'You are always glad to welcome me, and with you here I do not feel so badly about the house.'

"But," said the Fairy Queen, "I used my magic wand, and in three minutes and four seconds and two quarter-seconds the house was up again—and the old lady had both her home and her cat."

"That was a real fairy tale," the fairies and their friends all said.

"It was indeed," said the Fairy Queen. "It was about make-believe characters for a make-believe story, but that makes it a real Fairy Tale, eh?" And then they all enjoyed the Fairy Queen's fine banquet.

AUGUST 15: A Hospital Circus

THE circus was in the city," said daddy, "and every day the circus people and the animals had performed for thousands and thousands of children and many, many grown-ups. 'You know,' said one of the clowns, 'that I think it would be a good idea some morning when we haven't any performance and no parade and no practice performance, if a good many of us went to one of the hospital yards and performed for the children who can't get out and see us.' And they did! Every little child was either in a balcony bed or in a wheeled chair when through the big doors of the large hospital yard there came a parade—a real circus parade.

"And then the circus band struck up a fine tune and the clowns marched about and made jokes and giggled—oh, how they did laugh! And the children all laughed too and clapped their hands. The lady walked the tight rope with a parasol over her head, ponies ran around the yard, and there were some trapezes for those who swung and hung by their knees and their feet.

"The elephants did their act too—and the children fed them peanuts!

196

"But happier than any child, happier than any of the circus people who had come to make the sick children happy, was the merry, jolly old clown who had thought it all up!"

AUGUST 16: The Fire

"QUACK, quack, quack, help, help, help," shrieked and cackled more than one hundred thousand ducks at the same time. "Quack, quack, help, help, help," they kept on cackling.

"There must be some trouble over at the duck farm," said a man who was a fireman and who was sitting outside the firehouse in a town some distance away when he heard this quacking. He told another fireman that there surely must be some trouble at the duck farm.

"I think," said the fireman, "I will get out my spy-glass and see what I can make out."

For the quacking kept up and still it sounded very queer to the firemen.

"Don't you suppose," said the second fireman, "that one of the ducks has been hurt and the others are quacking in sympathy?"

"I don't believe," said the first fireman, "that one hundred thousand ducks would be so sympathetic at the same time. And they wouldn't make so much noise. I fear something has happened over there."

And he looked through his spy-glass in the direction of the duck farm.

"There. I see something like smoke," he said. "Yes, I'm sure I see something like smoke."

"Near the duck farm?" said the other fireman, getting up, and adding: "We'd better send out the alarm and get started."

"It's away from the farm that I see the smoke," said the first fireman, "but maybe the ducks are afraid it will reach them. It's one of those forest fires I think."

So an alarm was sent out in the town and the firemen rushed to the firehouse and got on their fire-clothes as they hurried away on the fire-engine.

How the horses did run! Still the ducks were quacking. The horses galloped, the men held on, and the ones who guided the fire horses drove as they had never driven before.

"It's a fire!" shouted the people on the farm. "A terrible forest fire! Oh, send for the firemen and the engines! Oh, send for help, help, help." And they telephoned wildly to the town.

But just at that moment, when the people on the farm felt that help could not come in time to save them and the hundred thousand ducks, along dashed the fire-engines and the brave firemen drawn by the splendid horses.

They rushed past the duck farm to the forest fire which was coming steadily nearer.

"Come men, come people," they shouted as they went by. And every one went rushing to help the firemen.

The dreadful forest fire was stopped just before it reached the duck farm, and the ducks cackled softly and happily, though still they were nervous from all they had been through: "We are safe, quack, quack, we are safe."

"How did you ever get here before we telephoned?" asked the people on the farm.

"Your ducks sent us the alarm," replied one of the firemen.

AUGUST 17: Friends of Animals

YEARS and years and years ago," said daddy, "there lived an emperor in India whose name was Asoka. He was the first man—in fact, the first person, I believe—to start a hospital for the cure of sick animals.

"He lived so many years ago that the way we know of much that was done in his time is by reading what the men who wrote histories have to tell us. Most of the good deeds which he did were written upon the rocks, 'way, 'way back, years and years and years ago. And upon these rocks were also written rules and directions for his people.

"Among many things which he did, in addition to building hospitals for animals, was to build hospitals for human beings and to see that they were looked after. He also had wells dug so people could drink when they were traveling through the country.

"He ordered the planting of trees so people could rest under their shade, and he spent all his time thinking how he could help others.

"But he was not the first person who tried to help others. He was the first one, though, to think of a hospital for animals and throughout the time he was emperor he saw that the hospitals for animals were kept in good condition.

"Animals with thorns in their feet were taken to the hospital. The horrid thorns would be taken out and soft, cooling liniment or ointment poured on and the animal would feel all right once more.

"Animals with sore throats, animals with colds, animals with broken bones and sprained ankles—all animals who needed attention and care were looked after in the hospitals founded by Asoka.

"If animals had written histories as well as human beings they would have written a great deal about Asoka and the wonderful things he did.

"But even though they could not write, for future people and future animals, of Asoka's goodness, and even though they couldn't thank him with words, they were grateful, as only animals can be grateful—very deeply, dumbly grateful.

"But the historians—the men who wrote about those times—speak of the goodness of Asoka and of how the people loved him."

AUGUST 18: The Orangeade

THEY talk about birds who go South for the winter and about butterflies and other little creatures who sleep all winter," said the Orangeade, "but my family might just as well not exist in the winter time."

"The same is true of me, too," said the Lemonade as well as the Iced Tea.

"But at the same time your families do exist because there are lemons and oranges and tea all the year around," said a little gnome. "And sometimes your families are about in warmer climates just as the birds are in warmer climates in the winter. But it isn't strange that you aren't wanted in the winter when it is cold, for no one wants a cool drink of orangeade or of lemonade and no one wants a glass of iced tea when there is a snow-storm and when the wind is blowing outside the windows.

"You can understand that, can't you?" asked the gnome.

"Yes, I understand that now," said the Orangeade, "and I don't feel unhappy any more. Ah, here come the tennis players. We must be ready for them!"

AUGUST 19: The Climbing Perch

I AM going to tell you this evening," said daddy, "about the Climbing Perch family before they came to the big aquarium.

"Far, far away in Africa they lived in a river, and were a very happy family. But one day the river seemed to be drying up so fast that they couldn't find enough water to live in. They had noticed it getting worse and worse every day for some time, and they had been hoping for rain. But this day it was so bad that they knew something would have to be done.

"'Well, even if the river dries up, it won't bother us,' said Granddaddy Climbing Perch, 'not in the very least.' And he gave a huge spatter-spatter with his tail.

"All the other fishes looked very much worried and their fins trembled with fear.

" 'Why, Granddaddy Climbing Perch,' said the old Mother Climbing Perch, 'do you want all the children to die?'

" 'I should say not,' replied Granddaddy Climbing Perch angrily. 'The very idea of your saying such a thing. I am surprised—yes, surprised, and very much annoyed.' Granddaddy Climbing Perch's fins wiggled with temper.

" 'I'm sorry,' said old Mother Climbing Perch meekly, 'but I didn't just understand what you said such a thing for, and why you don't seem to be worried that the river is drying up. You always used to love the children and tell them stories.'

" 'I do still love them, and I shall tell them a true story now of an adventure which will happen to us. Come around me, children!' And Granddaddy Climbing Perch flopped his tail very hard.

"All the fishes swam over by Granddaddy Climbing Perch and looked at him out of their queer, shiny eyes.

" 'Now, children,' he began, 'years and years and years ago, our great, great, greatgrandfathers were caught just like this in a river which had dried up. They decided that the only thing for them to do was to try to make up their minds to die, when the Fairy Queen happened along.

" ' "I will name you the Climbing Perch," she said, "and you will be able to go from pond to pond in the dry seasons. See if it is not so!" She waved her wand and disappeared—and sure enough all the family climbed out of the river—which was dry—and with their gills, which are like saws, they scrambled to the next pond, where there was water. We will do the same.'

"All the Climbing Perch family now knew the meaning of their family name, and off they started, led by Granddaddy Climbing Perch. They got to the next pond where there was water—but they hadn't been there for more than a week when that pond dried up, too, and they had to be off again.

"Would you believe it—but they had to change ponds five times before they could stay and make a real home! And they are the ones I saw to-day. Of all the fishes in the Aquarium they are the proudest because they had had such traveled lives—and they are very happy. Then, too, after all their hard work, they are glad to be in a big tank which looks as if it would never go dry!"

AUGUST 20: The Onion's Insult

"I HAVE been insulted," said the onion.

"Tell me what the insult was," said the carrot.

"Some one was going to help the cook get the dinner—some one who knew little about cooking but less about how to fix vegetables, and this person said she would peel the onions.

"She began to peel me first as though I were a potato and then she kept on peeling until the cook suddenly noticed what she was doing and said:

" 'Stop peeling that poor onion. It's all good to eat, and we will just cut it up in smaller pieces for frying.'

"Imagine," said the onion, "to hear of any one so ignorant about onions. That was said before you were brought out, Mr. Carrot. I was insulted! To think of not being understood better than that. Oh, it is sad, it is insulting, not to be understood."

"Cheer up," said the carrot. "It is not an insult when a creature is ignorant. You should just feel sorry for ignorance, and feel proud and happy that you were saved in time so you could do your part when the great meeting takes place between you and Mr. Beefsteak to-night at the big dinner."

"That's so," said the onion, "I will cheer up. It has made me feel better to talk to you. I don't feel insulted any more."

AUGUST 21: Harriet's Monkey

"A LITTLE girl named Harriet," said daddy, "was sitting on the front porch of her home one day when a hurdy-gurdy came along. An old man was wheeling the hurdy-gurdy and on top of it sat a monkey with a red jacket and red cap. His jacket had brass buttons on it, and on either side were two little pockets which jingled with pennies.

"Then the old man played a tune on his hurdy-gurdy and the monkey danced. He took off his cap and Harriet took out all the pennies in her purse—she had had seven—and gave them to the monkey.

"Into one pocket he put four pennies and into the other three. Then he took off his cap for more. But Harriet said: 'I have no more pennies.' The monkey did not seem to understand at first—but when Harriet shook her head and showed him her empty purse, he leaned his head on one side and pretended to cry. He took out a handkerchief from his pocket and he put it to his eyes as if to wipe the tears away.

"But soon, when the old man played another tune, the monkey began to dance around and seemed quite as happy as before.

"And the old man played yet again. But by this time the monkey was tired, so what do you think he did?"

"What?" exclaimed the children.

"He saw that opposite where Harriet was sitting, there was a rocking-chair—just like Harriet's. He gave a jump and up he got into the chair. Then twisting his tail around him, he began to rock and rock, back and forth, and how he did seem to enjoy it!

"As they were sitting there opposite each other—Harriet and the monkey—along came Harriet's mother. She was surprised to see Harriet's guest, and the monkey got right out of the chair and made a low bow. He began to do his tricks again, and he took the pennies Harriet's mother gave him. He also wept when she didn't give him any more!

" 'How'd you like to own a fine monkey like that?' asked the old man.

" 'Oh mother, could I?' asked Harriet.

" 'Well, he is a cunning little fellow,' agreed her mother, 'but what will daddy say?'

" 'Oh, daddy will think he is great fun,' said Harriet quickly, for she saw that her mother was really thinking of letting her keep the monkey.

" 'Is he a nice, quiet monkey?' asked her mother.

" 'Show how quiet you are,' said the old man. And the monkey laid down as if he were sound asleep.

" 'I think we'll keep him,' said Harriet's mother, and Harriet bounded up and down with joy. The monkey copied her and jumped up and down too, for he had taken a great liking to Harriet—and he made a polite bow to his former master, as he handed him some money from Harriet's mother."

AUGUST 22: Summer Corn

L ET me tell you," said Grandfather Corn, "the ways of summer corn."

All the ears of corn listened, which, of course, they could do quite perfectly, as they were all ears!

"I have grown very quickly. I am very big and full grown," continued Grandfather Corn. "I wanted to be like this, for in every cornfield some one must give this word of advice to little ears of corn.

"Advice, advice," said the ears of corn." We are going to hear advice."

"That's it, my bright little ears. I would say my bright little eyes if I could, but of course I can't."

"Too bad," said the little ears. "But never mind, we are not without ears, even if we haven't eyes and noses and chins."

"Eyes, and noses and chins are very silly and quite useless," said Grandfather Corn.

"Certainly for us at any rate," said the little ears.

"But for the advice," said Grandfather Corn.

"When it gets cold don't let any one encourage you into growing. We will give the people our fine selves as long as the warm weather remains, but not when it is cold. We're famous for being summer corn, and we will never let it be said of us that we were so coarse and hardened that we could stand the chilly days." And the little ears nestled in their silken beds and said they would certainly not try to grow in the cold weather for they knew they would hate anything that wasn't like summer warmth.

AUGUST 23: A Bee Story

THE worker bees," said daddy, "carry little pollen baskets and they bring in the pollen to the young. They also bring in some sweetened water which the little ones like very much indeed.

"Now and again on a very hot day a number of bees will stand at the front door of their hive and will fan in some of the outside air so as to cool the ones who must be within the hive. They always see that the hive is kept very, very clean. Oh, how neat they are.

"They have to guard against their enemy, the wax moth, too. The wax moth is a tiny gray moth miller who likes to get into the hive and feed upon the combs and the pollen stored away in the honey-bees' cells. If they are allowed there they will build tunnels through the combs and destroy them. The Italian bees, little gentle creatures, are fine about defending themselves, even doing better work than the usual honey-bees.

"The bees must go to many flowers in order to get all the honey that they need. They love clover, oh, how they love clover, which shows that they're not in the least bit snobbish, for clover grows wild in the fields, of course.

"The bees love buckwheat fields, and from many, many flowers and a great deal of gathered nectar and pollen, they get the amount of honey they feel they need for themselves for the time being, and to store for the future.

"They always work, they hardly ever play. Always they are

thinking of the day which may come when they won't have such an easy time gathering honey, and though they may seem to have all they need they think it is well to be thrifty and to be ready for a rainy day.

"How the bees love the sweet things of life, the flowers, the honey, the warmth, the summertime.

"But though they love the sweet things of life, they are never through working. Right through their little lives they work. They work too hard. They don't stop to enjoy their hard work as creatures should.

"Even when they have all the nourishment they need they go on searching for more for the storehouse. They do not flit about and enjoy life like the beautiful butterflies. No, they must always work. They've had no help from other creatures; they've never destroyed lives of other creatures in order to get food. Though they flit among all flowers they never become snobbish and love only the flowers which cost a lot to grow. They love clover, free clover, best of all."

AUGUST 24: Allie Baa's Portrait

A LITTLE girl named Melly," said daddy, "was having her portrait painted. The lady who was painting her portrait one day said to her:

" 'Now, you are such a good girl, and you keep so still while I am painting a lovely picture of you to give to your mother, that I wonder if there is anything you would like me to paint for you?'

"The little girl's face was in smiles at once.

" 'Oh yes,' she cried, 'I'd like to have my dollie painted.' And when Melly brought her doll the next time the lady said to herself, 'I think I will change the picture of Melly and have her holding her doll, as she is now.'

"And how differently Melly looked! No longer was she the little girl sitting stiffly on a chair, looking now and again at the window and longing to be out with her friends. She was not being good because she thought she should, but because she was happy having Allie Baa with her.

"She looked like a real little girl, and the lady was delighted. For before she had seemed unlike a child. She had looked so sad.

" 'Yes,' said the lady to herself, 'I will certainly have Melly holding the doll.'

"And then she did a painting of Allie Baa, and it looked just like her. How delighted Melly was! She showed the picture of Allie to her—but of course Allie never even smiled. She looked at it just as she looked at everything else.

" 'You dear, precious dollie,' said Melly, 'you don't care whether you have a painting of your dear old face or not. But it's a great comfort to your mother.'

"The lady was so pleased at the picture of Melly, and she was proud of herself that she had thought of having Melly bring her doll.

"When Melly's mother saw the painting she said: 'Whatever made you think of having her hold Allie Baa? Why, that is just like my dear little girl—just the way we always see her. How glad I am.' And the lady was happy, for she had made the real mother and the make-believe so pleased!"

AUGUST 25: Saving the Elm

YES, I was very, very ill," said the elm tree. "I didn't know whether I would ever get well or not. I had all sorts of things the matter with me. My wood was cracking and I was generally in bad shape.

"They talked about me, people did, and they said it would be a great pity to cut me down. They said I gave shade in the hot summer, they said I was very beautiful and they said I should be saved if possible. A lot of very clever tree doctors were sent for and they said that I could be saved. Oh, how happy that made me!" And Grandfather Elm swayed in the breeze and smiled.

"All the bad wood which had started in to hurt me was taken away. Then they fixed up the places where the old wood had been so it would keep in good condition in the future.

"I had steel straps put upon me in certain places to keep me from blowing over and fixed in such a way that I could sway and laugh and blow naturally with the rest of you.

"My, but when they said I was all right, how I did rejoice! I was so happy, so happy. For I am a well elm now!"

AUGUST 26: A Magic Lantern Show

THERE was a queer cry from outside the lighthouse—on the window ledge—and Teeny, the little daughter of the lighthouse keeper looked out. There, against the shutter was a sea gull and another was by him. The window ledge was very wide but they did not seem to be there from choice. Then Teeny remembered what a storm there had been the night before, and she thought that these sea gulls must have been hurt.

Teeny open the window and took the sea gulls inside. They were very young and they had been hurt. They had not been hurt very badly, but they had been very much frightened.

All day Teeny looked after the sea gulls. They grew quite tame, and as if they knew that Teeny was a little girl of the sea.

It was late in the afternoon when Teeny remembered that she had planned to have a Magic Lantern show.

"This will be fine," said Teeny to herself. "I have two of my audience. Usually I have to be audience and stage manager, too. Sometimes daddy and mother come, but they are busy at this time, and usually I am alone. Of course, I have lots of companions in the pictures that I show, and I leave them on the sheet which shows the pictures for a long time and talk to them."

Teeny took a great cushion and she put the sea gulls upon it. "To-morrow you will be strong enough to be set free," she told them. "I know you hate to be prisoners when you are used to flying over the great sea."

The sea gulls paid no attention to the magic lantern show, which disappointed Teeny a little. But still, they did make an audience, and that was quite a treat!

AUGUST 27: The Baby Ear

I AM so afraid I won't be eaten," said the baby ear of corn as it rested on the kitchen table in a fine house where lived a mother and a father and several children.

"Cheer up, baby ear," said the mother ear, "if you didn't get the chance to grow into a big, full-sized ear of corn, at least you have been able to live in a wonderful silken home, and that is more than many folks and creatures can do."

"What is it to live in clover?" asked the baby ear. "They say, out in the corn field, that some folks think it's fine to live in clover."

"To live in clover," said the mother ear, "means just the same as to live in a silken bed. In fact it means anything that is nice. People may live in clover and not be near a clover field, because they may live so happily and in such comfortable, cheery, pleasant homes that it's a perfect kind of life. Clover does not always need to mean clover. It may just mean happiness.

"Hark!" said the mother ear. They were being taken out of their silken homes.

"Look, children," said the mother of the children, "at this tiny baby ear alongside of a big ear. That is a most unusual sight. We'll let our youngest one eat this ear." And the baby ear was delighted.

AUGUST 28: How Arthur Saved a Little Girl

ONE day a lake schooner was making its daily trip," said daddy. "A boy named Arthur had paddled in his canoe to the head of the lake and was coming back home on the boat, for that had just made a nice length paddle.

"The boat was crowded with passengers. Many of them knew Arthur, and many of them had been rather mean and had said that Arthur spent too much time on the water.

"Suddenly some one gave a cry:

" 'Somebody overboard! Oh, oh!'

"And then every one became very much excited and cried and screamed. Arthur had not seen the person go overboard, but he rushed to the end of the boat where all the people had hurried and saw in the water just going down a little child in a white dress.

" 'She has been under twice now,' said some one.

"Arthur didn't say a word, nor did he scream, but in one dive he was in the water and had grabbed hold of the little girl. They were soon hauled in.

"And the people who had thought Arthur spent too much time in the water looked on, ashamed that all they had done was to scream, while Arthur had gone in the water and had saved the child's life."

AUGUST 29: The Huckleberry Pickers

TO-DAY I passed by a house and heard some little children talking to some other children who looked very ragged, hot and tired," said daddy.

"These children had been picking huckleberries and were going around this hot afternoon trying to sell them.

"They had stopped by this house where they had seen the little children playing. The mother of the little children had gone out for the afternoon, but they were having a party with a few of their little friends.

"They told the little poor children that they hadn't any money at all to buy the berries with, but they asked them to stay and play with them and that they were sure when their mother came home she would buy all the berries.

"The children could not resist the temptation. They sat down and had some lemonade and sponge cake, and, oh, it did seem so good after the hot tramp they had made looking for the berries. After they had had all the lemonade and sponge cake that they could possibly eat they all went wading in a little brook back of the house. They did so enjoy the lovely, cool water, and when the mother came home, there she found her children entertaining the little poor children.

"Of course she bought every one of the huckleberries, which pleased the little children so much.

"But what pleased them still more was that the mother added that if they came that way very often she would like to buy huckleberries of them, for her family was so fond of them, and that there would be lemonade parties too."

AUGUST 30: Mr. Sun's Birthday

THE children had seen old Mr. Sun on his way to bed. He had been as red as could be and very, very enormous. They wondered what Mr. Sun was up to, and were not surprised at all when daddy said:

"Mr. Sun had a birthday party this afternoon and the gnomes were invited. He told his guests to come just a little while before it was time for him to go to bed.

" 'Well,' said Peter Gnome, 'you don't suppose we would come after you had gone to bed, do you?'

" 'Oh, no,' said Mr. Sun as he grinned, 'but the party must begin at just such a time and end at just such a time. I have my own special reasons, so come as I've said, won't you, gnomes?'

" 'By all means,' said the gnomes.

"And just a little while before Mr. Sun's going to bed time, all the gnomes appeared on top of a high hill.

"Mr. Sun was shining brightly, but soon the gnomes noticed he began to get even brighter and brighter, and more red every second.

" 'You're looking magnificent, Mr. Sun,' the gnomes called out in admiration.

" 'So glad to hear you say that,' said Mr. Sun, 'for this is my birthday party!'

" 'Your birthday!' they cried out in amazement. 'Why, we never knew you had a birthday!'

As the bumble bees got nearer, they, too, saw they had made a mistake.

Page 182

For a moment Mr. Sun was hidden by a purple cloud.

Page 208

After a long time the lovely dawn fairies came out from their
sleeping places.

Page 229

So off they sailed, feeling just like birds with the delightful flying
motion of the ships.

Page 243

There would be fortune-telling, too, and Janet's mother had promised
to be the fortune-telling witch who would sit by her cauldron.

Page 256

Peter felt a little afraid at first that he'd fall.
Page 270

If he couldn't reach a thing, he'd climb on the table.

Page 282

They ate until they could eat no more.

Page 297

" 'Oh, oh,' said Mr. Sun, and he almost lost his fine color which he had been getting. 'Dear me, O Mr. Purple Cloud,' he called, 'let me hide my head in your best shawl—these little gnomes never knew I had a birthday!' And for a moment Mr. Sun was hidden by a purple cloud.

" 'But explain to us,' said the gnomes. 'We don't want to hurt your feelings. We're only too glad to be at your birthday party. We just didn't know about it—that's all. Won't you tell us, Mr. Sun?'

"And Mr. Sun again came out from the purple cloud and said:

" 'Why, you see when I change into this bright red robe of mine— then it's my birthday. Perfectly simple, isn't it?

" 'And as for having more than one birthday a year—that is true. I have them whenever I feel like it—but usually I have one when I'm going to work very hard for the next day, to make folks fine and warm, and the things in the gardens grow. You see, when I'm feeling so strong and well I think I ought to celebrate, so I give a birthday party.

" 'Every one admires me when I wear this robe, and it's just the same to me as if they were all saying that they wished me many happy returns of the day—for they all are hoping that I will wear the red robe again.' "

AUGUST 31: The Lost Dog

Y OU know I got lost," said Collie. "It was a dreadful experience. I really didn't know what to do. I had gone off for a trip and hadn't realized how far I had gone. And you know I'm very young.

"Of course, I would have found my way home in the long run, I know that. But it was everything to be helped as I was!

"I found myself in another small town where there was a very fashionable Inn. An Inn is a fashionable boarding-house, I believe, and is like a smart hotel, only smaller. Now, in this Inn, they didn't allow dogs.

"There were many elderly ladies there, and many of them were fussy.

"I came upon this place, and I was so tired. I thought to myself that the people might be friendly, and so I wagged my tail, although they didn't look the friendly sort.

"None of them had spoken to me, or anything like that.

"But when I wagged my tail and looked at some of them politely, they said to each other:

" 'What a lovely dog.'

"I thought that they might help me, and so I wagged my tail again and gave a low, friendly bark, and one of the ladies said:

" 'That dog must be lost.'

"Very gently I walked up near her, so I wouldn't frighten her, and I found that she wasn't frightened.

"Then I put my head in her lap and she patted me. And one of the other women said to her:

" 'Why, I never saw you pat a dog before. How do you know that he won't bite?'

"Of course that was enough to make me furious. As if dogs were all going to bite!

"But I kept my temper and the lady said:

" 'Oh, he is a beautiful dog and you can tell he is used to being petted. I am not afraid of him.'

"And then the lady called out the one who owned the Inn, and she asked to have me fed and a drink of water given to me.

"Then one of the very stylish and superior waiters brought me out a dainty meal and served me as though I were a fine paying guest, and called my meal 'luncheon.'

"Then they telephoned about to the neighbors and others, and asked questions about any missing dogs that had been reported, and they found out I belonged to my master, and they helped me to come home.

"In fact, I should say they brought me home, and it would have been a hard job by myself. But, oh dogs! It's good to be home!' "

SEPTEMBER 1: The Whippoorwills

IN the deep and dark woods, where there are many rocks, and where people seldom go, live the Whippoorwills.

The Whippoorwills guard their young if danger is near, but when they are little eggs they are not sheltered by a home-nest—the ground does well enough for them.

Perhaps Mother Whippoorwill thinks it is a mistake to begin by spoiling her children, but she is not a hard-hearted mother as this would seem to show. No, she is always ready to defend them from enemies.

Now, Mr. Whippoorwill is about the size of a robin, but he looks longer because he has great, long wings. He is covered with reddish-brown feathers, and sometimes grayish-white. He has a fine white collar and his quills are decorated with white. He has bristles all about his beak, which is very large.

Mrs. Whippoorwill is just about the same in looks, except she has a tan collar instead of a white one, and her tail is tan, too.

One night—for the whippoorwills love the night-time—a boy thought he would like to catch a whippoorwill and have him for a pet. He loved the wonderful song of the whippoorwill—which is a beautiful, rather sad note. The whippoorwills only sing when away from people, and they love to be by themselves. That is why they choose their homes where people will not come.

And he caught Mr. Whippoorwill. "Ah," he said. "I will be very good to you. You may have a big place to fly about in, for I have made it with wire in the yard. And you will have a little home of your own. I will not keep you in a small cage. That would be cruel."

The little boy hadn't thought that it would be cruel to keep the whippoorwill in any way—the bird who loves solitude—or being alone.

Every night after this he listened to hear his whippoorwill sing, but never a sound did he make. Then he thought is was because Mr. Whippoorwill was without his mate, and after a long time he caught Mrs. Whippoorwill.

Now he would surely have the glorious Whippoorwill singing every evening, he thought.

But not a sound did he hear. In fact, they seemed to have forgotten their note—they had left it behind in the woods.

You see, the Whippoorwill will not sing in captivity. He is utterly miserable then, and he longs to be back where he can be alone and away from creatures. Then, at night, when it is quiet and dark, we can sometimes hear his glorious note.

The boy did not know what to make of it, but at last he let them go. Oh! The joy of spreading their wings toward the dark woods! How wonderful it was! And to see the Whippoorwill children! To feel the dark cool woods, to sleep all day, to work all night!

"Ah," said Mr. Whippoorwill, when he was back in the woods, "I must see if I can find my note. I left it in the woods behind me."

"So did I," said Mrs. Whippoorwill. And to their great delight they found their notes again—they had just been quiet deep down in their throats, for they had left the woods, and their little bird hearts had been too sad for singing. The children joined in too. And the boy heard them all.

"They sing now," he said. "They don't like to be caught." And how glad the Whippoorwills were that the boy understood.

SEPTEMBER 2: The Monkey

A HURDY-GURDY, or hand organ," said daddy, "came to town one day when it was very, very hot. No summer day had been so sultry. Down the village street the old man played tune after tune as he stopped in front of different shops and houses.

"A monkey was with him and the monkey took off his cap and put the pennies which were given to him into his cap and then into his little pocket of the red coat he wore. He was all in red and he looked rather hot and uncomfortable.

"The man would make the monkey do tricks and the people who watched gave the monkey money. Later on the man took the money. For what could the monkey do with pennies! He could not go out and buy food. No, he had to take just what was given to him. And sometimes he did not get quite enough.

"And yet the old man was always greeted with smiles. No one asked him if he was good to his monkey. No one said that he ought not to be making the monkey work on such a hot day.

"They all just watched! Lots of people who had not been able to do any work to speak of all day—so hot had it been—now watched the monkey work.

"Trick after trick he went through, and his little hand clutched the pennies that were given to him in a sort of way, as if he wanted to say:

" 'I must hold on to these. I have to work so hard for them.'

"The hurdy-gurdy played pieces in front of the different places until at last they stopped before a little gray house.

" 'We won't stay here long,' said the man to himself. 'I don't believe we will get many pennies here.'

"Out of a window appeared the head of a little boy. His name was Bobbie and he loved animals of all sorts.

"He smiled when he saw the cunning little monkey with the red hat and jacket and the tune of the hurdy-gurdy sounded so bright and jolly and full of fun.

"He hurried down the stairs and ran out of the front door. What joy on a horrid, hot day to have a hurdy-gurdy and monkey in the village! What a treat! What a very great treat! He had three pennies ready!

"The monkey began to do some tricks, urged on by the man who had seen the pennies shining from Bobbie's hand.

" 'Show the little gentleman your fine tricks,' said the man.

"Bobbie was feeling so happy when suddenly he noticed the face of the little monkey. Oh, how pleading were his eyes, and Bobbie put his hand underneath the red jacket. The body of the little monkey was so hot.

" 'Aren't you ashamed!' said Bobbie. 'The very idea of making a monkey wear a hot suit on a day like this just because you think it looks fine!'

"The man pulled at the monkey's chain. 'Come along,' he said. 'We'll not show this gentleman fine tricks.'

" 'I don't want to see them,' said Bobbie. 'On a day when grown men don't feel like work, to make a little dumb animal go through trick after trick to get you money! Aren't you ashamed!'

"Somehow the man did not go away. He was so surprised at being talked to in such a way. He really did not know just what to make of it.

" 'I'll tell you what I'll do,' said Bobbie, who was half sobbing now with anger. 'I'll give you all the pennies from my bank. I have 63 pennies in all. Only, promise me to take off the monkey's red hat and jacket and give him a rest to-day and other hot days? To think of a man making money out of a little monkey when it's so hot his little back is burning and his eyes are begging to be allowed rest and a cool place!'

" 'I'll promise you,' said the man, as he took off the monkey's jacket and cap. 'But I won't take your 63 cents. You and my monkey have made me ashamed. I'm ashamed enough—I don't want the 63 cents.' But Bobbie did give the man and the monkey a nice, cool drink."

SEPTEMBER 3: Paper Dolls

A LITTLE girl named Milly," said daddy, "was very fond of paper dolls. Now one day when she had had three of her dolls a year she thought she would give them a birthday party and her mother told her to start off at once to ask her friends.

" 'You must bring your paper dolls too, and all their clothes, so we can pretend they are going to lots of things,' said Milly as she went to the houses of her friends. 'Bring them first dressed in their best as my dollies are dressed up now waiting for them.'

"And Milly told them to come in one hour. In just that time they arrived and brought with them their boxes of paper dolls.

" 'Come right along,' said Milly. 'The dolls are waiting for their party in the nursery.'

" 'We have brought them presents,' said Milly's little friends. 'Our dolls are giving them birthday gifts of new paper shawls and hats which we have made.'

"Of course Milly was delighted, but the greatest surprise of all was when they entered the door of the nursery.

"There around the neck of each paper doll was a pink piece of crinkly paper which reached out to the little table. In the center of this was a pink and white birthday cake, with three candles—one for each paper doll!

" 'Oh mother!' shouted Milly, 'what a gorgeous surprise!' "

SEPTEMBER 4: Larry's Labor Day

LARRY was five years old and he loved holidays. But the coming holiday—it was not Larry's. Nor had it anything to do with Larry. The thought of that bothered him. He wished somehow it could be different.

He had asked his father what Labor Day meant and his father had told him that it was a holiday set apart as a day of recognition of the laboring class. He had not quite understood what that meant but his father had explained that it meant a day set aside in honor of there being such a class as a laboring class, showing that to belong to the laboring class was something dignified and to be respected.

Larry knew then that it was useless for him to have a share in this holiday—a real, real share in it at least. This was different from Xmas and Thanksgiving and the Fourth of July.

But then a happy thought came to him. For the next few days Larry was very, very busy. Every one thought he was busily playing and making mud-pies and such, but not at all.

And on the morning of Labor Day they knew what Larry had been doing. He led his father and his mother and his grown-up sister and his fourteen-year-old brother to the very far corner of the garden which had always been set aside as Larry's mud-pie playground.

There he showed them a tiny garden set out with paths and borders of pretty pebbles. Growing in the garden were ferns which Larry had transplanted from the woods and a tiny red geranium stood proudly in a little bed by itself. It had come from Larry's nursery flower pot.

"You see," he said, "I wanted to have a holiday to-day—I mean I wanted to have a right to the holiday, as daddy talked about laborers having, so I've labor-ed too." It was rather a hard word to say but he managed it well.

"And now," he turned to his family, "don't you think I can have a little share in Labor Day too—a real little share?"

And his family said "Yes," and I think you'll agree with them too!

SEPTEMBER 5: In the Barnyard

"QUACK, quack," said Mrs. Duck, "these warm days do make me feel like swimming."

"They don't make me feel like swimming, grunt, grunt," said Grandfather Porky Pig. "They make me feel like lying down in the mud and resting and dreaming sweet pig dreams."

"What in the world are sweet pig dreams?" asked Mrs. Duck. "Yes, quack, quack, what in the world are they? I've never heard of sweet pig dreams though I have heard of sweet dreams."

"Sweet pig dreams and sweet dreams are the same," said Grandfather Porky Pig, "except that sweet pig dreams are the sweet dreams which a pig has. Do you see? I dream of being given too much to eat for I'm never given enough to satisfy my pig heart, and so I always pick up some more myself."

"I wouldn't speak of my pig heart, if I were you, quack, quack," said Mrs. Duck. "I'd speak of my pig tummy."

"Oh, very well," said Grandfather Porky, "I do not object. But I must be off for my rest as I want to feel fit for my next meal."

"Don't you always feel fit for your meals?" asked Mrs. Duck.

"Always," said Grandfather Porky, "but I like to talk that way. It amuses me," he ended with a laughing squeal and a twist to his tail.

SEPTEMBER 6: The Animals' Talk

"OF course it is true we do not speak the language people speak. We have our own way of talking, but that doesn't mean that we don't talk," said Larry, the monkey.

"It is just as absurd, I think, for people to say that of animals as it would be for the animals to tell American people that they can't talk because they don't speak like all the other people in the world, or to tell the French people that they can't talk because there are people who speak quite differently from them.

"When we are unhappy we make certain sounds and words of our own.

"When we are frightened we have other sounds to make. When we are pleased we have still others. When we are playing we have others again.

"And so have all the animals. The Bears have different kinds of growls for different things they mean to say.

"The Deer can talk, oh so well!

"The Chimpanzees and the Orang-utans are great talkers and they know a lot, too. Don't people know that? Haven't they ever seen and heard a Chimpanzee and his keeper talking?

"Then if they haven't, I just wish they would! And I wish they'd come and hear me when I chat with my keeper. He understands me.

"He knows what I want and why I want it, and when I want it. He knows whether I feel well or sick. He understands me perfectly, and I understand him.

"Dogs talk, as every one surely must know! And Mr. Siberian Tiger talks. He told the keeper how pleased he was the other day when the keeper rubbed his back through the side of the cage.

"He actually purred like a pussy cat!

"And the Wolves! How they talk whether they are here in the zoo or whether they are free!

"The Bears all talk. And the Rabbits talk. Their thumping sounds are words, oh yes, indeed.

"Mother Rabbit thumps the ground when danger is near; instead of saying 'Danger,' as people do, Rabbits thump their word 'Danger.'

"Beavers talk. Prairie Dogs talk, and one of them always guards when the rest are playing above ground and the one who is guarding certainly knows how to say 'Danger' when danger is near.

"The Striped Chipmunk talks, too. He can tell you that he is happy living about the rocky ground where he makes his home. He knows how to warn of danger, and he talks of the things he likes to eat.

"Dear me, all animals talk! Of course they do! And every sound they make means something. Our talks must be translated into the language of people if they're to understand what we're saying, but if they study us and our talk they'll be able to translate what we have to say."

SEPTEMBER 7: Doctor Birds

A LITTLE boy named Peter," said daddy, "had been very ill. His mother and daddy had been so worried about him that they had decided he needed a change of air. So his mother had taken him north, far, far from his home.

"Poor Peter! How long the days did seem sometimes.

" 'If he could only get interested in something,' said the doctor. 'He would then get well twice as quickly. Doesn't he like to read?'

" 'Yes,' said his mother, 'but he is lonely for his friends.'

"But one day on the ledge of the little sleeping porch Peter had, came a small bird.

" 'What a beautiful voice,' said Peter, after the little bird had given a glorious song.

" 'Twit, twit,' answered the little bird. 'Chirp, chirp, tweet,' which was his way of saying he was so glad Peter liked it.

" 'Mother,' called Peter, 'may I have some crumbs for this little bird? He has sung for me and has been here to call on me.'

"Peter's mother came rushing out with a bowl of bread crumbs and then she brought out some clear, cool water. The little bird looked so grateful and pleased, and he went off singing gaily. That morning seemed very short to Peter, and that afternoon the doctor said that Peter seemed very much better. The next day seven birds came and sang and had a delicious repast. And the following day a flock of birds came—all of many colors and they all had lovely voices. Peter grew steadily better.

"Peter suddenly thought that the birds would leave him, for the autumn would take these birds south. Sure enough, they began to grow fewer and fewer, but his first little friend was the last to leave.

" 'Oh,' said Peter, 'you've made me well. How I hate to see you go.' Peter was walking around now, but he always spent his mornings in the sleeping porch where the birds came. And Peter waved a beautiful blue silk handkerchief he had. 'Good-by little bird friend,' he called.

"But that afternoon when the doctor came he told Peter's mother that Peter was well enough to go back home, so Peter went back with his friends, 'The Doctor Birds,' as he called them."

SEPTEMBER 8: Nine Years Old

I'M nine years old to-day," chirped the canary bird. "That is a pretty good age for a canary bird, too. I believe I am to have a special piece of crisp lettuce and a new piece of cuttle fish bone as birthday presents.

"Then, too, I've heard that I am to have a bite of an apple, also. Ah, yes, it is fine to be nine years old.

"My mistress has been saying for some time that when to-day came it would be my ninth birthday.

"How good she is to me. I haven't been able to see for the past year or so. I found myself seeing things less clearly and less clearly.

"Finally I couldn't see anything. I can feel my way about my cage of course, and sometimes my mistress takes me out and pets me, and I sit on her finger and she kisses the top of my head.

"Then I give her little love pecks, too—my little bird kind of kisses.

"I have an idea when it is night because my mistress says 'Hush' to me several times over and kisses me several times, one time right after another for several moments, and then I'm put back on my perch.

"Then I put my head under my wing, which, of course, is the way I sleep. And next I put my head out for a moment and I hear her say: 'Good, Dicky. That's right.'

"Yes, I'm nine years old, and I've had nine happy years of bird life, so far."

SEPTEMBER 9: Evelyn's Story

YES, I know," said daddy, "I promised Evelyn I would tell her about the dolls I saw in the Old Natural History Museum in Washington the other day. There were dolls which belonged to the great-granddaughter of Major Bradford, who was an aide-de-camp to Washington.

"There were dolls and toys which belonged to children at different periods of time, years ago.

"Some of the dolls had blue eyes, and some had brown eyes. Many of them wore real lace and looked very fine and wonderful. There were toys too, and there were some sets of dolls' china which didn't look unlike the china Evelyn owns. There were many dolls and toys which belonged to children in 1870.

"So that any little girl who ever goes to Washington should go to see the dolls which used to be played with many years ago."

SEPTEMBER 10: The Gallant Rooster

AH," said Mr. Red Crown Rooster, "I have found a worm. First come, first served," he added.

"Then Miss Gray Hen looked at the worm and said:
"May I have it? I didn't eat much breakfast this morning, and I'd enjoy an extra meal."

"Indeed, it is a pleasure to give it to you, cock-a-doodle-do," said Mr. Red Crown Rooster, who was a gallant, mannerly young rooster.

SEPTEMBER 11: The Fairy Queen Story

THE little chicks were still half-way out of their shells and half-way in their shells," said daddy.

" 'See the broken shells we are leaving behind us,' said one little chick to his brother.

'Will we ever be able to get back in again?'

" 'I don't believe we will,' said another little chick. 'Oh, dear, there we have gone and broken our shells and we won't be able to go back when we want to. And we may want to, very much indeed. For we may feel very shy in the great barnyard world. And we may want to crawl back into our little dark hiding places.'

" 'Little chicks,' said a sweet voice, 'I am the Fairy Queen. I won't come too near to you so you can see me, but I am going to tell you something. You are growing out of your shells just as boys and girls grow out of their shoes and their suits and their dresses. They can't get back into them again, either, any more than you can get back into your shells, for that is growth, little chicks, and when you grow to get bigger and stronger you can't go back to your babyhood.

" 'A grown-up man can't go back into a little boy, a little boy can't go back to the way he was when he was a baby and had to be wheeled in a carriage, and neither can you go back into your shells. None of us can do such things, because it isn't Mother Nature's way, and Mother Nature's way is always the best.

" 'So don't feel sad, little chicks, because you are leaving your shells for good. It only means you are growing up into big chickens.' And they all felt happy again."

SEPTEMBER 12: The White Oak

WE have sturdy, strong trunks and arms," said Old Mother White Oak, "and we have such good roots that we can stand storms.

"We are very popular with the men who gather lumber and the people who care for trees. And we live to a very great age. Oh, we become so old!"

"Then we've a long, long, time to live, eh, Mother Oak?" asked the little Oaks.

"You may live to be more than two hundred years old," said Mother Oak. Yes, you will probably live to be far older than that."

"How wonderful," the young Oaks whispered.

"We belong to a very great and mighty family of Oaks. By that I mean that there are many different kinds of oaks; like us in many ways and again unlike us in a good many ways.

"They say that there are three hundred different kinds of Oak trees!"

"Oh dear, what lots of Oaks," said one of the young Oaks. "How thrilling to belong to such a very big family."

SEPTEMBER 13: Wasted Moments

THE gold watch was talking to the silver watch and the gun-metal watch.

"Well, I'm bright in a way," said the gold watch, "because I am of gold. But I will tell you first of all why I have done dreadful things—such as to lose and gain time in a reckless way.

"I was made to look expensive. I cost a lot of money—that is, I cost a good deal of money. The creature who made me, and the one who had me made were more anxious to make me look well than to have me act well.

"They didn't care what happened to me once I was sold and they sold me for less than they usually would sell a gold watch for because I was so cheaply made inside.

"Of course in truth I was very expensive, for I wasn't worth my price and that makes an object most tremendously expensive.

"Well, you see, my works were very poor. I was nervous and not well and strong and so I couldn't go steadily. One day I'd feel very fine and I'd go dashing ahead, trying to make up for lost time. That, of course, a poor watch can never do. It has never been expected of a watch and so a watch shouldn't try to do it.

"Time goes right on no matter what we may do. But you see I would be so silly. I would go ahead so fast that it was as bad as though I lost time.

"Many were the times when I felt so down-hearted that I just dragged the hours away—and lost lots of time. The whole trouble was that I was trying to pretend that I was something I wasn't. And that never does. If a creature is what it is and isn't trying to be something else, then it is all right.

"I was trying to act like a fine gold watch and I was really a poor gold watch. I was a humbug, but it wasn't my fault. It was the fault of the people who made me. Anyway, now I am here to be fixed up so I can be what I pretend to be—a timekeeper. But there are people who don't appreciate moments! Oh, wasted moments are such a pity when people could make so much use of them in working or playing—anything but wasting them! That is what I think is the greatest pity of all."

SEPTEMBER 14: Welcome, the Dog

THERE was once an old, old lady who lived all alone," said daddy. "Her only companion was a big dog whose name was Fred.

"But one day Fred got sick. Oh, he was such a sick doggie. He could scarcely wag his tail when his mistress asked him how he was. He just looked at her out of his big eyes and made queer little sounds in his throat, which in dog language meant, 'Don't worry, kind mistress. It makes me sad to see you so unhappy.'

"But Fred only grew worse and worse. The dog doctor came, and said Fred was dying of old age. Poor faithful Fred! How he did hate to leave his mistress. He seemed to know how much she would miss him.

"A week passed by and at the end of a long night when Fred had dozed off and on with his head in his mistress' lap, his breathing stopped. And over his shaggy fur the old lady's tears fell hour after hour.

"Now one day, some little while after Fred had died, the old lady was sitting by her window looking out on the village street. There at her door was a big dog—he looked very much like Fred but he was young and he jumped and bounded.

" 'Scratch! Scratch,' went his paws on the door, and the old lady slowly got up and let him in.

" 'Whose doggie are you?' she asked.

"The dog looked at her for a moment, jumped about and then licked her hand, as if to say, 'I am yours, if you will have me.'

"She brought him some milk to drink, and gave him a bone. While he was playing with his bone, she put on her bonnet and shawl.

" 'Come with me,' said the old lady. 'But you mustn't go too fast.'

"And along the village street they went—the dog going off on short runs, but always coming back to join his new mistress.

"From house to house, from store to store, they went, and the old lady's question was always the same, 'Do you know from where this dog came?'

"And always she got the same answer, 'We have never seen the dog before. But he looks like Fred. Maybe he is one of Fred's grandchildren—you had better keep him.'

" 'I shall name you Welcome,' she said to the dog, 'for you were very, very welcome to me. I was so lonely.' And several tears fell from the old lady's eyes—but now they fell from joy."

SEPTEMBER 15: The Children's Museum

"T HE other day," said daddy, "when I had to be in Washington on business, I found a little spare time in which to visit the children's miniature museum in a building known as the Smithsonian Institution. Now, in this museum, where there were different kinds of birds and insects and trees, there was a description of the bird or of the insect, and of its ways. Among the insects and spiders were some scorpions and the thousand legged creature. Mr. Thousand Legs is very long and has lots of little legs underneath him.

"Of course he must have lots and lots of little legs when he is called Mr. Thousand Legs.

"Then I saw Mr. Tarantula from South America. Mr. Tarantula can catch birds. Then Mr. Giant Walking Stick was there with long feelers coming from his head. He, too, had been brought from South America.

"He had some little feelers, too, and three pairs of legs which are almost enough for any creature.

"He was grayish white in color.

"Then," daddy continued, "there were examples of different kinds of trees and of the different creatures who lived in the trees, and of how they could protect themselves by the color of the nests they made, and by the safety habits they had.

"For example, the Brown Creeper creeps over the bark of trees which have much the same coloring as his feathers.

"The Wood Pewee has a nest, bending down, in the tree, shaped and fixed so that it almost looks like a part of the tree.

"Then the bird called the Least Tern always lays its eggs among the pebbles on the beach and the eggs and the babies are much the same color as the pebbles.

"In that way the Least Tern can protect the eggs from the Sea Gulls who would steal them if they thought they were eggs instead of pebbles.

"Mrs. Night-hawk's ground nest is made to look like dead leaves and just like the ground. It is hidden that way. And it made me think yet again how clever the birds are."

SEPTEMBER 16: Prince, the Horse

I HAVE a true story to tell you," commenced daddy, "of a horse who wouldn't be sold!

"The horse's name was Prince, and he belonged to a farmer who had six nice little children.

"One day along the road came a man in a big wagon, driving two horses. The children didn't like the looks of the man though they didn't quite know why, until he said: 'That's a fine horse you drove to town yesterday. I'll buy him from you for three hundred dollars.' Now the farmer was not rich—he was really poor, and he needed three hundred dollars more than he needed Prince.

"'Well,' he said at last, 'I'll sell him to you.'

"The next morning when the farmer got up—very early—for the children had said their good-bys to Prince, and none of them could bear to see him go—he went over to the stable and hitched Prince to the wagon.

"Prince gave a low 'Whinny-whinny,' and licked his master's hand.

"'Oh Prince, Prince, don't do that,' said his master half choking with tears.   And Prince neighed softly.

"They started off, the farmer holding the reins loosely, as if he couldn't bear to guide Prince to the town.   Prince knew where he was going and went ahead.   But every few minutes he would turn around, and look at his master, and there were real tears in his big eyes. 'Prince,' shouted his master, 'you're worth more to us than that money!   Turn around!'   And Prince neighed joyfully this time, as his master turned him around, and said, 'Home, Prince, we're going home!'"

SEPTEMBER 17: The Deer

F AR away," said daddy, "some men went hunting."

"'We hope to get a couple of deer,' they said.   'And of course, we'd like it better if we could get more.'

"They thought they were going out for a great deal of fun and they planned what they should take to eat and what a glorious grown-up picnic they would have.

"They went hunting on the first day of their trip, and there, sure enough, was a deer.   Oh, such a lovely deer!   His eyes were soft brown in color and very large and beautiful.

"He had left his mate to go hunting for food and here he was caught by the men.   He could not run.   He just stood there for one awful moment, his great eyes looking at the men.

"'Oh men,' he was trying to say, 'oh great, big men with guns, don't shoot me down.   I do no harm.   I am gentle.   I have a mate. I don't want to be shot.   Oh men, you men with guns!   You are so powerful, so strong.   What can I do?   But have pity on me.   Think of me killed and enjoyed by you as food, and my poor mate crying away by herself in the woods.'

"'Sometimes,' said one of the men, 'I cannot bear to shoot one of these lovely creatures.   They look so sad.   And this one is struck still with fear.'

"'Oh, nonsense,' said one of the other men, 'you always get this way on the first day of our hunting trip.   Think what good venison we will have.'   For venison is the meat of the deer.

"And the man's kindness fled from him and a loud bang-bang ended the beautiful deer's life—the deer with the big brown eyes which begged and pleaded for kindness—not for gunshot.

"The next day the men were off shooting again. They had what they called a great deal of luck. In truth it means that they killed some of the woodland animals and could feed on some of the meat.

"They saw deer in great numbers but none of the family of the poor deer they had killed on the first day.

"On the fifth day of their trip they saw the doe who was the mate of the deer. She, too, had beautiful soft brown eyes and with her a lovely fawn child.

" 'Oh look,' said the men, 'there is a doe. And a fawn with her.'

" 'There is a fine against us if we kill a mother deer,' said one.

" 'Who will know?' said another.

"Now the man who had shown a little bit of kindness on the first day by feeling badly to kill the deer was the one who spoke next. To be sure, he had not felt badly enough to have prevented the killing of the deer, nor had he gone home and given up hunting. But he was like those people who haven't the courage to say they don't want to do a thing when they know and feel it is cruel and wrong. They just go on doing it to be thought fine and manly.

"But to continue with the story. The man spoke and this time he meant what he said.

" 'I cannot bear to kill that mother doe and her lovely fawn. She is running from us, and I, for one, won't try to get her.'

"The mother doe and fawn had vanished and were safe back in the woods. Oh, how her heart was beating. 'It was those men who killed my mate,' she was saying to her fawn child.

"And the fawn nestled close to her mother and licked her head to tell her how much she was still loved by her child.

" 'Yes,' said the mother deer, 'I am all alone without my mate, but I have you safe with me.'

"But for days and days the mother had great trouble in keeping her child safe from harm. For it was the time when the men were around with the big guns and the look in their eyes to kill the creatures of the woods and forests.

"And when the men from the hunting trip I have told you about went home, one man vowed he would never join them again. And he kept his word. Neither did he eat any of the venison, for he could not get from his mind the thought of those great brown eyes begging for pity from the strong men with the guns. And something deep within him must have told him of the lonely mate left in the woods, for never again did he go hunting."

SEPTEMBER 18: A Black Cat

A LITTLE girl," said daddy, "owned a beautiful big black cat. The little girl's name was Carrie and the cat's name was Mrs. Coal. One day Mrs. Coal's eyes were shining very brightly and she rubbed up against Carrie as if to say:

" 'I am so happy,' and how she purred.

"From the look in Mrs. Coal's green eyes Carrie knew that she wanted her to follow somewhere.

"Way back in a storeroom lying on an old worn-out mattress were five little bits of fuzz.

"Mrs. Coal looked at Carrie and then licked the tiny little bits of fuzz with her big tongue. 'My little kittens, my babies,' was what she was saying in cat talk."

SEPTEMBER 19: The Oysters

F ELLOW Oysters," said a little oyster, "it was cold last winter. What is more, it was freezing cold. And what is still more, the water was frozen over, oh so strongly, and so securely.

"I have heard that our relatives were so hard to get that they were very, very expensive. They cost too much and so very few went into people's mouths."

"Great, great, great," all the oysters shouted with glee.

SEPTEMBER 20: The Elevator

T HE elevator," said daddy, "had stopped at the ground floor of a building and as it was during a time of the day when the people were not using it very much, it had plenty of time to rest.

" 'Yes,' it said to the ground floor, 'pretty soon the rush will begin. Very few people get down to their business before this, very few indeed, and very few come just around this time.

" 'But in a very short time they will be coming. They'll rush and they'll be so affectionate with me.'

" 'My dear elevator,' said the ground floor, 'when people rush at you in the morning it is not because they love you so but because they are almost late to business or are afraid they will be.'

" 'Oh dear,' said the elevator, 'I thought they loved me so. Still it makes no difference. I am but an elevator and I haven't feelings, so I shall recover from what you have told me. Anyway I never get so high up people can't reach me.

" 'Now there are some creatures who, when they reach high and lofty positions won't notice those who are down below them. But not your friend the elevator.

" 'No, no matter how high I go, up to the highest floor of this high building, I never fail to think of the people down below on you, ground floor, and down I come for them. I never forget the people down below even if I do go up high in life!' "

SEPTEMBER 21: The Fog

I Want a change," said one of the drops of water in a river. "And so do I," said one of the drops of water in a near-by lake.

"I want a change to the air," said a little brook, and a tiny stream said, "I want to be up in the world for a little while."

A few drops in the big ocean not far away heard the murmurings of the river, lake, brook and stream and said in roaring, rumbling tones: "Let's have a change. One, two, three, now all together go!"

Then up in the air went the drops from the ocean, river, brook and stream that had wanted a change and a great fog was over all.

SEPTEMBER 22: The Land of Nod

YOU must go off to the Land of Nod," said a mother to her little boy whose name was Douglas, and before long Douglas saw a Goblin standing before him.

"We must visit the circus of the Land of Nod," said the Goblin, And off they went to see the circus.

It was just like a regular circus. There were clowns, a band, ladies in pink and yellow and blue who rode on white horses and little black ponies. There were bicycle riders and trapeze performers, and there was even popcorn!

"What does it all mean?" asked Douglas. "The Land of Nod has everything."

"Of course," said the Goblin. "For the Land of Nod is the land of wonderful dreams—dreams of things that really happen in this wonderful world. And come again," added the Goblin, for Douglas was opening his sleepy eyes as it was bright daylight.

SEPTEMBER 23: The Homesick Chicken

NOW one of Mrs. Turkey's children," commenced daddy, "had been stolen by a great big rat. So Mrs. Turkey said to herself: 'I think I will take a chicken and look after it. Mrs. Hen won't mind. She has so many to look after as it is. It will probably be a great relief to her to have one less.'

"Mrs. Turkey talked on in this way and she called the chicken she liked best.

" 'Come here to me,' she said, and she tried to make her voice sound as a Mother Hen's would sound.

"The little chicken came running to the side of the turkey and seemed to be quite happy and contented. The turkey fed the chicken when she fed her own children and she looked after him all day long.

"But when evening came and the turkeys were ready to go up to the tree to roost as they always do when night-time comes, the poor little chicken wished he had not left his own mother.

" 'I was very bad to leave my mother,' he whispered in a fretful little voice.

" 'Come on up the tree,' said Mrs. Turkey, who had reached the topmost branch. 'I am ready to go to sleep and all the turkeys are. We want to put our heads under our wings. We are very sleepy.'

" 'But I can't get up there,' said the chicken.

" 'Try,' said Mrs. Turkey.

"The turkey children began to laugh at the poor little chicken who couldn't fly to a branch of the tree.

" 'Gobble, gobble, gobble,' they said. 'Can't you fly?'

"And the little chicken stayed on the ground below looking very unhappy.

" 'We can't keep awake any longer,' said the turkey children.

" 'Go to sleep, my loves,' said their mother. 'You are good children and know how to roost in a tree and have a good night's rest.'

" 'I could roost and have a sleep too,' moaned the chicken, 'if you'd come down low.'

" 'Now this is annoying,' said the Mother Turkey. 'Didn't I give you good things to eat and look after you all day?'

" 'Yes,' said the chicken.

" 'And didn't I let you play with my splendid children?'

" 'Yes,' said the chicken again.

" 'Well, can't you be grateful and come to bed like a good chicken. Show you are fine enough to belong to a turkey family.'

" 'But I don't want to belong to a turkey family! I am a chicken and I am used to the ways of chickens. I wish I were back home.'

" 'Well, go home then, you little silly,' said Mrs. Turkey. 'It's the last time I pay a compliment to a chicken by asking to bring him up as one of my own. You're not able to fly up to this branch. Shame!'

" 'I'm very thankful for the pleasant day you gave me,' said the chicken politely, 'but I really must be going now. For I'm just a little bit homesick and I want my Mother Hen.'

"Here the chicken began to cry, and from a short distance away the turkeys heard a 'cackle, cackle!'

"Along the ground half walking and half flying as best she could, came the Mother Hen.

" 'Ah, here you are, my naughty chicken,' she said, but so happy was she to find her child that she didn't scold any more.

" 'Oh, take me home to the chicken roost,' said the little chicken.

" 'Yes,' said the Mother Turkey. 'I do not care for your child.'

" 'You had no right to take him away,' said Mother Hen. 'If you weren't so high up I'd thrash you with my wings.'

" 'I'm afraid you couldn't in the first place,' said Mrs. Turkey politely, 'and in the second place you should be glad I'm 'way up here, because your child couldn't fly this far and so got homesick.'

" 'Oh, I'll never leave home again,' said the chicken as he reached the chicken roost, which was just right for him. And the Mother Hen cackled a happy. 'Good Night.' "

SEPTEMBER 24: Mrs. Duck's Dinner

THE Ducks settled themselves comfortably for Mrs. Duck's dinner party. Mrs. Duck's husband came forth from one end of the pond with an enormous tray and his tray was filled with bugs which the ducks love.

Oh, no, Mr. Duck didn't carry the water-lily-leaf tray. He pushed it ahead of him through the pond with his long bill. And then all the Ducks gathered around and picked out the bug they liked the best. So altogether it was a most successful dinner party.

SEPTEMBER 25: Doll Children

A LITTLE girl named Helen," said daddy, "gave her dolls a wonderful tea party.

"She asked her four best friends to come and bring their dolls. Altogether there were twelve dolls at the party.

The dolls had stiff little chairs to sit upon and they behaved very well indeed. In fact none of them fell on their faces as sometimes dolls are apt to do.

"And the little girls stood behind them and gave them make-believe things to eat on little dishes. Then when the dolls had finished their tea the little girls had cambric tea, bread and butter and sponge cake. And that was the best of all!"

SEPTEMBER 26: The Leaves

T HE reason we are so glorious," said the autumn leaves which had just turned into lovely colors, "is because we want to make a beautiful going-away bow of farewell."

SEPTEMBER 27: The Dawn Fairies

O NCE a little boy had heard of the dawn fairies," said daddy, "and was so eager to see them that he got up long before daybreak—in fact, before the fairies themselves were up, for they sleep when it is really dark. This little boy hid in the trunk of a tree. After what seemed a long time to him the lovely gray dawn fairies came out from their sleeping places, and he heard them laugh their low bell-like laughs. Suddenly one of them realized that some one was around and caught sight of the little boy. 'Oh dear,' shrieked the fairy; 'there's a huge person near us!' at which all the fairies scattered.

"From that day the fairy queen has been careful that no one else should see the dawn fairies, and so they all dress in invisible costumes."

SEPTEMBER 28: The Dream

O NE night," said daddy, "a little boy named Julius had a dream in which he joined a circus and so successful was he as a bareback rider that when he awoke he said, 'When I grow up I shall join a circus. I'll be a great rider.' For his dream had seemed very real!"

SEPTEMBER 29: The Monkey's Collar

"GYP, the monkey," said daddy, "was ill. He had hurt his right foot and it had been bandaged by the doctor.

"Gyp had been very good while this was done and had taken his medicine like a little man, or rather, I should say, like a little monkey.

"But how the bandage did annoy him! He had to stay quite still and not move his leg at all. That was so hard! He tried to keep still and yet he longed to play, for the nice liniment which had been put on the bandage quickly made the horrid foot feel so much better.

"Yes, he was quite sure that if he hadn't the bandage on he would be better. And so he tugged at the bandage and got it off.

"Then how the foot did hurt! No longer was it protected by the soft rags and the soothing liniment! Whew, how it did hurt! And Gyp did not know what to make of it.

"He felt very sad to think that his foot was really no better, and there, he had thought it was just about well. He cried a little, for even though he was a very brave monkey the pain was so hard to bear.

"Now, his master came along and saw what had happened.

"'You have taken off your bandage,' he said.

"The monkey did not say anything, but he curled up by his master and tried with his eyes to say:

"'The foot aches, the pain is very bad, master.'

"'I understand,' said the master. 'But we must have a fresh bandage.'

"The master sent for the doctor again, and once more a bandage was put on Gyp's foot, and once more the foot began to feel much much better.

"After a little while Gyp said to himself: 'I am sure it must be really well this time. It feels better than ever. In fact, there is no horrid pain there now.

"So he yanked off the bandage and once more the pain set in. This time he howled, and quickly his master came to him.

"'Oh, Gyp,' he said, 'you've worked off that bandage again. Oh, Gyp, why did you do such a thing?' And Gyp looked very sad. For he felt he had been naughty from the tone of his master's voice, and yet he hadn't meant to be. He just had thought his foot was all well, and the bandage did get in his way and made him stay so still—so awfully still for a monkey to stay.

"'We'll have to have another bandage,' said his master.

"Pretty soon the doctor came again.

"'What!' he exclaimed. 'You don't mean to tell me that the monkey has taken off his bandage again? What a bad monkey.'

"Gyp hung his head in shame, but his master understood. 'Gyp didn't mean to be naughty,' he said. 'We must be patient with him, for he wants to get well.'

"And Gyp, who was watching the other monkey, his chief friend and companion, playing and jumping and swinging, would have told the master and doctor if he had known how that he certainly did not want to be ill.

" 'Once more, doctor, just once more,' said the master. 'This time the bandage won't come off.'

" 'How do you know it won't?' asked the doctor. 'In fact, I don't see why you don't say that you know it is bound to come off.'

" 'You bandage it nicely, doctor,' said the master, 'and in a moment I will come back.'

"The doctor bandaged the foot and the monkey was very patient. The doctor was really kind and talked in gentle tones to Gyp while he was caring for the foot. That kept Gyp from being frightened. How fine the bandage and soothing liniment did feel! He knew he would be all well soon!

"Just then the master came back carrying a little round collar—it was rather wide and yet it was not at all heavy and rough. He put it around Gyp's neck, just holding in Gyp's arms enough so that he could not reach his bandage. The wide collar got in his way. But Gyp understood, and when the foot was all well, off came the collar which had helped so much."

SEPTEMBER 30: Mr. Fox's Marketing

"MR. FOX was spending his time near a fine barnyard," said daddy. "But one day when Mr. Fox was hovering near-by, the farmer spied him.

" 'Bang, Bang, Bang,' went the farmer's gun.

" 'Oh me, oh my,' said Mr. Fox. 'This is no place for me to hunt. There is a horrid man with a gun around here. How very inconsiderate of him when I want to do my marketing and when I like his chickens so much. He should be flattered to think I like his barnyard.'

"But the farmer wasn't flattered in the least, and off went the gun again.

"Mr. Fox ran for all he was worth and got safely back to the woods.

"When he reached his home, Mrs. Fox said, 'Well, and what luck to-day, my dear?'

" 'None at all,' said Mr. Fox. 'That marketing place is no good.'

" 'Why not?' asked Mrs. Fox as she raised her head.

" 'Because, my dear,' said Mr. Fox, 'there is a man around with a gun.'

" 'Oh dear,' shivered Mrs. Fox. 'Did you hear the gun?'

" 'Indeed I just escaped being killed.'

" 'Oh, my love,' said Mrs. Fox. 'Well, we still have some chicken left, and to-morrow you'll just have to find a new market—that's all!' "

OCTOBER 1: Gypsy, the Cat

G YPSY was a cat," said daddy, "who had been so named because she had been picked up one night when she was all alone, and when she certainly looked as if she had had no home for weeks and months. She certainly looked as if she had led a gypsy's life—wandering and homeless, and she seemed happy indeed to be taken by little Marian to her nice warm house.

"Marian got home just before dinner time. 'Ah,' she thought to herself, 'Gypsy will have a nice dinner—not just a meal she has had to pick up as best she could. It will be a real meal, and she will have her milk in a fine saucer.

" 'I have brought a cat home,' said Marian to her mother. 'I have named her Gypsy as she is a poor little waif cat, quite homeless and friendless.'

"Right away Gypsy was given a nice warm bowl of milk. And then Marian's family sat down for their dinner.

"Gypsy sat upon a bookcase. 'Maybe she thinks she looks wise,' said Marian. And Gypsy blinked her eyes and purred as if to say, 'I am a wise cat. I know I have a good home. And I have the sense to look happy.'

"While Marian and her family were eating Gypsy would look at them from time to time, but every time any of them turned to look at her, she would put her head to one side and look off into space.

"She seemed to be saying, 'Maybe I have been a waif but I'm very proud. And I will not appear to be a beggar.' "

So from that day on, Gypsy always had some milk before Marian began her dinner. She never begged for food, for she was a Gypsy cat with a great deal of pride!

OCTOBER 2: The Make-Believe Elephant

"L UCY," said daddy, "had her home in a big city apartment house."

"Down in the main hallway, on a stand there, was an elephant. Not a real elephant, for of course a real elephant could hardly find room on a hallway stand, to say the least. This one was made out of stone and he was exactly the same color as a real, live elephant.

"Now often Lucy would come in from dancing class, or from play, or from school, and she would wonder what it would be like to be a stone elephant, and she used to feel very sorry for the elephant, always standing in the hall.

" 'I know,' she would say, 'that the elephant isn't a real, live one, but just the same, it does seem funny to be always in the same place, day after day.'

"And then one evening when Lucy was asleep the Dream King sent the elephant to call on her.

" 'I know,' the elephant began, without even waiting for Lucy to make a curtsy as she might have done if he had only given her time, 'that you have often wondered about me.'

" 'I have,' said Lucy, 'it is true.'

" 'But,' said the elephant, 'you mustn't, for I am very happy. The reason I am happy is because I haven't the brains or the feelings to be unhappy because I am always in one place.

" 'If I were a real elephant I would want to go out in the sunshine, I would want to eat, I would even want to play baseball; perhaps I would march in parades. But I'm not a real elephant—I'm only a make-believe one, and I haven't any feeling at all—no, not a scrap of feeling.

" 'And I haven't any brains. I couldn't even smile at you if you were awake. It's the old Dream King who is helping me to smile now.'

"And Lucy noticed that the elephant was smiling, such a funny, droll, stone-elephant smile.

" 'No, Lucy,' the elephant continued, 'you need never feel sorry for me because I am always in one place. I am like a table or a chair or a bed—except I am made in the shape of an animal.

" 'It is nice to be a stone elephant if one has always been one,' it said, 'and I suppose it is nice to be a little girl if one has always been one,' and it waved its trunk and was gone."

OCTOBER 3: Canary Cloudy Wings

C LOUDY WINGS thought he would like to see the world," said daddy. "He had always had a good deal of freedom but he thought he would like more.

"So this little canary flew out of a window. He wandered about and flew from bush to bush. Soon it began to rain.

"Cloudy Wings stood under the tree but the rain dripped down over his little body and his bright yellow feathers were all wet.

" 'Oh, how cold it is,' thought Cloudy Wings to himself. 'I can't shake off this water as I do my bath water, because it all comes on me again. And my little Master always puts me in the sun to dry after my bath. If there is no sun I am put near a stove or where I can slowly get good and dry. This is awful!' And he gave miserable little sounds.

"Of course in the meantime, McLean, his Master, was almost frightened out of his poor wits. What could have happened to Cloudy Wings? He saw that a window had been left open, and he knew the bird must have gone out. He kept the window open hoping Cloudy Wings would come back, and he sat by the open window, shivering in the dampness, saying to himself, and trying hard to keep back the tears:

" 'Oh Cloudy Wings, come back! I want you so! Please come back, Cloudy Wings!'

"Poor Cloudy Wings, wet and miserable, saw a round glass house, and beat his wings against the panes of glass.

"An old man was inside looking after his flowers, for the glass house was a conservatory of flowers and plants. When he saw the poor little wet bird he opened the door and took him in. Cloudy Wings sat in his warm hands while the old man smoothed and dried the little wet feathers.

" 'You belong to the little boy down the road,' he said to himself. 'I've seen you in the window. I always could tell you by your gray wings.' So back in the old man's pocket Cloudy Wings went to his Master, and never again did he leave his home."

OCTOBER 4: The Abused Pencil

A BOY named Gerald," said daddy, "was finding it very hard to do his lessons. School had commenced and yet the days were so lovely it was hard to study.

"He could not draw a map and he was supposed to have one drawn for the next day. He found it so hard to remember just how the places looked on the map and he was supposed to do it from memory.

"He gave up trying the map after a few moments. Then he sat and chewed the end of his pencil. Perhaps in a moment or two he would think of all the places he was supposed to mark.

"He decided he would do his arithmetic but he could not manage the sums. They were all so extremely hard. Much worse than they had been in the spring, though in reality they were a little easier. The teacher had known the children had had a long summer and it would take them a little time to get back into their work.

"He tried to do the sums but couldn't. What a pity the book had no answers in the back! And he began to chew the end of his pencil again while he tried to think.

"Before long he felt he could not do his lessons for he was too tired and they were entirely too hard. He was dreadfully afraid he would be put back with the boys a year younger than he was, and yet he couldn't do such difficult lessons.

"How ashamed he would be to be put back! Oh dear, what could he do? He must simply tell the teacher the lessons were too hard. But then he felt sure she would tell him to go back into a class where they were easier.

"He put his head down on his arms. The soft autumn breeze was blowing. It had been a warm day and two bumble-bees were buzzing and talking very near him. They were having some sort of a talk about the sweetness of the honey in the honeysuckle vine.

"Just then he saw his pencil. The end of it was wrapped up in cotton wool and gauze.

" 'Gracious, pencil, what is the matter?' asked Gerald.

" 'I shouldn't think you would ask me what is the matter,' said the pencil as it squeaked in a sad little voice.

" 'Why not?' asked Gerald. But the moment he had asked the question he knew the answer.

"The pencil answered him just the same. 'You know I am to do your work. I will work but I must be guided and directed. I cannot think. A pencil is not supposed to think. A boy is supposed to do that. I merely write down what you think is correct, and goodness only knows I often feel very badly when I have to write down all sorts of wrong answers.

" 'And when I won't think for you,' continued the pencil, 'this is the way you abuse me. Think! Don't bite me to pieces. And I'll tell you another thing. You may bite me in two, but never, never will I do your thinking for you. I am not supposed to and I won't.' The

235

pencil was certainly very emphatic, Gerald thought, and he decided he would not argue with it.

" 'I was a lovely red pencil with black lead,' the pencil continued, in an injured tone, 'and now I am all bitten to pieces. One of my ends is almost useless, and I will break when the lead is used very much further. Oh, dear! And I was such a nice pencil!' It sighed and seemed very mournful.

"Just at that moment the cotton wool came off the pencil and Gerald saw that he had been sleeping. The pencil had been badly bitten, but Gerald, now wide awake, put his mind to his studying, and found the lessons were not so hard after all!"

OCTOBER 5: The Onions

W E are far more useful than you are," said the seeds of the lettuce which were just peeping above the ground in a box, showing their little green heads. They were in a schoolroom.

"I can't help that," said the geranium plant. "I was never meant to be useful. I try to be bright and cheerful. I wish I could be useful but every one can't be just the same as every one else. Neither can plants all be the same. Some plants are meant to become food and some plants aren't. But we all have our own reasons for being here."

"I don't see," said one of the onions. They were very small but were also coming up in a box of their own. And after the onion had said that, it kept quite still just as if it had completely finished talking.

"You commenced to say something," said the lettuce. "Why not finish?"

"Sometimes I get too discouraged to finish," said the onion. "We all feel that way at times."

"And why?" asked the lettuce.

"For you it is different, little lettuce leaves," said the onion. "You are a salad when you grow up. You are considered a luxury and a treat."

"Don't people enjoy eating you?" asked the lettuce.

"Yes," said the onion, "they often enjoy eating us. But they won't give us any praise for it. They eat us when they're off by themselves as if they were a little ashamed of eating us.

"I have often heard folks say," continued the onion, " 'Oh, I am ashamed to admit it, but I do like fried onions.' Then another will say, 'Just imagine, little Freddy likes to eat raw onions when they are small.' Oh, things like that cut us so," said the onion. "We like

236

to be eaten. All vegetables do, but we would like to be appreciated."

"If you weren't appreciated and liked," said the lettuce politely, "you wouldn't be planted and grown. They use you all the time— to season food and to make things have a nice taste."

"Ah," said the onion, which was doing all the talking for the family, "that is true. But listen to what they always say. They explain that they like to put a little onion in the soup—not so the soup will taste of onion—oh, mercy, no—but just to give it a little flavor. That is what we do. We flavor many a dish, but we don't get the credit. Life is full of trials," ended the onion.

OCTOBER 6: Trixie's Burglar

IT was night time and Trixie the parrot," said daddy, "had her head under her wing. Sometimes she slept this way, just as a canary bird would sleep. But often she would huddle up on her perch and doze off with her head drooping down a little on her chest.

"All of the family were asleep when Trixie seemed to hear in her dream a strange sound. She pulled her head from under her wing and looked about her with sleepy eyes.

"Did she see some one way off in the corner? Trixie was frightened. She did not quite know why. She was never frightened of people, but this person stayed where it was so dark, and did not light a light— only a little one that flashed quickly and went right out again.

"When her master came downstairs late at night, he always turned on the light. But Trixie thought she had better be polite. This was probably some very queer guest and she must be nice, for all the family were asleep.

" 'Hello,' said Trixie. The man grumbled to himself. 'He didn't answer me,' thought Trixie. 'I must speak again.' And this time she shrieked, 'Hello.'

" 'Will you keep quiet?' said the man in a frightened, low voice.

" 'No,' answered Trixie, 'never still.' Now Trixie had said this in a very loud voice, and from upstairs Trixie's master heard the parrot. 'She never says that except when some one is here,' he said, and he went downstairs.

"As he reached the room where the parrot was he saw a man hurrying off—hurrying off before he had had a chance to get anything, for he had spent his time since Trixie had spoken putting a large coat over the parrot's cage.

"The window had been left open and a burglar had come in, but Trixie, the parrot, had been the cause of his going out."

OCTOBER 7: An Autumn Party

A TRUMPET sounded through the woods," said daddy, "and then the voice of Mr. Giant was heard saying, 'Come, all the fairies, to the bonfire party. Come, brownies; come, elves; come, gnomes; come, bogeys; come, goblins; and come, Witty Witch!'

"At that all the creatures came flying and running and rushing to the bonfire party. The invitations were delivered by Mr. Wind to those who were any distance away. They told stories, they sang, and they ate roasted corn. And later on, when Mr. Moon had come up to see what was going on, they danced. And how like fairyland they all did look, for they all wore gorgeous costumes of the early autumn colors."

OCTOBER 8: A Little Dog

A LITTLE gray dog named Soot," said daddy, "was out for a scamper when he saw out in the lake, far out from the shore, an upturned canoe and two girls trying to swim with all their clothes on to the shore. They could swim—yes, but how long could they keep it up?

"Oh, dear, how badly Soot did feel to be so small. He could not rescue them. He was so very tiny. But he had a voice and he could run on his little legs. So back into the village he tore as fast as he could, barking, barking, barking.

"He ran to some men and he stood around them barking and jumping up and down; his little face looking very sad and worried.

" 'Something must be wrong,' said one of the men. 'Let's go and see. This dog never acts like this as a rule.' Soot led them down by the water and there they saw the upturned boat and the two girls trying so hard to swim to shore. The men rushed to one of the boat houses on the shore of the lake. Everything had been closed up, for the boating season was almost over and very few people went out in the autumn. The men broke open a boat house and they took a launch out into the lake. They just reached the two girls in time. In another three minutes they could not have kept up any longer. They had called for help but the wind had carried their voices in another direction, and the only one who had seen them was Soot, their real rescuer!"

OCTOBER 9: The Little Red Hen and the Grain of Wheat

A LITTLE red hen once found a grain of wheat. "Who will plant this wheat?" she said.

"I won't," says the dog.

"I won't," says the cat.

"I won't," says the pig.

"I won't," says the turkey.

"Then I will," says the little red hen. "Cluck! cluck!"

So she planted the grain of wheat. Very soon the wheat began to grow and the green leaves came out of the ground. The sun shone and the rain fell and the wheat kept on growing until it was tall, strong, and ripe.

"Who will reap this wheat?" says the little red hen.

"I won't," says the dog.

"I won't," says the cat.

"I won't," says the pig.

"I won't," says the turkey.

"I will, then," says the little red hen. "Cluck! cluck!" So she reaped the wheat.

"Who will take this wheat to mill to have it ground?" says the little red hen.

"I won't," says the dog.

"I won't," says the cat.

"I won't," says the pig.

"I won't," says the turkey.

"I will, then," says the little red hen. "Cluck! cluck!"

So she took the wheat to mill, and by and by she came back with the flour.

"Who will bake this flour?" says the little red hen.

"I won't," says the dog.

"I won't," says the cat.

"I won't," says the pig.

"I won't," says the turkey.

"I will, then," says the little red hen. "Cluck! cluck!"

So she baked the flour and made a loaf of bread.

"Who will eat this bread?" says the little red hen.

"I will," says the dog.

"I will," says the cat.

"I will," says the pig.

"I will," says the turkey.

"*I* will," says the little red hen.   "Cluck! cluck!"
And she ate up the loaf of bread.

OCTOBER 10: A Devoted Dog

BOBBIE was a small fox terrier. He was black and white,"
said daddy. "Or perhaps I had better say he had a white
body with black spots.

"He belonged to a little girl named Lily and he was very, very fond
of her.

"One day Lily's mother said: 'How would you like to visit your
cousins?' Lily thought it would be splendid. On the following day
the trunk was brought down from the attic to be packed. Bobbie saw
it and knew that he was not going to be taken on the trip. If he had
been going too, Lily would have acted very differently.

"He sat by the trunk and cried! And all day long he wouldn't move.
Early the next morning the trunk was carried away to the depot by
an expressman, and poor Bobbie howled.

"Lily kissed his little black-spotted ears and she, too, cried but her
cousins did not want Bobbie brought too.

"After Lily had left the house Bobbie would not be comforted. He
would not eat, and all day long he would look up the road to see if
Lily was coming. The next night there was a sudden scamper and
a wild bound. For far away Bobbie had heard the sounds of wheels
and he felt Lily was there. Yes, she had come right home. She had
missed her Bobbie. And never again were they apart."

OCTOBER 11: A Bird's Secret

THE Fairy Wondrous Secrets told me to talk to you when
you were asleep," said the canary to his little mistress Cora.
"Then tell me how it is you can get along without teeth,"
said Cora.

"My beak takes the place of teeth," the canary explained. "It is
very sharp, and I can eat all I want.

"When you see me at the cuttlefish and the sugar, I am really sharpening my beak—just as though it were a knife. Now that is something creatures cannot do with teeth. Whoever heard of people
sharpening their teeth?

"But that is what we do all the time with our beaks—we birds. Yes, we also sharpen our beaks on the bars in our cages. And the birds outside find plenty of tools for sharpening. We are never bothered about eating anything we wish to have. If we feel like it we sharpen up in time and then how we do enjoy our food."

OCTOBER 12: Columbus Day

OCTOBER twelfth is not celebrated as a holiday because it was the day when Christopher Columbus was born, but because it was supposed to be the date upon which Columbus first stood upon the ground which forms a part of the continent of America. The exact date of his birth is not known nor the exact place.

Columbus took many voyages in his life-time; he discovered many islands and made for himself a great and lasting name in history, but he never knew he had discovered a new continent! Always he thought that those places he had touched were parts of Asia.

And it seems quite sad to think of the times we've been applauded (and often, very justly too!) when we've recited well or played the piano well, while Christopher Columbus, who discovered America, did not even know of the great deed that he had done. Never had he any realization that in a new continent they would erect monuments to him, nor that in schools they would give pageants about his trip, his discouragements, his successes.

And his little son Diego, whom Queen Isabella made a page at the Spanish Court, could not boast to the others and say,

"My father has discovered a new continent, which is more than can be said for most fathers, and most people for that matter!"

For neither did little Diego know; and it has always seemed such a pity. It would have been so splendid a thing for any little boy to have been able to say!

OCTOBER 13: The Camels

IT always strikes folks as funny," said Sophia Camel, "that we look our best in the winter time and not in the summer time when the zoo is filled with people and when so many come to ride us.

"But we don't care about our looks. We have our family ways.

241

And one of our family ways is to molt our hair after the long winter is over.

"We can't change our ways to suit people, even if we would like to change them."

"We can't, indeed," said Sally Camel. "And though they may think it a pity we don't dress up in the summer time they will have to take us as they find us and be satisfied."

OCTOBER 14: A Naughty Cat

JOTA, the cat," said daddy, "was always complaining. First Jota would leave her milk as if she didn't like it at all and then she would upset her little dish filled with bacon.

"There was really nothing in the world the matter with Jota except that she had been spoiled.

" 'I have some nice milk for you to-day,' said the cook. 'It has just come and it is good and warm.'

"Now Jota was thinking of the mice she had heard scampering in the cellar. She didn't want the milk. She would much rather have mice. And when cook lifted her up and carried her to the corner of the kitchen where she had put the bowl of milk, Jota scratched as well as snarled.

"Oh, how badly the cook did feel! Not because the scratch was such a bad one. No, that amounted to very little, but she felt so hurt that Jota could have scratched her. She had always been so good to Jota.

"Jota hurried to the cellar. Yes, now she smelt the mice! Ah, what a scamper she would have. She did not want milk. No, she would have mice. She sprang for a mouse. What! It had vanished. Then she tried for another as it was hurrying across the floor. She missed the second one. She tried to catch three others and each time she missed them.

"Jota for once in her life was thoroughly and absolutely ashamed of herself. She had not been able to catch the mice and she had once been famous for her powers as a mouse catcher.

"Yes, she had grown lazy and useless. She had been stupid too. That was all because she had not been unselfish and nice, but had been horrid to every one. And it had spoiled her. She could not catch mice!

"Jota was a very sad cat as she slowly climbed the cellar stairs. She went back into the kitchen and there she drank the milk she had been so rude and horrid about before.

" 'Oh, you were thirsty after all,' said the kind cook. Jota purred and jumped into the cook's lap, trying to say:

" 'I know I have been horrid but please forgive me now.' "

OCTOBER 15: The Chipmunks

THE chipmunks were having a fine time the other day," said daddy. 'Hurry up, hurry up,' said old Father Chipmunk to the younger ones. 'We want all the nuts we can get for the winter.   There will be a long, long, time to eat, and we must hunt now.'

"Mother Chipmunk was down in her hole in the ground.   The squirrels always have their homes in the holes of trees but the chipmunks like the ground better.   She was teaching all the very little ones that they must only drink dew-drops. For they are like the rabbit family, and think that water which has touched the ground is very dangerous to drink.   They will only drink fresh dew-drops and rain water from leaves and flowers.

"All the little chipmunks hurried and scurried about, and pretty soon Father Chipmunk said, 'I will offer a prize for the one who gets the greatest number of nuts.   Hurry, scurry!'

"Chippy Chappy won the prize.   'It is a house I made out of nuts —a nice little house of special kinds of nuts,' said Father Chipmunk, and Chippy Chappy can eat a room whenever he feels hungry!   But now, all of you hurry, and hide your nuts!'   And off they scampered to their little homes with their winter food."

OCTOBER 16: The Fairies' Trip

THE queen of the fairies said," began daddy, "I have a scheme.   We will visit the clouds."

"At that the loveliest airships appeared. They looked almost like clouds themselves, so filmy and white were they.

"So off they sailed, feeling just like birds with the delightful flying motion of the ships.   And up to the silvery clouds they went.   When they got in the clouds the cloud fairies—you know there are fairies who live in the clouds all the time—took them all around and showed them their homes.   And such homes as they have!   They have the most marvelous palaces, with courtyards and exquisite scenery all about.

They have tall mountains where they always go for their parties. Everything is such a beautiful color too, for the cloud fairies are very fond of pale grays and blues and silver.

"Then the fairies from the woods suggested to the cloud fairies that they should return their visit and come to earth.

" 'We would love to do that,' said the cloud fairies. So off they began to fly from the clouds. They needed no airships but do you know what happened?

"As they began to drop great big drops of rain fell to the earth, and then the heaviest kind of a rainstorm began for the earth people, for of course when the cloud fairies move the rain is not held any more and it falls to the earth.

"But the fairies from the woods didn't mind, as the big trees always protect them, and the cloud fairies only let the rain fall where there were no trees. So the afternoon was one of greatest pleasure for both the wood fairies and the cloud fairies."

OCTOBER 17: The Lion Babies

I HAVE a true circus story to tell you this evening," said daddy. "It's to be a strange story, because it is to be about a mother dog who looked after some lion babies."

"A mother dog who looked after lions?" shouted the children.

"Yes," said daddy, "and you remember I said it was true.

"One time in the circus a mother Lioness grew very, very sick.

" 'I am afraid she will not live,' said the Keeper.

" 'But whatever will happen to her dear little Lion Babies?' asked another man.

" 'I'm sure I don't know,' said the Keeper. 'We will just have to do the best we can. I have watched her with them a good deal and perhaps I can look after them.'

" 'She is so fond of them,' said the other man. 'What a pity it is she can't live.'

"The Lioness seemed to know she could not live. Over and over again she kissed her little Lion Babies with her tongue. And when she opened her mouth, her great, cruel teeth could be seen—but the little babies didn't know their mother had teeth—so gentle was she with them.

"And the Lion Babies nestled close to their mother, and by the little, soft growls they made, they were trying to say, 'How we love you, mother! Your fur is so warm, so soft. You are so good to us, mother. How we love you!'

244

"And then the Lioness held them closer. And with one of her paws which could have crushed and killed a creature if she had so wished, she fondled and petted her babies.

"Slowly as she talked to them in her low, growling way, she began to see ahead. Her eyes gazed far out of the bars of her cage.

" 'What will happen to my babies when I am not here to look after them?' she was thinking. Her eyes stared and stared into space—beyond the people who passed by every little while to watch the beautiful mother Lioness and the little Lions.

"And she began to think so hard that she almost forgot her babies. She was searching with her eyes way, way out into an unknown world, and wondering, wondering all the time what would happen to her lovely brood.

"The Lion babies nestled closer. Mother was letting the cold in! And again she fondled them, while from her eyes that so often looked treacherous and wicked, great tears fell down on their soft, warm fur.

"The next morning when the Lion Babies woke up there was no mother Lioness. They couldn't imagine what had happened. They saw the big man always around their cage, feeding them, talking to them in soft, kind tones, but their lovely warm, soft, furry mother, where was she?

"The day went on and still she didn't come! Oh, such miserable little Lion Babies as they were! The Keeper did all he could for them —but he couldn't feed them anything to take away that queer feeling they had. For it wasn't hunger—it was loneliness! And the Lion Babies found that no food filled that place!

"But the next morning when the Keeper came to look at the Lion Babies, there outside the cage was the big, woolly sheep dog. She was licking the paws of the Lion Babies and they were once again giving their low growls.

"When the dog saw the Keeper she jumped up and down as if to say, 'Let me care for the Lion Babies.'

"The Keeper saw that the Lion Babies were quite gentle with the dog, and he seemed to know that they wanted to be together—so he let the dog in the cage.

"Day after day the dog stayed with the Lion Babies, except when she came out now and again for a run. And the dog brought up the little lions—and when they were big enough for the circus they always had the dog with them."

OCTOBER 18: Max's Escape

A LITTLE dog," said daddy, "was one of five beautiful puppies living in the country with a very proud and happy mother.

"But, sad to tell, it was not very long before the mother dog heard her master saying to a friend of his, 'I simply cannot keep so many dogs. There is no room for them—not even here in the country. You see I have as many animals now as I can possibly manage.'

" 'Well,' said the friend, 'I will take a puppy for you. I can keep one easily in our city house. There is plenty of room. I will take the little white one with the brown right ear.'

"So the little dog named Max was taken to the city. He was dreadfully homesick and one day when he was being taken for a walk led by a leash he escaped.

"Such adventures as he had. He remembered the trip he had taken with his new master. First they had gone on a ferry boat across some water—and then on a train. So Max ran and ran until he reached the railroad station. He got through the gate when the guard wasn't looking and he jumped up into the baggage car just as the train was pulling out.

"On and on he rode until he saw some water and a great boat—just like the one he had been on before. What should he do? Jump? The train was going fast, but it stopped where the ferry boats were. And so Max reached home and his mother—and somehow or other room was made for him by his first master."

OCTOBER 19: The Fire Bell

I N a big city school," said daddy, "there were several thousand children. Pretty soon the school bell rang and all the children went to their different classrooms.

"They had not been there long when a great bell sounded through the school. It was different from the usual school bell which brought them to their lessons, and it filled them all with fear. The teachers looked frightened too, but they were all very quiet.

" 'March out, slowly, in single file,' said the teacher of each classroom. 'There! A little faster, but no shoving. We must all see how calm we can be. It is only when we become frightened that there is danger.' And in this way every one tried to be calm, even though every one felt so nervous.

"For the bell had been a fire bell. And they had all known it. Soon every single one of the children was out in the big courtyard and they had at last reached the street. The teachers were all out too, for they had all 'kept their heads' as the saying is."

OCTOBER 20: The Rain

WE heard some people talking and they made us very angry," said the Rain Drops. "They said, 'Oh, it's raining cats and dogs.' And we would never rain cats and dogs, never, never, never, at any time at all."

The King of the Clouds laughed hard. "Well do I remember when it used to make me mad when people said those things," he chuckled. People often talk in that foolish way."

"Whatever do they mean by it?" asked the Rain Drops.

"Nothing, nothing at all."

"Then they don't imagine we will really rain cats and dogs?" asked the Rain Drops.

"They know you really won't," said the King of the Clouds. "When they say that you are raining cats and dogs they mean that you are raining very hard and furiously."

"But, Cloud King," said the Rain Drops, "there were some other people and they said that it was raining pitchforks. Now can you imagine us doing that? We wouldn't rain pitchforks for anything. They'd hurt people and children and animals, and while we do love to splash and have our jokes, still we would never do anything mean such as rain pitchforks."

"Of course you wouldn't," said the King of the Clouds. "They say that in just the same way as they say it is 'raining cats and dogs.' That also simply means it's raining very, very hard. So go back and play." And the Rain Drops were much relieved.

OCTOBER 21: Grandfather Pine Tree

TWO little pine trees had been planted by two big ones. They were so tiny, and the two big ones known as Grandfather and Grandmother Pine Tree were very, very tall, even for pine trees.

"We seem so tiny," said the little pine trees. "Will we ever grow to be as tall as you are?" And they tried to lift up their heads and see the tops of the big pines, but it was almost impossible.

247

"Listen," whispered Grandfather Pine Tree. "You will surely grow to be tall, so do not get discouraged. And more than that, you will be happy. You will be awake all the time. You will see what I have seen each year.

"There will be snow soon and then there will be the springtime, when the flowers will peep above the ground and will say a good morning to all the world, and the leaves will follow the blossoms on the trees.

"Then will follow the warm summer and the children from the white house down yonder will bring old rugs and books, and will come up under us. They know we'll keep them cool.

"You must grow to be strong and tall and you'll find that it's one of the most interesting of things in the world to be a pine tree. And most especially, to be a pine tree here on this hill overlooking the garden and the white house where two children, a little boy and a little girl, are always happy—all the year around, just as we are, in the winter, spring, summer and autumn."

And the two small pine trees decided they would try their hardest to grow and see as many lovely things as their grandfather and grandmother saw each year.

OCTOBER 22: Jack Frost's Evening

JACK FROST, and the Frost Brothers," said daddy, "were off for a good time. 'We'll have the most wonderful party,' said Jack Frost.

" 'What will we do?' asked the Frost Brothers. They were always ready to do anything Jack suggested, but they never thought of the things to do first.

" 'We'll celebrate,' said Jack Frost.

" 'What will we celebrate for?'

" 'Because the wind has gone to sleep and we can do our work in peace. Oh, such work as we'll do!'

" 'First you say we'll have a celebration, and then you say we'll work. Whatever do you mean, Jack Frost?'

" 'I mean,' he said cheerily, 'that we'll have both a celebration and that we'll do wonderful work too. For work and play are all the same to me. I feel like singing a song about it.' And off he started singing, dancing around as he sang these words:

> I'm so happy, I'm so gay,
> I like to work, I like to play.
> Whichever it is I do not mind,
> So long as the wind is still and kind.

"They put many of the flowers to sleep for the winter. Then the Frost Brothers helped Jack Frost make his wonderful pictures and this was what they called the celebration. They worked all night, and when morning came, people looked out and saw their windows covered with frost. 'Jack Frost must have been around last night,' they said."

OCTOBER 23: Beans and Peas

A CAN of beans and a can of peas were talking. They had just been opened and had been poured into large bowls in the kitchen. "Last summer," said the peas, "a young man came from the city. He wanted to work in the garden, he said.

"Well, of all the funny workers he was the funniest! But the funniest of all—that is—it was the funniest to us, was that he didn't know us at all."

"He didn't know you," exclaimed the beans.

"No," grinned the peas, in their vegetable way, "he didn't know whether we were flowers or vegetables. He looked at us from a little distance away and he said:

" 'Are these flowers or vegetables?' "

"Think of that," exclaimed the beans.

"Yes, he didn't know peas," said the peas.

"Well," said the beans, "we've heard of creatures who didn't know beans, but we've never heard of creatures who didn't know peas."

OCTOBER 24: Tiger West's Food

T IGER WEST," said daddy, "had been off on a number of trips with his cat friends who lived down the street.

"Now Tiger West lived in great grandeur. He had a special bed of cushions and a blanket to curl under. He had a rug of white, soft, fluffy material which he could lie upon whenever he wanted. And he wore a beautiful bow to match his mistress' gown.

"His master was a very rich man, and Tiger West was used to the best of food. But he had missed adventures and when he became friendly with the cats down the street he certainly did have enough. He narrowly escaped having horrid cold water thrown on him from an upper window one time, because he had been getting some goodies out of an ash tin. 'Meow,' he said to himself, 'what a joke it would be if the master could see me with my whiskers quite dirty and my beautiful fur ruffled up. Well, I know how to make myself look like a gentleman cat when I am ready to go home.'

"Days passed and Tiger West still went on trips with his cat friends. One day there was to be a meeting on the back fence of the cats of the neighborhood, and Tiger West was asked to be present. Now, Mr. Black Cat was very different looking from Tiger West. Mr. Black Cat's fur was not handsome, and he had a thin look, not at all becoming to a cat. He looked as though he had to hunt for his food and had to exercise entirely too soon after eating. Tiger imagined he must have been chased away after every meal he took.

"Still Mr. Black Cat was a leader in the cat neighborhood. He was President of the Night Singing Club, Vice-President of the Ash Can Visitors, Secretary of the Hunt Mice Club, and Treasurer of the Garbage Guild. He was always chosen as the judge of all the trials held in the cat neighborhood and for this reason he was always called 'Your Honor.'

"Now it made Tiger West very much annoyed to hear such a common cat called by such a fine name. 'Do you like strawberries and cream?' he asked.

" 'Never ate any,' said Mr. Black Cat.

" 'I do,' said Tiger West, 'and I eat them in and out of season. My master always gets them for me, or else he gets something else that is nice for my breakfast with cream.'

" 'It doesn't satisfy my hunger to hear what you have had to eat,' said Mr. Black Cat.

"Still Tiger West wanted to show that he amounted to something and was better than Mr. Black Cat. 'I never eat any kind of meat on a chicken but the tenderest white meat,' he said. 'And I am particularly fond of ice-cream. I like all the best food, and I get it too.'

"Mr. Black Cat raised his back and snarled. 'This cat,' he said, tries to be superior to us. Let's put him out of the club.'

"The cats were chasing Tiger West now, but he got away from them and back home. 'How foolish I was,' he said to himself as he began to drink a bowl of rich milk, 'to leave a home like this for such terrifying adventures. But my curiosity is satisfied, and now I will stay home and live in luxury as I should.' "

OCTOBER 25: Autumn Leaves

A H," said the autumn leaves, "now is the time of the year for our great and wonderful party."

"Are you going to have one soon?" asked Mr. Wind.

"We hope to have one very, very soon," said the leaves as they blew about.

"The reason I asked," said Mr. Wind, "was because I did not want to have any other engagement on the day that you give your party. It would be the sort of a party I would enjoy and I trust you will invite me."

"Well," laughed the leaves, "we couldn't very well have the sort of a party we want without you. We want your help in the races and jumps and scampers. We need you to say, 'Ready, Set, Go.' We could never go without you, Mr. Wind. And so we talked about this party right before you, hoping you would show a great interest."

And Mr. Wind came to the party and helped to make it a huge success.

OCTOBER 26:   Old Mother Hubbard

OLD Mother Hubbard,
    She went to the cupboard,
To give her poor dog a bone,
But when she came there
The cupboard was bare,
    And so the poor dog had none.

She went to the baker's
    To buy him some bread,
And when she came back
    The poor dog was dead.

She went to the joiner's
    To buy him a coffin,
And when she came back
    The poor dog was laughing.

She took a clean dish
    To get him some tripe,
And when she came back
    He was smoking his pipe.

She went to the ale-house
    To get him some beer,
And when she came back
    The dog sat in a chair.

She went to the tavern
    For white wine and red,
And when she came back
    The dog stood on his head.

She went to the hatter's
  To buy him a hat,
And when she came back
  He was feeding the cat.

She went to the barber's
  To buy him a wig,
And when she came back
  He was dancing a jig.

She went to the fruiterer's
  To buy him some fruit,
And when she came back
  He was playing the flute.

She went to the tailor's
  To buy him a coat,
And when she came back
  He was riding a goat.

She went to the cobbler's
  To buy him some shoes,
And when she came back
  He was reading the news.

She went to the sempstress
  To buy him some linen,
And when she came back
  The dog was spinning.

She went to the hosier's
  To buy him some hose,
And when she came back
  He was dressed in his clothes.

The dame made a curtsey,
  The dog made a bow;
The dame said, "Your servant,"
  The dog said, "Bow, wow!"

OCTOBER 27: A Talk with the Sun

A LITTLE boy named Melville," said daddy, "had heard that day that every one should make hay while the sun was shining.

" 'Make hay while the sun shines,' was what Melville had been told. The one who had told him this was his teacher in school.

"How could any one make hay in the winter time and the sun shone in the winter time as well as in the summer time? he thought.

"He wondered about it more and more as he felt the warmth of Mr. Sun shining into his window. He was sitting curled up in a big arm chair.

"How he wished he could ask Mr. Sun what it meant. Of course he could ask his teacher to-morrow. There must be some meaning to it, or some catch to it which he didn't understand."

"Mr. Sun looked very pleasant and as though he would be quite willing to tell Melville if only Melville knew how to ask him so he would hear.

"How nice and warm Mr. Sun was. More and more sleepy did Melville become, and after a few moments he was sound asleep. Then it seemed as though Mr. Sun came and sat on the window sill. 'It is true,' said Mr. Sun, 'that one can only make hay when the season allows it, and the season doesn't allow it when it is winter, most assuredly.

" 'But the expression, "Make hay while the sun shines," has nothing to do with the seasons.

" 'It is simply an expression meaning to take advantage of the good weather or the good time or the good season and prepare for ones which aren't so good.

" 'For example, when daddies and mothers are well and strong they try to save a little money for the days when illness may come. That is making hay while the sun shines, for they're saving during the time when they get a chance to save.

" 'When children study when they're young they're making hay while the sun shines for they're taking advantage of the opportunities they have which will make them wise when they're men and women.

" 'When people are wise and take advantage of time it is making hay while the sun shines, for it is not losing time. The expression, as you see, means taking advantage of good times to prepare for bad times, and it started by some one telling some one else to see about the hay while the sun was shining, for the rain might come, and then it would be too late.

" 'And,' continued the sun, 'it is a wise saying, a very wise saying, indeed.' "

253

OCTOBER 28: The Squash

I T'S all right to be a winter vegetable or to be a summer vegetable, and it's all right to be any kind of a vegetable at all a vegetable wishes to be," said the squash, "but it's sad above everything to be a squash."

"And why so?" asked one of the potatoes.

"Because there is something flat about being a squash.

"Just think of the family name, for example—squash! Doesn't it sound flat and squashed and trampled upon and walked upon and squashed down flat? It has such a hopeless sound!"

"It does sound that way," said the potato. "But still you aren't all trampled upon and squashed down flat. In fact, I don't know that I ever saw folks going around and trampling upon you. To be sure, your name has a flat, trampled-upon sound."

"And, oh, dear," said the squash, "we're such a dull sort of family. There is no interest to us. We're not fascinating and pretty, like the tomatoes, and we're not even loved by some and hated by others, like the cucumbers.

"They are interesting, for they have both friends and enemies.

"Now we haven't any who really love us. Most people think we'll do and that we do no harm and that we're all right, but no one even gets excited over squash. It is indeed sad to be nothing but a squash!"

OCTOBER 29: Jack O'Lantern

I WAS made by a very fine boy," said Jack O'Lantern. "I was a little nervous when he was cutting out my nose for fear he'd give me a crooked nose.

"But he didn't. I have a fine nose, haven't I?"

"Indeed, your nose is a thing of beauty," said Billie Brownie.

"And my eyes are nice, eh?" asked Jack O'Lantern.

"There is nothing the matter with your eyes," grinned Billie Brownie.

"Good," said Jack O'Lantern.

"And," he added after a moment, "I do hope you feel like admiring my mouth. It is such a nice big mouth."

"It is a nice big mouth," laughed Billie Brownie. "Yes, I think you're a fine fellow, and I love the head piece of a bit of green stalk you wear at the top of your head. It makes you look quite dashing.

"And I'm sure your candle will shine through beautifully when it is lighted," Billie Brownie added.

"And then I will go Hallowe'en calling," said Jack O'Lantern. "What joy that will be!

"Yes, I will go calling on many people, and I will sit on their doorsteps all by myself with no one to tell me what to do and no one to tell me how to act.

"For I will know how to act. I will smile at the people and that is why I am glad my mouth is big, for if I hadn't a big mouth I mightn't look as though I were smiling. I mightn't look as though I were grinning my best grin.

"I tell you, Billie Brownie, I'm a cheerful fellow."

OCTOBER 30: Daddy's Hallowe'en

I AM going to tell you," said daddy, "of the things I did when I was a boy at Hallowe'en time. "First of all I used to love bobbing in a tub for apples. I wore a bathing cap so if it was a cold evening my mother wouldn't be afraid I'd get my hair wet and catch cold because she knew how far down I'd dive into the tub of water!

"And we all did the same. The girls needed the bathing caps on their heads more than the boys did and they certainly could dive with hair all held in so dry and safe by their caps.

"Then we would play games and one of our favorite games was to run races carrying peanuts on knives.

"Two at a time would race against each other. The end of the race would be a big bowl set on the floor and we would start off at the other end of the room.

"Then we would each have a lot of peanuts and we would carry as many as we could on our knife until we had gotten rid of all of them.

"We had to take all the peanuts to the bowl without letting any drop off.

"It was most exciting, for though none of the other children could push us or joggle us they could make funny remarks to us and we would start laughing and sometimes our knife would shake and we'd drop the peanuts and have to start all over again.

"Sometimes we would only take one at a time because we could get them all to the bowl more quickly that way in the long run.

"Sometimes the one who starts off fastest does not win, you know. And then of course we went calling each with a Jack O'Lantern, and how mad we were at those who hadn't enough fun in them to like these Hallowe'en callers!"

OCTOBER 31: Hallowe'en

THE preparations for the party to be given at Janet's house that Hallowe'en evening had already begun. Already they were hanging apples attached firmly by strings from a doorway and as soon as the guests came and the tricks began they would all try to bite these apples, which would swing so annoyingly away from them!

And there was going to be a dish of flour in the kitchen after supper and the children were all going to try to find a twenty-five cent piece hidden there. They were going to hunt for it with their teeth! And there were apples bobbing in a great tub of water. And these had to be caught by the teeth too. Some of these held pennies!

There would be fortune-telling, too, and Janet's mother had promised to be the fortune-telling witch who would sit by her caldron which was now being made of red cheese-cloth. At the bottom of it, barely hidden, there would be a flashlight which would be kept going all the time, of course!

Oh, the party was going to be splendid. Janet knew that. And yet—and yet—she wished she knew why they had a party—not that she didn't want a party! But just why was it for this evening with the strange name. What did Hallowe'en really mean? She hated to ask for she felt she should know and that she would be laughed at for not knowing.

"Why, Janet," her mother said that afternoon late as she caught sight of Janet's little worried face, "this isn't the time to look sad when we're having a party! What is the trouble, my darling?"

There was something in the understanding, sweet way that her mother asked her that made Janet ask what she thought was so foolish a question.

"Mother dear," she began, "just what does Hallowe'en mean?"

"October thirty-first," her mother said, "is the vigil of All Saints' Day, or Hallowe'en, for Hallow means to devote time to holy purposes and e'en is short for evening. So that it means the evening before the religious day which is known as All Saints' Day.

"But Hallowe'en, while coming before a religious day, has always been an evening of festivity and frolic and fun for children. In all countries they celebrate it—it is a real children's evening—though in various countries the children have their own little ways of celebrating.

"Our way, though, is used by children of many countries and we have make-believe witches just as they have, for in the olden days in the old countries those who were superstitous or given to imagining things not so, thought witches came out on Hallowe'en."

And somehow, Janet never enjoyed a party so much, for it was so nice to know just what the day meant and to know too that in many countries children on this very evening were having a celebration of such a weirdly wonderful kind!

NOVEMBER 1: The Brownies Help

A LITTLE girl, whose name was Kitty, was very anxious to win the prize," said daddy. "I shall work so hard over it," she said to herself, and she refused an invitation to walk with her friends that afternoon.

"She put her hand to her head and thought hard—but she couldn't think of anything to write! She dipped her pen into the ink-well and only made two smudge spots on the paper in front of her.

" 'Oh,' she sighed, 'I wish I had gone for a walk. I feel so sleepy— and staying in the house all afternoon is so silly!' She really was much annoyed with herself and soon she put her head down on her desk and went sound, sound asleep.

"Pretty soon the two smudge spots grew larger and larger. They seemed to get round and funny and fat—and she almost saw them grinning at her!

"Soon she saw that around one spot was a wide band of white on which were written the words:

" 'I'm Mr. Pen and I'll write you a story.'

"And around the other spot was written:

" 'I'm Mr. Ink and I'll write you a story.'

" 'But I don't want two stories,' cried Kitty. 'I only want one. If I write two they will think I want to have two chances while every one else has one. That will never do.'

"But the round, smudgy spots proved to be Billie Brownie and Bennie Brownie, and it was around their hats that the words were written about Mr. Pen and Mr. Ink.

" 'We are going to whisper to you the most marvelous of stories,' they said. And they grinned and hugged each other with delight.

" 'She'll win the prize,' said Billie Brownie, and his brother Bennie laughed and said:

" 'She certanly will.'

"And then they told her, while she was napping, the most wonderful story you can imagine. 'I won't forget it, will I?' she asked. And the two Brownies laughed and said:

" 'Forget one of your stories? Never!'

"And then Kitty stretched out her arms until one hand was taking hold of Mr. Pen and the other was bringing Mr. Ink's Home—the inkwell—forward on the desk.

"'Ah,' she said, as she rubbed her eyes and looked at the paper in front of her. 'What a nice sleep I have had. I feel so fresh and just like writing a composition. I am so glad I didn't go out—for I know just what I want to write about.'

"Kitty wrote all the afternoon and the very last thing she did was to make a nice, neat copy of the composition. When it was all ready and tied with a little piece of blue string at the top, she put it away in her desk drawer until the time came to hand it in.

"Of course, she won she prize and the teacher said that it was because her composition showed she had taken time to think about it, but Kitty knew it was because of the Brownies!"

NOVEMBER 2: The Butterfly and Bumble-Bee

"GOOD-BY," said the golden butterfly. "It is late for me to be out and I must leave now. I have come around because it is what they call Indian summer.

"That is when another week of summer comes in the autumn when people have almost become used to cold weather."

"I must still do a little more work in this warm sunshine," the bumble-bee said; "you know it has been said of us that we improve each shining hour."

"But," said the golden butterfly, "how do you know you're improving each shining hour? Aren't the hours all right as they are?"

"Yes," said the bumble-bee, "that may be so, and they may be all right spent idly by some people. I don't suppose the hours care so very much, though I have heard they hated to be wasted, and we will never waste them."

"But they like to give pleasure and to have people take rests and enjoy themselves, too," said the golden butterfly. And as he waved a golden wing in farewell he said to himself, "Bumble-bees overdo things. They work so hard that they've forgotten how to play! And that is the saddest thing about their lives."

NOVEMBER 3: The Furnace

"HA, ha," said the Furnace, as the pieces of coal were being shoved in; "ha, ha," he laughed. "So they're becoming anxious to have me working again.

"And I believe they never gave me a moment's thought all summer long. I'm sure they didn't. I feel quite certain of it.

"And then they wonder why at times I act crossly and queerly and why I get upset at times. I try not to, but of course when I get thinking of how no one gives the poor old Furnace a thought all summer long, then I can't help but get upset.

"And when I get upset they all grumble about me, as if I mustn't get upset, no matter how I may feel.

"Well, it's a bit unfair. But I try to rise above it and give them heat and no smoke; warmth and no trouble.

"I suppose things aren't appreciated until they are needed. I've heard that window-shades or blinds or whatever one wants to call them have been so good about hiding the light from people's eyes when they were sleepy, and then when they are old and had holes in them, they were horribly complained about, though never a 'thank you' did they get when they were doing their good work.

"And no one ever says:

"'Ah, what a good pair of socks you are, my dear,' or, 'What a lovely pair of stockings you are, Nice Pair.'

"Yet so soon as a hole comes, how they grumble!"

"You're very useful," said a piece of coal, "but you aren't the whole thing. We're all needed. Matches are needed. Sticks and paper are needed when you are started. Sone one is needed to watch over you.

"You require a great deal of watching. You must have a nurse, or furnace man, or watcher of some sort looking after you.

"So, Furnace, you mustn't become too conceited." And the Furnace thought the coal was right.

NOVEMBER 4: The Elephant's Bath

"STEVE, the elephant," said daddy, "wanted to take a bath. He was in the big theater when he had this wish, for he did an act every afternoon and evening on the stage.

" 'Yes,' Steve said to himself, 'I feel the need of bathing. I'd like a good plunge in the real water—a river for example, just as I would have if I were free.

" 'Of course, the first thing I must do,' he continued, 'is to get out of that side door there and get on the street. Then I will go a-looking for a river.

" 'I know there are plenty of rivers, for in my five years of circus life I've seen quantities of rivers. Yes, there must be one not far from this theater. It seems to me on one of my marches that I remember seeing it.

" 'In fact, I feel quite sure I remember seeing a river at the other end of the long street we marched through.

" 'At any rate, I will go and have a look.'

"So Steve started to go through the door at the end of the lower part of the stage where he was staying waiting for his act to go on. There would be other acts first and then he would come.

" 'I'll be back in time,' he said to himself, 'but if not I'll be just having a holiday. Of course, usually holidays are given to people and animals, but this time I will take my own holiday all of my own accord.'

"Instead of undoing the door or opening it in the usual way Steve walked along pushing the door in front of him and taking it right off its hinges.

"When he got out on the street he looked about him. The children were just coming from school.

" 'Well, hello, children,' he said, as he waved his trunk around. Some of the children had peanuts with them and some of them had pennies so they threw delicacies to Steve and said:

" 'Oh, aren't you a nice big elephant.'

"But when their mothers saw that the elephant was walking along they called to their children to come right in the houses.

" 'He is nice,' the children called back.

" 'You can't be sure,' said their mothers.

" 'Now isn't that annoying,' said Steve. 'Here I am feeling as friendly as friendly as can be, and the mothers want their children to come away from me and to go into foolish houses.

" 'I don't want to go into houses. They needn't bang their doors so tight shut. Haven't I just left a house and don't I want a bath?

" 'I don't take a bath by going in people's houses. I've heard of the size of their bath tubs. They wouldn't do for me.'

"Steve suddenly discovered a river at the end of another few blocks.

"He hurried along, waving his trunk as he went, and oh, what joy it was to him, to take a real swim in a real river. By the time he had finished his keepers had come after him, but he didn't mind going back again to do his tricks in the theater for he had had a bath in a real river!"

NOVEMBER 5: Waving and Dreaming

LADDIE lived out in the country on a farm and not far away were the railway tracks," said daddy. "How Laddie did love to see the great long trains go rushing by and curling blue smoke coming from the engine!

"He would sit on the back porch of his home and watch and watch the trains as they went by, and every day there were sure to be trains passing five different times. Laddie was always there on the back porch, just as regularly as if he had to be there.

"And every time a train would pass Laddie would wave and as he waved he would think of the people in the train and how they would go on and on into wonderful parts of the land, new parts he had never seen.

"Often people would wave back to him and then he would smile and feel just like an adventure, too, for he had made friends with these wonderful people rushing by on adventureful travels."

NOVEMBER 6: The Clever Fire Horses

THE fire," began daddy, "was in a deserted barn on the very outskirts of the town. It was quite near some houses and an inn. So the firemen wanted to do all they could to keep fire from spreading to the houses, for there was quite a high wind. No one minded if the old barn burnt, for it really was of no use to any one, and the owner of it never bothered to keep it up at all.

"But the fire-engine horses made an awful fuss. They heard, what the firemen didn't hear, one of their own kind crying for help in horse language.

"They tried to break from the engines and kicked their heels and made a lot of commotion. They shook their heads and made all sorts of funny sounds.

"Finally one of the firemen said:

" 'I have a suspicion that the horses hear something in that barn, and I am going in to investigate, for maybe there is something alive inside. I have never known these horses to make a mistake.'

"So he went in through a broken window, and when he got inside he found a horse trembling with fear at seeing the flames.

"The old fireman unbolted the back door of the barn where the fire had not as yet spread and led the horse out. Then you should have seen the fire-engine horses. They were so happy that the old horse had been saved.

"But just at that moment an old man came running out of the inn and crying: 'Oh, save my horse! He's in that barn!'

"And when he saw that his horse had been saved he went over and put his head on the horse's mane, and the horse neighed contentedly.

"The old man had stopped at the inn for the night, and there they had told him he could safely keep his horse in the old barn.

"'Oh, I am so grateful to you!' said the old man to the firemen. 'I love my horse like a very real friend. How can I ever thank you?'

"'We're not the ones to thank,' said the fireman who had gone in the barn when the fire horses had seemed so excited. 'Our horses saved your horse's life.'"

NOVEMBER 7: The Two Roses

HAVE I ever met you before?" asked the yellow rose of a beautiful pink rose. The pink rose was of a very exquisite color and though the yellow rose had seen many pink roses it was sure it hadn't seen one of just that very same shade.

"I don't believe you have," said the pink rose, "for I am a new kind of a rose. I haven't any thorns on me—that is, I only have some way, way down by the bottom of my stem. That is what they have trained my family to do. It took a good deal of training and teaching to make us like that and last spring when my grandmother made her appearance she was the first one to have succeeded in being almost thornless. It was a great day for grandmother!"

NOVEMBER 8: The Moth Balls

HOW funny moths are," said the first Moth Ball. "When most creatures go to the country or the seashore in the summer the moths prefer to stay if they can, in great heavy coats and furs and tam-o'-shanters, and so forth.

"It is really most ridiculous. One would think they would prefer it where it was cool."

"Still," said the second Moth Ball, "we do not go to cool spots in the summer. We stay right in with the warm clothes."

"That is so," the first Moth Ball answered, "but we have our work to do. Our business keeps us in warm clothes in the summer-time, and you'd think moths would stay away, when they can see there is no hospitality offered them."

"Oh, well," the second Moth Ball said, "I suppose there are some creatures who will never take hints and perhaps it is just as well.

"For if moths took hints there would be no need for moth balls."

"True," the first Moth Ball ended as it was shaken out of a heavy coat about to begin its second winter.

NOVEMBER 9: Good-Winter

A S you know," commenced daddy, "when the little creatures who go to sleep for the winter are about to begin their long, long rest they wish each other a good-winter just as we would say a good-night to each other, and Billie Brownie hurried off to make his good-winter calls on some of his friends.

" 'Well,' said Billie Brownie to Mother Grizzly, 'I wish you a good-winter.

" 'If you were only going to have a night's rest of course I'd only wish you a good-night and pleasant dreams.

" 'But as you sleep for the winter I wish you a good-winter and pleasant winter dreams.'

" 'Woof, woof, thank you,' said Mother Grizzly.

"And Billie Brownie left Mother Grizzly to tuck her children into their nice beds right by her in the old family den.

"He was very fond of Mother Grizzly.

"Then he went to call on the Ground Squirrels.

" 'Hello, little Ground Squirrels,' he said, as he saw them after he had traveled a little distance in his Brownie motor-car.

" 'Are you on your way to bed?'

" 'We are indeed,' they said. 'Our parents went to bed at the end of the summer but we were allowed to stay up longer.

" 'It is such fun to be allowed to stay up a little longer once in a great while. Good-winter, Billie Brownie.'

"For they said good-winter to Billie Brownie, too, as they would not see him during the winter, although he would not be asleep.

"They would be the ones asleep!

"And then he called on Mother Black-Bear, the Prairie Dog family, Willie Woodchuck and his family, and many others and to all he wished pleasant winter dreams."

NOVEMBER 10: The Horse's Complaint

WHEN I went out to-day," began the horse, "the farmer had a new checkrein for me. It held my head way, way up in the air and it was so hard for me. My neck ached and throbbed, and still the farmer drove me along and never paid any attention.

"I just longed to have him wear it for five minutes and see how he would feel. But we had not gone so very far when a lady stopped and spoke to the master.

" 'That check rein is very tight,' she said.

" 'Oh no,' said the master. 'He is used to a rein like that. He always keeps his head up that way. He is a fine, well-bred horse.'

"That's true,' said the lady. 'But that is no reason why you should make him suffer.'

" 'He doesn't suffer,' said the master. And all the time my neck was aching, aching, and, oh, how I was longing to get my head down a little. The rein held it up, and never for a moment could I get it down.

"Before another word was said, my check rein was loosened, and then joy of joys, I put my head down. I moved it around, and twisted it, and I shook it! It was glorious.

" 'There,' said the lady. 'Don't you see he likes his head down? He doesn't want it forced up beyond where he would hold it naturally. That is a very cruel rein.'

" 'You know nothing about horses,' said my master as he put the check rein back.

"There was my head back in its cruel check rein again, and on we drove. Oh how long that drive to town and back seemed to-day. And though I wish the master no harm, how I do wish he could be driven into town just once—with his head way back—held—so he couldn't move it—couldn't let it down for a second! Then he would know what it means to a horse who has too tight a check rein."

"Then he would know," neighed the other horses. "Oh, if masters could only wear check reins too, so they would know just what they are like," they added.

NOVEMBER 11:   The Fox and the Rabbit

ONCE upon a time a fox and a rabbit were neighbors, and one fine spring morning the fox asked the rabbit if he would go hunting with him.   The rabbit said, "I do not think I can go with you to-day, as I shall be very busy."

But when the fox had gone, the rabbit, who really had nothing to do, sat in the sun and enjoyed the beautiful morning air.   After a while he spied the fox returning from his hunt, and he thought out a scheme whereby he might secure possession of the fox's game bag.

He went a little way into the forest, and lay down as if he were dead.   When the fox came up to him, he touched him with his paw, and said to himself, "Here is a nice fat rabbit for which I will presently return, and add to my larder."

When the rabbit saw the fox go on, he got up, took a short cut ahead of him, and lay down as before.   Seeing, as he supposed, another rabbit fast asleep, the fox said to himself, "Fat rabbits seem to be very plentiful this season; I will take this one home with me."   Then he thought he would go back and get the other one; so he put his game-bag down on the grass by the stump of a tree, and started back.

When the rabbit saw that he was alone, he took the bag and hid it in a thick clump of bushes.   Then he ran behind a tree, and waited to see what would happen.

The fox returned with a disgusted look on his face.   He, a fox, had been fooled, and when he saw that his game-bag had been taken, he became very angry indeed.   A cunning trick had been played upon him, and he looked about to see if he could find the culprit.

The rabbit was very proud of the fact that he had outwitted his neighbor, and, seeing the look of anger and disgust on the fox's face, laughed so loudly that he betrayed his hiding-place.   Fortunately for him, his burrow was close by, and he reached it only just in time to escape the fox, who would have made short work of him if he had caught him.

While the fox was watching for the rabbit to come out, a boy passing by saw the game-bag in the clump of bushes, and, picking it up, threw it over his shoulder, and walked off with it.   And so neither the fox nor the rabbit had the game.

NOVEMBER 12: Window Castles

THE children want to look out of their windows and you're in the way," said Mr. Sun to Master Chilly and Jack Frost's other brothers.

Chilly and the others began to move a little and as they moved their castles disappeared with them. The children were getting up now and were calling to each other. "Oh, look at the wonderful pictures on the windows. There are castles too! Aren't they beautiful!"

Chilly and the other Frost brothers and workers were delighted. "You see, Mr. Sun, they like us."

"Well, maybe they do," said Mr. Sun, "but I can't help you stay around. I must smile and talk in my usual way and it's too warm a day for you to like."

Slowly the frost castles left the windows, for they were taken away by the Frost Brothers after Mr. Sun had talked to them as they will never teach any one else the mystery of their work.

NOVEMBER 13: The Autumn Paint Club

COME on, now," said Jack Frost to his brothers. "It is time that the Autumn Paint Club finished up some of its work. Nutty Chum, Chippy Chappy, and Sharpy and Bright Eyes and others of the squirrel family will be glad that we have come, for we will improve the nuts and they like the nuts, oh yes indeed!

"Then we will please the children, too, for they like the chestnut season. Oh, yes, that is the truth! They do like the chestnut season.

"But ah, Frost Brothers, the night is almost here. Let's get started.

"Remember, you all know just what you have to do! You all know which of you must paint the windows with the magic Frost paint brushes this evening, and you know which of you must whisper to the flowers the little Frost word, 'Obey!' You all know what you must do."

"We all know," said the Frost Brothers.

"I feel just like work," said Master Very Cool.

"So do I," said Master Chilly.

"I feel like it, too, I should say I did," agreed Master Heavy Frost.

"Good," said Jack Frost. And you're a fine worker, Master Heavy Frost. You make creatures obey you!"

So off went the Frost Brothers, and the next morning when the people awoke they said what a heavy frost there had been, but Jack Frost was chuckling to himself as he said: "The Autumn Paint Club did fine work last night!"

NOVEMBER 14: Mother Brown Bat

AH, children," said Mother Brown Bat, "it will soon be time to go to bed. And we shall sleep well, for bats are good sleepers. We shall sleep especially well if it is to be a cold winter. Ah, my children, what marketing trips we have made. I have not had to call in a neighbor to take care of my babies when I went out. No, my babies hung onto my neck and came along, too.

"What times we used to have catching bugs and other delicious delicacies we found about at night. What meals we used to have.

"We used to have beetle pudding quite often and gnat salad. Do you remember, my Bat babies?"

"We remember, Mother Brown Bat. But," they said, " we are no longer babies."

"That is true," said Mother Brown Bat, "and you are able to look after yourselves; but I still call you babies, for it is hard for a mother to realize her children are grown-up and you do grow up so quickly.

"Sometimes we went about in the very, very early mornings and often we started out before it was really night. But we took great care, for we kept away from people. People have such a curious habit of not liking bats."

"That is hard to believe," said the Bat children.

"I think so," said Mother Brown Bat. "I should think they would like bats, and especially the members of our family, for we are so small and dainty and so clever in the way we hang on to the trees when we

267

sleep, rather than fussing about housekeeping and bed-making all the time.

"Housekeeping takes up too much time for a Mother Brown Bat and the Mr. Brown Bat and the little Brown Bats wouldn't half appreciate it either.

"So she doesn't bother to do a lot of work for no reason at all, for none of us miss a home life. We're perfectly happy as we are and with our own ways and habits."

"Perfectly happy," agreed the Bat children. "We're perfectly happy, Mother Brown Bat."

NOVEMBER 15: The Magic Slate

THERE was once," said Witty Witch, as she sat in the center of old Mr. Giant's cave, and told stories to the elves, brownies, gnomes, goblins and many of her other little friends, "a very naughty little gnome.

" 'I think slates are the nicest things in the world,' he said. 'Anything we write or draw on them we can rub right out again. I guess I'll be like a slate myself. I'll do what I please and then I'll rub it out.'

"Of course he didn't quite know how he was to do that. Rubbing out chalk marks on his slate he found to be quite a different matter from rubbing out mean and naughty actions!

"Still he said to himself that he would never do the same naughty things again, and that he was sorry, and that was just about the same as rubbing them out.

"He always pretended in school that he knew the answer to every question. Then, when Professor Gnome would ask what he had written, he would say, 'Oh, I'm sorry, Professor, but I didn't know you wanted me to keep the answer on my slate. I rubbed it out.' For then, he thought, he had shown he knew something by writing on his slate—even though he did not write the answer at all, but simply something quite absurd.

"One night he was very tired. He had been playing hard and had quite forgotten about his lessons. He had also knocked down a little creature smaller than himself, but he had said to himself that he was sorry for that. He really hadn't meant to be so rough.

"Suddenly before his eyes he saw Professor Gnome, only he looked much bigger than he did in school. He was carrying a big slate.

" 'This is a slate which cannot be rubbed off by your sponge, little gnome,' he said. 'I have the magic rubber for it which the Fairy

268

Queen gave me. You can now do your lessons correctly on this slate and when I think they are well done then I shall take your slate and rub it clean.'

"And the little gnome seemed to be back in the school-room now and he had written something on his slate—just to pretend he knew the answer—and then he tried to rub it off before Professor Gnome saw it. But it wouldn't rub at all. And all the class laughed at him for knowing absolutely nothing.

"Next it was recess time, and the little gnome he had knocked down was crying. He had bumped his head as he had fallen, and the bump kept growing larger and larger until at last his head had gone entirely, and there was only a big bump left!

"Oh, how the gnome felt. 'I shall always remember that I can't rub out everything I do,' he said. 'My magic slate will teach me a good lesson, for I'll be so ashamed when I see all my mistakes right in front of me until I have made them really and truly right.'

"It was only a dream, to be sure," said Witty Witch, "but from that day on the gnome worked and played as though everything he did and said could not be washed off unless everything was right."

NOVEMBER 16: Peter's Trip with the Man in the Moon

THERE was once," said daddy, "a little boy named Peter who had always longed to see the man in the moon. Every night when there was a full moon he would sit at his window and look at the funny, jolly face of the old man until he became so sleepy he would have to go to bed.

"One night he sat watching so long that he fell asleep by the window. It was not long before he saw the strangest thing. The moon seemed to be growing larger and larger, and soon it was back of a tree near his window. He could see quite plainly the jolly old face of his beloved man in the moon looking jollier and fatter than ever. The old man grinned from ear to ear at Peter, and in a moment or two he spoke.

" 'Well, Peter, here I am. Now how do you like me?' And as he spoke he chuckled and laughed.

" 'Oh, I think you're wonderful!' said Peter, with wild enthusiasm and joy.

" 'So you think I'm wonderful, do you? Ha, ha! Well, that is a joke! But there certainly isn't any one else just like me, that's true enough. So maybe I'm wonderful because I'm so queer. What about that?'

" 'Oh, no,' said Peter, 'you're wonderful because you're so fat and jolly and because you're always laughing and seeming to have a good time.'

"At that the old man in the moon laughed some more and said: 'Well, you're a funny little chap too. All folks don't think it's such a compliment to be fat, but I do. It's the way I am, you see, and it's best to be satisfied with the way you are, isn't it? If you really like me then I'll take you off in my chariot of mist to visit the stars, and you'll call on all the bright queens of the stars, who sparkle so you can see them from down on the earth.'

"So off went Peter with the man in the moon for the most gorgeous trip. They visited all the stars, saw the bright fairy queens who live in them and all the little elves and brownies. And then the man in the moon showed Peter where he stayed in the sky and how he moved every week so that all the little boys and girls in the world could see a full moon every month. And Peter could see down below all the wee little houses (they looked so small from where Peter was) and the earth, which looked very funny and small, too, from up in the moon. Peter felt a little afraid at first that he'd fall, but as he'd never heard of the man in the moon having a tumble to earth he felt comforted. Alas, all too soon the journey had to end, for Peter heard the distant sound of a breakfast bell.

"As he yawned he realized he'd been sleeping all night by the window. But, oh, such a gorgeous sleep as it had been!"

NOVEMBER 17: Dinah

HER name was Dinah," said daddy, "and she was a gorilla. A gorilla is a relation of the monkey family, you know, and looks something like a chimpanzee.

"She had had quite an interesting life as she had lived in Africa when young, and then she had been captured and had been tamed and had been very friendly with her owner, and after that she was brought over to this country and given to a Zoo in a large city.

" 'I don't expect to stay here very long,' said Dinah. 'I do not care about living to a great old age, as some creatures do, and I do not like captivity. I am different from the ourang-utan and the chimpanzee, who are so friendly with the keeper.

"I do not object to the keeper, but life bores me. There are some creatures who are always happy, and if they aren't always happy, they are happy most of the time. So look at me while you can. Now is your chance to see the gloomy gorilla.' "

NOVEMBER 18: Winter Sleepers

BILLIE BROWNIE had still many of his calls to make in order to say good-winter to his friends who were going to sleep for the winter.

"Goog-a-room, goog-a-room, goog-a-room," said Grandpa Frog from the near-by pond; "come, little frogs, come all, and sleep in the beautiful mud. The cold weather is coming.

"It was bitterly cold last night, little frogs."

Then he saw Billie Brownie.

"Good-winter," croaked Grandpa Frog.

And the toads and the frogs all squealed and croaked,

"Good-winter, Billie Brownie, good-winter!"

Then Billie Brownie went to call on the Jumping Mice.

"That frost last night was a hard one," said little Miss Julia Jumping Mouse. "I'm going to bed to take care of my mouse beauty sleep."

"Ha, ha," laughed Miss Jenny Jumping Mouse, "who ever heard of a mouse going to bed early to get her beauty sleep?"

"I can't stop to talk it over with you. I'm too sleepy," said Miss Julia Jumping Mouse.

"Good-winter to all of you," said Billie Brownie. But as he walked away from all his friends who were going to sleep for the winter, he said to himself:

> "To sleep for a night
> Is quite all right.
> But to sleep half a year
> Is really quite queer.
> But of course we're all different,
>   As different can be,
> And what is natural to you
> Might seem very queer to me!"

NOVEMBER 19: Toody Ruggles' Luck

A NUMBER of rich ladies," began daddy, "at the seashore one day last summer had been throwing pennies from a bridge into the water for a lot of poor boys who were diving for them. The water was quite a good deal over their heads, but the little boys were marvelous divers and swimmers, having always lived by the water. The ladies kept on throwing pennies time and time again to see the wonderful dives the little boys were able to make. They would dive straight down into the water and stay down ever so long and then come up, each one holding a glittering bright penny.

"But, alas, a dreadful thing happened. One of the ladies in throwing pennies dropped a most beautiful diamond ring off from her finger and into the deep water.

"'Oh, dear,' she cried in dismay, 'that was the ring I valued most and cared more for than any piece of jewelry I had. I shouldn't have worn it, though, for it was much too loose for that finger. Whatever shall I do without it? I was so fond, so fond of it!'

"At once the little boys offered to dive for it, for it had been by the throwing of pennies to them that the lady had lost her much prized ring, and they wanted, of course, to get it back for her.

"So again and again they dived, but as none of them had seen her drop it they couldn't judge where it had been dropped.

"Now, Toody Ruggles was perhaps the best little diver of all, and yet even he had been so far unsuccessful, but at last he thought he saw it shining down among some weeds. The lady, however, had just about given up hopes of ever seeing her ring again when, lo and behold, up came Toody, his wet little face wreathed in smiles, carrying the beautiful ring. The lady was overpowered with joy and gave Toody a most wonderful reward.

"Oh, how happy Toody Ruggles was! At home he had one little sister who was very fragile and delicate. As their parents were very poor, Toody was trying his best to help the family with their bills by selling newspapers and carrying suitcases from the station. Lately, though, the doctor had told him that his sister must have plenty of fruit to build her up and to make her regain her strength, and this poor Toody was unable to afford.

"But now he had the wonderful reward from the lady, and all the other boys were delighted that Toody had been the lucky one.

"Toody at once began to give his little sister delicious fruits. Soon the color came back to her cheeks, and she grew well and strong. So Toody's worry that he might lose his beloved little sister was over, and through his good luck their little home once more became very, very happy."

NOVEMBER 20: The Limpets

"A LIMPET," said daddy, "is a little shellfish. They're very, very small, perhaps a shade smaller than a snail, and they cling to the rocks which are their homes. There are always hundreds of them fastened on the big rocks on the coast by the sea. They live on seaweed and the salt water.

"When I was a boy we spent some time in a town by the sea. We used to play off a bank called 'Greenbank' because in the summer time this bank was always so very green. Below this bank there were countless big rocks. We could hide behind these rocks, and no one could see us. We loved that because it seemed so mysterious to hide like that. We could see the bank above us, and then, miles and miles, as far as we could see, was the ocean. The rocks were covered with seaweed, and they used to be very slippery. Sometimes we would play hide-and-seek back of these rocks.

"The rocks that were half in the water would be covered with the limpets. One big rock had great numbers of them on it, and we always called the rock 'Limpet Rock.'

"One Saturday about six of us had taken a big basketful of lunch and had gone down to Greenbank to spend the day. There had been a terrific storm the night before. We looked for our Limpet Rock the first thing, but we saw not a sign of a limpet. How funny, we thought; that surely is the rock! What could have become of the limpets? They were quite used to storms, and surely they couldn't have been hurt by the storm of the night before! Suddenly we spied them.

"There they all were, looking very unhappy and clinging to little pebbles and rocks in the low water. Before the day was over, though, the limpets had attached themselves to another big rock. So we called this rock the 'New Limpet Rock.' Once the limpets had fastened themselves to the new rock, they were just as happy as before, for they can change homes more easily than any other creatures and be happy.

"So I think we should admire the limpets because they are so brave and cheerful when they are driven from one home and with practically no fuss they set about and get a new home right away."

NOVEMBER 21: The Rescue

A LITTLE girl named Fannie," began daddy, "was walking across a city street carrying a very small black poodle dog in her arms.

"Suddenly the poodle dog, whose name was Gyp, saw another dog on the other side of the street. Evidently Gyp thought the other little dog would be nice to talk to, so he jumped with one bound out of Fannie's arms.

"Fannie gave a scream of horror, at which the policeman, standing near, flew to the rescue. Had he been a minute later the little dog would have been struck by a street car.

" 'Oh, you've rescued my little dog!' Fannie cried. 'You are so brave and wonderful!'

"Gyp, who had been very much frightened at his narrow escape, was breathing little short, quick breaths from the fear of a moment before.

"But at the same time his little tail was wagging for all it was worth, as he wanted to show the big policeman how much he thanked him, for he knew the policeman had saved his little dog life."

NOVEMBER 22: The Old Man in the Woods

A LITTLE boy named Bobbie had a sister named Agnes," said daddy. "They had few neighbors, as they lived in a very small place where there were only a few houses. Near their house were long stretches of woods. They had never been to the other side of the woods nor had they ever really walked very far into the forest, for it was said in the little hamlet where they lived that a queer old man had a hut about a mile and a half through the long lonely road. But one day the children decided they'd venture forth to see this old man.

"Off they started, and after walking quite a distance they came to a funny little hut with smoke coming out of the chimney. When the old man saw Bobbie and Agnes he called out in a happy, excited voice: 'I'm having visitors! Hurrah!'

"He took the children in his hut and showed them some wonderful picture books. He told them how delighted he was to have visitors, as he knew he was thought queer, but really he wasn't at all, except that he loved to live in the heart of the woods. So the children promised to see him often, and he promised to show them more picture books, and before they left he gave them each a big piece of delicious apple pie."

NOVEMBER 23: The Queen's Pin

O NCE when I was a little boy," began daddy, "I heard an interesting story that a pin told. Now, you may think that a pin could not tell such a very good story, but this was an exceptional pin, belonging to a very grand person.

" 'Having been made into a beautiful crown shaped pin of superb pearls,' said the pin, 'I was put into a show case in a very beautiful jewelry shop. People would notice me above all other pins in the case and pick me out as being by far the most beautifully set pin. All the pearls which belonged to me were very, very lovely ones. But I was so expensive that people could just look at me and could not afford to buy me.

" 'The jeweler was so proud of me that he really did not care whether I was sold or not, for my beauty attracted so much attention that it was a help to his business. You see, people would ask one another if they had seen me, and if they hadn't they would come right to the shop to look at me. Then, though they didn't buy me, they would be sure to buy something else in the shop.

" 'But at last a marvelous carriage drove up before the door. It was drawn by four horses, and there were two fine coachmen and two very pompous looking footmen sitting up on top of the fine carriage.

" 'The jeweler was all in a flutter. Never before had he seen such a wonderful carriage. And out of it stepped a very handsomely dressed lady with a lady on either side of her, who both guarded her very carefully.

" ' "The queen—the queen has come to my little shop!" cried the excited jeweler, and all the other shoppers stood by and made low bows.

" 'But I didn't bow. I didn't think a crown need bow.

" 'The queen had heard of me, and she had come to buy me. The jeweler, with trembling fingers, fastened me in my little blue velvet box, and off I went, carried by the queen.

" 'When we reached the palace I felt very much at home, for everything was so beautiful there. I must confess, though, that I did feel a little nervous that first evening when I was worn by the queen with so many other exquisite jewels.

" 'Oh, but such times as I did have! The court dinners and balls and receptions were so dazzling, and I adored them. But, best of all, I loved the parades and seeing all the crowds of people cheer and wave their handkerchiefs to the queen. And the bands were so exciting!

" 'But the proudest moment of my life was really when the queen gave me to a young lady as a token of her appreciation of the lady's brave soldier daddy.' "

NOVEMBER 24: Eagle's Thanksgiving

O F course," said Daddy Bald Eagle, "Thanksgiving Day is a day when the turkey is shown a great honor. But I would like to have something to say for Thanksgiving Day, too. Thanksgiving Day is a day when people are thankful. They are thankful for their homes, thankful for their country, thankful they belong to their country and that they have so many blessings.

"And the Eagle would like to say he is thankful, too.

"Yes, I would like to say how thankful I am that I am chosen as the national emblem of the United States. I would like to say that I shall never cease to be thankful that this honor has been shown to my family."

NOVEMBER 25: Thanksgiving Day

IT was a holiday and it was Thanksgiving Day. From the moment Melly got up she felt in a "holiday" spirit, she said. And everything and every one seemed to feel the same way too.

First she went in quite early in the morning to see her mother who was sitting up in bed, waiting for her little visitor.

Her mother was wearing a dear little blue jacket and a blue cap and was looking so pretty.

She had a nice little chat with her mother and then she went back into her own room to get dressed.

Yes, every one in the house seemed to act and feel as though the day was a holiday as it most certainly was.

And oh, such a Thanksgiving dinner as they had.

First they had corn soup and then they had turkey and many vegetables and then they had apple and celery salad. Next they had two pies to choose from, or to take a piece from each, and they had ice-cream too, and every kind of a nut and piece of fruit was in the fruit dish.

In the center of the table was a little bit of a pumpkin. It was a real pumpkin but it was very, very small.

On top of the pumpkin Melly's mother had put some tiny carrots and baby potatoes and some little snowberries from the snowberry bush.

They did make the table look so gay and pretty. After dinner Melly and her family played the good old game of "stagecoach." You know the game?

The different people in the room who are playing the game take the names of the people supposed to be in the stagecoach, such as the driver, the little boy traveler and his mother and so on.

Every time the word stage-coach is mentioned each person playing the game must get up and turn around and the last person who sits down when doing this goes on with the story-telling.

Of course the one who is telling the story must tell all of the trip this imaginary stage-coach took.

And of course the names of all the characters must be mentioned often, for every time a character is mentioned that one who is taking the part of the character must get up and turn around.

So Melly and her family played this in the afternoon.

And when it became dark they lighted the lights and the fire was poked up so that is blazed most beautifully.

They had supper in front of the fire and though each one had said he couldn't possibly eat another thing after such a dinner, they all managed to eat something.

And when Melly went to bed that night she said: "I believe in Thanksgiving Day! And I have so much to be so thankful for! More, I'm sure, than anybody else has."

NOVEMBER 26: Thanksgiving Day

IN 1620 as we all well know," said daddy, "a 'little band of Pilgrims' came to this country, brave, fearless souls who had already met with difficulties and were not afraid to face more. They had already tried to cross the Atlantic but their ships had leaked and they had had to go back.

"But they would have nothing to do with such a word as failure —and this is I think in itself an inspiration to all of us when we feel discouraged and as though we were failing in what we were trying to do—and so at last the Mayflower left Plymouth in Devonshire, England, and anchored on the American coast on November twenty-first.

"Here they were going to have freedom, and though the trip had been a terrible one and though there were only a hundred of them all told to keep up each other's spirits, they did not lose heart.

"They had planned to land on the New Jersey coast, but driven as they had been by gales and storms they found themselves on the Northern shore of Cape Cod, New England. Finally they chose Plymouth for their colony. Then came a terrible winter when over half of their number died, but in the spring those who had lived through the winter still would not use the word failure—and decided to stay on.

"And then, at last, came harvest time, and hope and great thankfulness was in the hearts of these people. So that in the autumn in 1621 they set aside a day in which they gave 'solemn Thanksgiving to the glorious Hearer of Prayers!'

"The first national celebration of Thanksgiving was in 1789 when George Washington named Thursday, November 26th of that year, as a day to be observed in which to give thanks for the blessings of the year.

"It was Abraham Lincoln who recommended that the last Thursday in November should be observed as a day of Thanksgiving.

"And every since then it has been observed each year all over the country, and not from time to time in the different states according to whether their governors proclaimed it as such. Formerly that had been the custom.

"So it was Lincoln who gave us this day as a National holiday and day of Thanksgiving for every year. But it was because of that little group of people so many years ago that we have so much for which to be thankful.

"Sometimes it is hard to think that such terrible days followed one after the other, for the country is so big and prosperous and cultivated now. But everything has to be begun. And it seems to me that our present-day joyous Thanksgivings are just what those people, so full of pluck, would have wanted us to have. For people who could be so brave and who could endure so much for what they believed was right, could not help but have hearts full of love and capable of great happiness."

NOVEMBER 27: Good News

I'VE been here in the zoo for some time," said Daddy Buffalo, "and of course I do not keep up very well with the news outside of the zoo.

"But to-day I heard of some news and it was very good news. I will tell all the buffaloes about it. I heard that they were protecting the buffaloes more and more all the time, now.

"I was told that they didn't go after buffaloes to kill them but that they brought some of them to a zoo and people learned of their ways and of their habits and became interested in them, and others they left quite free. Surely that is good news for buffaloes."

NOVEMBER 28: The Newsboy's Dog

THE town authorities came to a poor little newsboy who owned a dog and told him they would have to take his dog unless he paid for a dog license. But the little boy hadn't enough money and he did not know what to do, when some kind people overheard the conversation. They told the men that they had plenty of money and quickly paid for the license of the little brown dog. The boy then almost cried for joy.

So the little dog wagged his tail when his master told him to thank the kind people, for he saw quickly that his master once more was happy.

NOVEMBER 29: The Gun-Metal Watch

A VERY rich and spoiled little girl," said daddy, "owned a gun-metal wrist watch. It kept very bad time, and she had it mended again and again.

"One day she went and had it fixed for the very last time, she said, and several days afterward the watch would not go for more than a half hour at a time. She took it back to the watch mender and was told that the only thing that could be done would be to have new works put in it. She said the watch wasn't worth that and she was so annoyed that she threw the watch into the first ash can she saw.

"Well, there passed by a very poor little girl. On top of the ash can she spied a paper with funny pictures, and she grabbed the paper out of the ash can, and then, to her amazement, she saw the little watch.

"She ran all the way home to show it to her daddy, for her daddy had often mended watches for people just as favors, as his real business was that of a fruit dealer.

"When her daddy saw it he said:

" 'This watch has been fussed with so much that it is no wonder it refuses to go. I will see that it goes.' And sure enough he did.

"The watch went beautifully, and the little poor girl wore her gun metal watch with the greatest pride.

"Every one had to ask her the time, of course, every few minutes so she could look at her watch, and if they didn't ask her the time often enough she would tell them of her own accord.

"Now, the little rich girl was given a gold watch as a present from her daddy, but it didn't give half the pleasure that the little gun-metal watch gave the little girl whose very own daddy mended the watch for her."

NOVEMBER 30: Barnyard Thoughts

I CAN celebrate Thanksgiving time," said the pig, "for I am so thankful I do not live in the city." And then the pig squealed this song:

"Grunt, grunt," he said, "I'd think it a pity.
If I were forced to live in the city.
There would be no nice mud in which to dig,
A poor place indeed for a sensible pig!"

"Quack, quack," said the ducks, "and what is more there'd be no place to swim,
In the city we'd lose our life I'm sure, and certainly our vim."

"And," said the cow, "I agree with you too!
In the city I'd not have the spirit to moo.
There'd be no green meadows and nothing to chew,
Oh, what in the world would a poor cow do?"

And all the animals began singing, and talking, grunting, squealing and quack-quacking.
And all of them said, in their different kinds of ways:

"We'll never, never leave the farm, we'll stay here all our days!
We'd hate it in the city where they say it's crowded so,
We'll never add to the crowds, we say; to the city we'll never go!"

"That is a fine chorus, grunt, grunt," said the pig, "and a fine song of Thanksgiving."

DECEMBER 1: The Toy-Shop

WHY, here we are again," said the first toy to the second toy as they looked at each other on a counter in the shop, for they had met before in Santa's workshop.
"Oh!" continued the first toy. "A child is coming to look at us! Oh, there are ever so many children coming into the shop, and there are grown-ups too, and their voices—oh, aren't their voices nice! They sound so merry and so happy and as if they loved each other and the whole world.
"I'm being bought, I do believe," the first toy added.
"Oh, so am I," said the second toy. "I'm going to be wrapped up."
"We must be going to be presents from the mothers and daddies of the children as Santa will come to get most of these toys just before Christmas."
"Good-by," said the second toy; "merry Christmas "
"Merry Christmas," said the first toy. "Oh see! How the children are standing outside that window looking at the tree with all our friends upon it!
"Wouldn't you think the window would break? See their faces right against the window pane."

And as Santa Claus heard the reports of the pleasure of the children over this year's toys, he smiled to himself and said:

"That is all I want as a reward for my work!"

DECEMBER 2: A Story of the Fireplace

JACK and Evelyn and daddy were watching the dance which was taking place in the Fireplace. They saw the beautiful costumes the Fire Fairies wore and they saw them blaze and flame and then become quiet. "They're eating their supper now," said daddy. "The Fire Fairy cooks have finished everything and now they are all enjoying the goodies."

But soon the flames began to die down and only a few little flashes of light and fire were seen from time to time.

"Those flashes and flames," said daddy, "are some of the Fire Fairies who are still wide awake enough to ask the Fire Witches questions. For the Fire Witches tell bedtime tales. Soon the Fairies will be sound, sound asleep. They love to be put to sleep by the Fire Witches."

The flames died down entirely and only a little smoldering went on in the Fireplace.

"The witches are saying good-night," said daddy. "Then they too will go to bed. But the ashes that will be left—nice warm ashes— they will be the pleasant dreams that are left behind for the Fire Fairies."

The fire had gone out! Only some ashes could be seen, but in one corner a few red coals had appeared.

"What are they?" asked the children.

"They're the King and Queen of the Fireplace and they've come to see that their people are all fast asleep. Then they will go to sleep, but they will first whisper a 'Thank you' to the Witches who tell the marvelous stories." And just as daddy said that, the children heard a faint, crackling noise, and then they knew that every creature of the Fireplace had gone to sleep in their warm ashes of pleasant dreams.

DECEMBER 3: The Pig Who Had No Table Manners

I HAVE a fairy tale to tell you this evening," said daddy, "of a little pig who left his mother to visit the fox family.

"The foxes, as you know, are very careful about their table manners and also extremely proud and were quite disgusted with little

Piggy Look-a-do's table manners, for instead of saying 'Thank you,' he'd just grunt when anything was passed to him. He swallowed his food without chewing it at all. He would reach across the table, and if he couldn't reach a thing he'd climb on the table, much to the horror of all the other animals. Well, in fact, he behaved so badly that all his other nice mannered playmates simply would not have anything to do with him and just called him 'pig.'

"Even Br'er B'ar couldn't like him because of his bad manners, and finally he just had to go out and root in the ground for something to eat. Of course when he did that he ruined his lovely little clothes, his white shoes and trousers became all muddy, and his little speckled coat got very rusty looking.

"Piggy Look-a-do realized that he was losing his good looks, for the little pink nose looked white and his eyes very dull. At nighttime he returned to his mother. She had made a nice turnip stew for dinner. But when she saw how sick Piggy Look-a-do was, she sent him straight to his room, and invited in the squirrel's children, who were really hungry.

All that night Piggy Look-a-do tossed and turned with bad dreams. When he woke up he promised himself to become a good little pig who could count his blessings. And he did!

DECEMBER 4: Jimmie's Airplane

A LITTLE boy named Jimmie," said daddy, "wanted a toy airplane for a Christmas present.

"Well, Jimmie wrote a letter to Santa Claus not long ago, and he wrote the following:

" 'Please, dear Santa Claus, give me a little toy airplane. For when I'm a big man I want to go up in the air in a real one! I'd love to fly and so I'd like a little airplane which would fly around the room as I've seen them do in the store. The store at the second corner after you pass my house has one. It looks like a nice one, too.

" 'Wishing you a merry Christmas, your loving friend Jimmie.' And Santa has reserved the airplane for his little friend Jimmie, I've heard," concluded daddy.

DECEMBER 5: The Christmas Dog

A LITTLE girl named Peggy," said daddy, "wrote a letter to Santa Claus, and this is what she said:

" 'Dear Santa Claus: I would like a rag doll and a doll which says Mamma and Papa, and can shut her eyes. I also want a book and a set of paints, and please, dear Santa, bring my mother and daddy a doggie to guard the house. I want a doggie too, but mother and daddy also want one, so we could all share one doggie.

" 'Your affectionate little friend,

" 'PEGGY.

" 'P. S.—Please give my love to your Reindeer and a great deal of love for you, dear Santa Claus.

" 'PEGGY.'

"She put her letter down by the fireplace and the next morning it was gone, for she had addressed it quite correctly to 'Mr. Santa Claus, By the Fireplace.' As he was on the lookout for letters such as these around Christmas time, of course, he got it safely.

"Now Santa Claus loves to get letters. His mail around Christmas time is tremendous. But the more he gets, the more he chuckles and laughs to himself. 'Oh this is splendid,' he says, as he opens letter after letter. Days went by and Peggy kept wondering what Santa Claus would bring her for Christmas. She thought of writing him again about the doggie, for her mother and daddy would say so often.

" 'It would be a great protection if we only had a dog. This house is rather far away from the rest, and then we would be safe. Besides, a dog is such a companionable animal and the children would love him.'

"Somehow, she didn't like to write again to Santa Claus, but just before bedtime each night, she would whisper up the chimney—'Please, dear Santa Claus, don't forget the doggie—and the doll, and the paint box—and—and,' but by this time her mother had led her off, for she would have gone on talking and talking to Santa Claus. And if she had kept on talking and missing her sleep, she would have been too tired to enjoy Christmas Day when it came.

"At last it was Christmas Eve. Again Peggy called up the chimney, and she put her stocking first on one side and then the other. And by her stocking hung four smaller ones, for Peggy's little sisters and brothers.

" 'Good night, Santa Claus, Merry Christmas. My love to the Reindeer,' called Peggy for the last time. And the younger children called out too, 'Good night, Santa Claus, give our love to the Reindeer.'

"And off they all trotted to the land of dreams which they had to pass through before Christmas morning would come.

"The next morning, bright and early, Peggy and her sisters and brothers were up looking at their stockings. Such goodies as they found! Peggy got her rag doll, and a doll who could shut her eyes, and say 'Mamma, Papa.' And she got a set of paints and a fine book.

"Her sisters and brothers got the presents they had asked for, and they had such fun over the oranges in their stockings. Several of them were covered with black soot which Santa had dropped coming down the chimney! They loved to think of how Santa Claus had picked out these very oranges himself.

"But when the first excitement was over, Peggy thought to herself, 'There is no doggie.' But then she thought Santa Claus was not supposed to get her everything she asked for. So after brushing away a tear which had fallen she began to laugh and play and say, 'Merry Christmas,' over and over and over again, to her mother and daddy, her sisters and brothers. But in a moment or two they all thought they heard a whimper outside the front door. 'I shall see what can be outside,' said Peggy, with beating heart. She opened the door! And there stood a little white dog, shivering miserably in the cold. 'I have no home,' the little dog's eyes seemed to say, and as Peggy held him closely to her she said, 'I know Santa Claus sent you here, and I wish you a Merry Christmas! And this is to be your home, Doggie dear!'"

DECEMBER 6: The Pride of Toys

O H, I'm so proud," whispered little brown Teddy Bear.
"You're no more proud than I am," said a little white lamb. "Please pinch me—so—and then I will say: 'Baa-Baa-Baa.' Ah, that will make some one happy."

The toys were in Santa Claus' toy-shop and they were getting very much excited. There were still some to be finished—in fact, there were many to be finished, but none of them were worried, for they knew perfectly well that Santa Claus never left any toys unfinished.

That was the wonderful part of Santa Claus. He could be rushed and hurried and he could be so busy that you wondered how it was possible for him to do so much and you might think, if you didn't know, that some of those many, many things wouldn't be done. But the toys knew, for the tools which Santa used to make them with whispered to them many secrets.

"He may be busy," the tools always told the new toys, "but he'll finish you and you'll go to the children on Christmas day."

"How proud I will be," whispered the Teddy Bear once more, "if I am put on a tree. They say that Santa hangs toys on Christmas trees. But then I would be just as proud if I were put in a stocking. How I would love to peep my head out from the top of a stocking and see the children as they come downstairs early Christmas morning! In fact, I would be proud no matter where Santa put me, or how he gave me. It's a great big and wonderful pride to be a toy made by Santa Claus which is given to a child on Christmas day."

"That is what we all feel," said the other toys.

DECEMBER 7: Christmas with the Squirrels

WHEN Christmas day comes all the little squirrels," said daddy, "meet near the largest tree, which they pick out for the occasion. Then there is a wild scramble up the tree for the branches, where the squirrels perch themselves, and finally the feast begins.

"After they have finished their scrumptious Christmas dinner they play 'tag,' 'hide-and-seek' and many other games, which make the branches wave around as they jump from one tree to the other. Prizes are offered by the older squirrels for the sports and games which are played. The prizes are usually extraordinarily big nuts or very red apples. Sometimes, too, kind children just before Christmas put nuts in the trees where the squirrels can find them. That makes the squirrels very happy, and they call these nuts their Christmas gifts."

DECEMBER 8: How to Address Santa

WHERE is Santa's home," asked Evelyn, "for we must know where to write him?"

"He lives way up North," answered daddy, "but any letter directed to 'Mr. Santa Claus, the Chimney,' will reach him, for he has special reindeer collecting his letters from the tops of chimneys several weeks before Christmas. You must put them on the hearth, and on the envelope you must put a speck of soot, for that is the stamp you use for the letters which go to Santa Claus Land."

DECEMBER 9: A Letter to Santa Claus and the Answer

I SAW such a poor little boy to-day," began daddy to Jack and Evelyn. "He was looking in a shop window where there were loads of toys, and as he looked great, huge tears dropped from his eyes and trickled down his face.

"I spoke to him and asked him where he lived, and for a moment he couldn't speak, but between sobs he began to tell me of his life. He was very ragged and quite dirty.

"He told me his daddy had died in the summer and that a few months afterward his mother had married a horrid, cruel man who hated him and called him 'little nuisance.' The stepfather didn't like to work, and as soon as he had used up his wife's savings he told the little boy he would have to beg or steal his food, for he wouldn't be bothered with him.

"The little boy said that he had always had a happy home, a good warm fire and plenty to eat when he came home from school, and he simply would not beg or steal. One night he came home, of course bringing nothing. His stepfather saw he could neither make him beg nor steal so he forced him to leave the house. His mother was so afraid of his stepfather that she did not say a word. Now, he had been away from home for two weeks. He spent his nights with a little school friend, but he could not stay there much longer, as the boy's parents were so poor they could hardly keep their children. He dreaded the cold, but what he felt more than anything was that Santa Claus did not know where he was and that he would have no Christmas."

"Let's write Santa a letter right away," said Evelyn, "and tell him about the little boy. What's his name, daddy?"

"His name is Harry Armstrong, and tell Santa to bring his presents here, for I've told him he can do odd chores for us and stay here for as long as he likes."

So Evelyn wrote: "Dear Santa—A poor little boy named Harry Armstrong is afraid he'll have no Christmas. So please, dear Santa, send him a warm suit, an overcoat, a sled, some skates and lots of candy. Your loving Evelyn."

Jack and Evelyn had just gone to bed when daddy walked into their room with a note and a stamp of soot on it. Evelyn hurriedly opened it and read aloud: "Dear Evelyn—I won't forget about Harry Armstrong on Christmas, and you were very dear to think of some one else who wanted a Christmas. Your friend, Santa Claus."

"Hurrah!" shouted Jack and Evelyn together.

DECEMBER 10: Betty's Dream

OH, mother, I had such a dream," said a little girl named Betty. "I dreamt I saw Santa Claus in his shop. Oh, he was the most beautiful old man I ever saw in all my life—and oh, mother, his eyes! How they laughed. And he was making—think, mother—he was making a rag doll! The very sort of a doll I hope he will give me for Christmas and he was smiling at the doll. And I saw the whole shop and all the toys—and everything. Oh, I hope Santa brings me a rag doll."

Now the Dream King had sent this dream to Betty, and it **was as** real as a dream can be. But it was absolutely real that Santa Claus was making a rag doll and that that rag doll was going to be found Christmas morning in Betty's stocking, for the Dream King had told Santa Claus it was what she wanted and that was why Santa Claus had smiled so—because he knew how the dolly was going to please Betty!

DECEMBER 11: The Snow Man

THE Brownies and Gnomes thought it would be a fine scheme to make a snow man," said daddy. "Billie Brownie made his feet first of all, and so they made him on up until his head was all ready.

"Then of course, he had to have a hat, and Peter Gnome made him a very handsome high one.

" 'We have forgotten something,' said Billie Brownie.

" 'What?' they all asked.

" 'A pipe for his mouth,' said Billie.

" 'To be sure,' said Peter Gnome. 'A snow man isn't a real snow man without a pipe. We'll make it right away.'

"So they got some twigs and some wood, and with their little pen knives they all made pipes. The very best pipe of all was chosen for the snow man, while the other pipes they put around on the ground beside him.

" 'For,' said Peter Gnome, 'he ought to have a little collection of pipes.'

"He was the tallest snow man ever made and he looked so jolly and happy. He reached so far up that when it grew dark Mr. Moon came out and said:

" 'What is it I see? A man who is almost tall enough to talk to me. What fun!'

"And how he grinned when he found out the man had been made of snow!"

DECEMBER 12: Sharpy and Chappy

SHARPY, the squirrel, with his friend Chappy were watching some children as they filled bags with candies and nuts. "We want to make a noise so they will notice us," said Sharpy.

"Perhaps they won't like us," said Chappy. "And some don't enjoy noise."

"They look as if they liked it," shrieked Sharpy. "Listen to the children. I don't believe they will hear us."

But then Chappy and Sharpy began to scamper over the porch and as they shrieked at each other, sometimes as if they were scolding and sometimes as if they were laughing, the children shouted, "Oh, there are two squirrels!"

Sharpy and Chappy looked their very best, or tried to, standing on their hind legs and looking very sweet and cunning as they begged. Their little mouths were moving all the time as if they were quite ready. "We have quantities of nuts to-day," said the children, "as we're getting our Christmas presents ready. Isn't that fine?" And I can assure you that Sharpy and Chappy thought it was fine, too, as they were given all the nuts they could eat.

DECEMBER 13: Christmas Letters

STILL the letters keep coming," chuckled Santa Claus. "And every year it seems to me as though I received a larger mail than I ever had before.

"But it can never be too large for Santa Claus.

"And the precious dears! What memories they have. They know just what they want! They don't forget!

"They think old Santa remembers too when they have told him one thing and then just add a little postscript or another letter without explaining to him just what their last letter was about.

"They think he can remember and keep them all straight, even though he may get several letters from the same child in many, many cases.

"They think he can remember their names from year to year, and they're right. Yes, the blessed little dears are right." And Santa Claus chuckled to himself as he stroked his beard and by the burning coals of the great stove in his workshop he read the letters which had just come.

"Dear Santa Claus," was the beginning of every one, or at least almost every one, though some of them began, "Dear, dear Santa Claus," and "You precious old Santa Claus," and a number of other nice beginnings like that, which made Santa Claus very happy.

But every letter made him happy, for every letter was just a little different and he liked all the children to be different and not to be just alike.

"I hope you remember me," one read, "for I wrote to you last year and the year before. The year before that I was too young

288

to write, but my brudder wrote for me? Do you remember my brudder's letter that he wrote that year? He said that he guessed the next year I could write you a letter, for I could then write my name.

"And my brudder was right and the next year I did write you a letter."

Some of the spelling wasn't just like this, but this is the way it sounded as Santa Claus read it aloud. He was all by himself, except that his collie dog, Boy of the North, was sitting by him on the floor, but he read it aloud, for he loved to hear the sound of the words the children had written and picture them as they looked while writing.

And he didn't care about the spelling.

"Of course," he said to himself, "they must go to school and learn how to spell, for they would feel dreadfully when they grew up if they didn't know more than they do now!

"But when they're writing to Santa Claus it doesn't make so much difference. They can take a little holiday then. And even when they make a blot and then write down by it that it is a kiss I know that they do mean to send a kiss to me, even if the blot itself was accidental!

"Well, I must go on with this letter."

He went on with the letter and this was what he read:

"My brudder won a gold medal in school the other day. He is getting to be so smart, dear Santa, and I know you'll be pleased to hear it. You sent me a picture once Santa when I was very little of a boy who was very cold on his way to school with his coat all wrapped up tight around him.

"In school he won the gold medal. It was the day they gave the prizes, and coming home from school the picture showed the boy with his coat open wide, and the gold medal pinned on, and he didn't feel the cold the least bit!

"Do you 'member, Santa Claus? Brudder was like that the other day."

Yes, he remembered that picture and how pleased he was to think the boy, a boy he had always liked so much, had won a gold medal.

And on he read the letters. Some were letters just full of news of what they all were doing in the different homes, of what they were going to do, and in some they wrote of the new sisters or brothers who had come since Santa Claus had last been written to.

Of course they told him what presents they wanted and they all said they hoped he wouldn't get too tired, and they all, every single one of them, told him how they loved him and wished him a Merry Christmas, too.

And that made Santa Claus so very, very happy.

hair, and the cart was painted a bright red. Oh, how delighted the little boy was, and he closed the closet door and went back to his playroom very happy.

"As no one had seen him look into the closet, the next day he thought he would take another look. What was his horror to find that the horse and cart had disappeared, and no sign of it was anywhere to be found. He cried himself to sleep, so ashamed did he feel.

"The next morning he decided to write to Santa Claus. So he said, " 'Dear Santa Claus—I know I was a naughty boy and looked when I was told not to. Please forgive me and give me back the horse and cart and I will never be a bad boy again.'

"He put this note up the chimney, and the very next morning he found this lovely answer:

" 'Dear Teddy—I am sure you are sorry, and am certain you will never do such a thing again. So on Christmas morning when you get up you will find the horse and cart awaiting you. Your old friend, Santa Claus.' "

DECEMBER 18: Blue Sky and Sun

"WHERE are you going—all dressed up?" asked the Blue Sky of Mr. Sun.

"I am going to a coasting party," he said.

"And pray tell me, how can you go to a coasting party?" asked the Blue Sky as a smile in the shape of a little silver cloud came over it.

"And why not?" asked Mr. Sun.

"I'd hardly say," continued the Blue Sky, "that coasting was exactly one of your talents. No, not exactly. Now confess! You can't coast. So why do you go to a coasting party? It would be as funny as if the Blue Sky went a-skating."

"Ah, but don't you see?" said Mr. Sun.

"Just because you're so extremely bright there is no reason why you need think you're the only one who sees. I can see perfectly, thank you, and on a clear day like this I'm at my best."

"But you don't see—truly—" persisted Mr. Sun.

"Then explain to me how you can go to a coasting party," said the Blue Sky.

"There! That's something like! Now that you've asked me the necessary question I can tell you my story."

"Must you always have the necessary question, Mr. Sun?"

"Always," replied Mr. Sun.

"Well continue," said the Blue Sky.

"It's this way," said Mr. Sun. "You see there are many children in the world."

"That isn't news to me, Mr. Sun."

"I'm only telling it to you to begin with."

"Begin with something I don't know," said the Blue Sky.

"How do you suppose I can tell just what you know and what you don't? I never went to your school."

"Oh well," said the Blue Sky frowning a little, while three small clouds came over it, "go on with your story any way you please."

"Thank you," said Mr. Sun. "Some of these children are giving a coasting party this afternoon, and what do you suppose they said?"

"I've no idea," said the Blue Sky. "I don't see how any one could guess. Children are apt to say so many different things. They seem to know so many words and games and stories and all sorts of things."

"Yes," said Mr. Sun, "they're bright little things, that's true."

"You talk about them, Mr. Sun, as if they were Stars. Bright little things indeed! How funny you are!"

"Well they are little and they are bright, aren't they?

"Very well," said the Blue Sky. "Do go ·on with your story."

"I don't get half a chance," said Mr. Sun looking a little dull for a moment.

"I won't say another word," said the Blue Sky.

"And these children said, 'We do hope Mr. Sun will come to our coasting party.' Now then! I was asked to come by the children. A great honor—and I'm going. Yes, I'm going to shine with might and main over that party. They'll keep so warm! They'll have such a good time, and they'll be so glad that they asked me!"

"I don't think it's such an honor," said the Blue Sky, "for they're just making use of you."

"I like to be useful," said Mr. Sun.

Now just at that moment the children appeared for their coasting party. "Oh see the bright Sun," they exclaimed. "We wished for the Sun and here he is. Such fun as we'll have now."

And then one of them added, "And the Sky is all blue—it's a wonderful day!"

"Run away, Clouds," said the Blue Sky. "These children like me too."

"Ha, ha, ha," laughed Mr. Sun. "So you will do as the children ask, eh?" And the whole big face of the Blue Sky was without a cloud or a frown!

And the children had a Blue Sky and the Sun for their party.

DECEMBER 19: Christmas Time Joy

BA-A-A, Ba-a-a, Ba-a-a," said the lamb Santa had just finished making, as he gave it a little squeeze.

"Fine!" exclaimed Santa Claus. "That's right."

"Suppose," whispered the lamb, "the child who gets me wouldn't know where to look, or where to press, what then? She'd never know I could make those sounds."

"She'll find out, never fear," said Santa Claus.

And the lamb smiled its little toy smile for it knew Santa Claus always spoke the truth. And that night the stars all over the world seemed brighter as they looked down upon the Earth for they knew of the joy so soon to come in so many thousands and thousands of homes.

DECEMBER 20: Santa in Eskimo Land

IT was a Christmas morning, and Santa hadn't come," said daddy. "The little Eskimaux who live so far up north had been too excited to sleep.

"Finally one of the daddy Eskimaux said: 'I'm afraid something must have happened to Santa Claus. The storm last night was so wild. Let's get some of the dogs and sleds.' So a number of the bigger boys and some of the men began to get ready. They bundled up so much that all you could see was their eyes. The storm had let up, but the snowdrifts were like mountains. They had just started when a tinkling of bells was heard, and what should they see but eight beautiful reindeer and old Santa Claus dressed in a red suit with great big furs. On his back was a huge bag which was almost overflowing, so full was it.

" 'Merry Christmas, Santa Claus!' shrieked all the little Eskimaux.

" 'Merry Christmas to you all!' said Santa, and the reindeer shook their heads and tinkled their bells, which was their way of saying 'Merry Christmas.'

"Poor Santa's mustache and eyebrows were frozen, and his face was very, very red from the cold. But, oh, it was so jolly for them actually to have Santa with them! They had never before been awake when he had come even though his visit to them was always his last.

"As soon as he had warmed his hands and had seen to the feeding of his reindeer and patted them for their bravery he undid his pack. And such a Christmas as they all did have!

" 'You know,' said Santa, 'I'm glad there was such a storm, for this is my very first Christmas party!' "

294

DECEMBER 21: Santa's Toy-Shop

I THINK the children will have a pretty good Christmas this year," chuckled Santa Claus to himself, as he looked over his toy-shop, and the reindeer knew from Santa's chuckles that soon they would be starting off.

DECEMBER 22: A White Christmas

THE snowflakes saw Santa as he was making ready for his journey and some of them danced on his great red coat and sat for a few minutes on his white beard and his white eyebrows.

"Hello, snowflakes, glad to see you," said Santa Claus. "So King Snow has allowed you to be the honored ones to give us a white Christmas?"

The snowflakes danced about and some of them peeped in windows and saw great, tall trees ready to be trimmed. And they saw sleeping children. When the next morning came all the children shouted, "Oh, it snowed during the night! And we will have a white Christmas." Then how happy the snowflakes were.

DECEMBER 23: The Tree and the Stockings

I AM getting so excited I can hardly wait," said the Christmas tree. "The daddy of the children brought me to the house because he said it would be a great help to Santa Claus to have me all ready.

"I know Santa Claus will give me the most beautiful of decorations, for I've often heard my family talk of the wonderful Christmas trees there have been. Ah, how handsome many of my relations have looked, and I can hardly wait until Santa Claus comes to see me."

"You're not any more excited than we are," said three stockings which hung up by the side of the mantel-piece.

"I belong to Dot, age four," said the white stocking.

"I am hanging up for Jimmie, age eight," said the tan stocking.

"And I am for Betty, age six," said the black stocking.

"I'm for all of them," said the Christmas tree.

"That's so," agreed the stockings. "But even if we're not for all of them, but each stocking for one child, we're just as excited as we can be."

"Have you ever been here before?" asked the tree.

"Yes, we're used every Christmas. We're kept just for Christmas. That's all we do all the year. We're put up the night before, on Christmas Eve, and down we come on Christmas morning, but between then and Christmas morning the most wonderful things happen! Ah!" and the stockings waved a little as they talked of their evening and morning of pleasure.

"It's far better than being around all the time and getting worn out. We're very fortunate stockings!"

"You are indeed," said the Christmas tree. "But for my part I am willing to be around for one season of the year and to have a glorious time then. Oh dear, I am so excited! I can hardly wait!"

"Patience, dear tree," said the stockings. "Santa Claus will soon be here."

"You don't think he will lose his way," said the tree. "I never heard of his losing his way from any of my relations. But perhaps he might forget about this house."

"Santa Claus forget a house where there are children! Dear me, tree, but you don't know Santa Claus. He never, never forgets! He's Santa Claus—and that's reason enough why we won't be forgotten."

DECEMBER 24: The Two Little Mice's Christmas Eve Party

A LITTLE mouse had heard when he was hiding in holes in the corners of the rooms that all the little boys and girls in the world once a year had a Christmas tree full of goodies," said daddy. "A dear old person named Santa Claus trimmed the tree for them and filled the stockings which they hung up by the fireplaces.

"The little mouse didn't see why he shouldn't have a Christmas, too, so he told another little mouse what he had heard. Together they planned what they would do. They would bore two little holes into the parlor where they had heard the tree was to be. There they stayed every night, keeping very quiet. They heard the children talk about what they hoped Santa Claus would bring them and saw them constantly send notes up the chimney to him.

"Of course the mice had to keep very quiet, as they didn't want to let the children know they were there, and with a great deal of self denial they stayed out of the pantry, living for their very own Christmas party.

"At last Christmas Eve came. They saw the children in their little nighties hang up their stockings by the fireplace and then trot off to bed.

"Before long the mice heard strange noises on the roof, and then a little soot began to fall down the chimney. Soon they saw a jolly old man appear, with white hair and a white beard, from the chimney, and they nudged each other, whispering, 'That must be Santa Claus.'

"Sure enough, it was Santa Claus, for he had a big bag of presents with him, and at once he set to work. At first he trimmed the tree. He had plenty of silver trimming and candles; but, best of all (thought the mice), he strung popcorn over the tree and made it look as if the snow had fallen over it. Then he tied candy canes and candy animals of all sorts on the branches. Next he filled the stockings, and how the mouths of the two little mice did water as they saw all sorts of nuts, raisins and big rosy-cheeked apples going in! The toys didn't interest the mice, as they were longing to get at the things to eat.

"Before long Santa was through and quickly disappeared up the chimney. And then—the mice began their feast. And, oh, what a time they did have! They ate until they could eat no more, and they thought Christmas the finest time of the year, for never before had they seen food still before them which they weren't hungry for!

"The next morning when the children saw so many nutshells and bits of popcorn lying around they knew that some little mice must have had a party, but they didn't set a trap, as they thought it was fine that the mice had had a Christmas party too."

DECEMBER 25: Christmas Morning

"CHRISTMAS comes but once a year! Christmas comes but once a year!" shouted the children as they hurried down stairs on Christmas morning. They sat down on the floor as soon as they reached the library. And each one took a stocking which had been hanging in front of the mantelpiece. Every stocking was well filled. And each stocking stuck out queerly so that no one could guess what was in it. After the stockings had been looked at and the oranges and apples had rolled out of the toes, the presents were taken from the tree. Before long they began to feel hungry, for they hadn't waited to have breakfast first. They ate Santa's wonderful oranges, and the children's mother said to their daddy:

"Dear me, I wish I could find such big juicy oranges as Santa Claus does. He's a better shopper than I am!"

"He's a wonder," said Dot and Jimmie and Betty together, and then every one took his or her orange and paraded into the dining-room, singing once more,

"Christmas comes but once a year!"

DECEMBER 26: Santa's Telescope

DID you ever hear of Santa Claus' telescope?" asked daddy. The children shook their heads.

"He has the most wonderful telescope—more wonderful than any other, and he can see through it miles and miles and miles.

"Every Christmas morning he sits at the window at the extreme end of his toy-shop and looks through the telescope. He sees into the different homes and he watches the children as they take their presents and open them, and empty their stockings.

"'There,' he said to himself last Christmas, 'it is just as I thought; little girls will never grow tired of dolls and boys will always like trains.

"'And they enjoy a good game, too, for the winter evenings. And, ah, I see that boy at his skates! He asked for a pair in his letter to me—that is, he asked for them in six different letters he wrote me. He really can hardly wait to start using them. I do believe he would like it if the floor were suddenly covered with ice!

"'And how that little girl is hugging her doll! I thought the one I made with the golden curls and the eyes that opened and shut would just about suit her. She told me the kind she wanted in her letter. What a help those letters are! They tell me what they want, and they tell me so many more nice things, too. They tell me how much they are looking forward to my visit, and that they hope I'll have a Merry Christmas, too. The dear little people! As if I could help but have a Merry Christmas when I look through this telescope and see their smiles! How happy they do look! How their eyes sparkle.

"'And if ever I see a child scowl or look cross—oh, dear—how sad it does make me! There! I just saw a little girl look very cross because she thinks her brother's set of soldiers are better than her paper dolls. Oh, that makes me very unhappy!'

"But Santa's faithful dog, Boy of the North, put his head in Santa's lap and licked his hands.

" 'Oh, Boy of the North, you will not see me unhappy! I feel happy again. The little girl is not scowling now. Something or some one must have whispered in her ear that it was making me sad!

" 'Now I see a little girl who has been so sick this fall. She has that nice white lamb with the blue ribbon around its neck that I gave her. And how she does love him. What joy it is to have this telescope!' And again this year Santa will look through his telescope!"

DECEMBER 27: Christmas Letters

SANTA CLAUS was talking to his dog, Boy of the North.
"You see I get so many letters—hundreds and hundreds of letters. I love them so much and I read them many times. But if I kept them I would have to build houses and houses to hold them all. So I have a yearly bonfire, as you know, Boy of the North.

The ashes from the letters of the children keep me warm all through the long winter months. And in the summer I have to have a fire to help make the toys and to keep us warm. For it's cold here in the summer too.

"Yes, these ashes are used for the bottom of my fire in my big stove in the toy-shop and in my little house alongside. And I never have any trouble with my fire because it is started with these wonderful letters which keep going until next year. When we put fresh wood on the fire it starts up anew, because at the bottom are these ashes. Only I can have such a fire, so you see what a lucky old chap I am."

And Santa Claus started the bonfire of the letters children had written to him which made him so happy to read and which kept his fire going all through the year, and Boy of the North wagged his tail as the fire was started.

DECEMBER 28: Homes without Chimneys

WHEN they began to build these great, big apartment houses, years ago, Santa Claus was on the lookout," said daddy. 'Now,' he said to himself, 'I must think out a way to get to the children who will live in those big buildings.'

"The people went on building, and they were so interested in watching the floors grow—one went right on top of the other—that they seemed

299

to forget all about Santa Claus and his one trip of the year, which is worth more than anything else that happens.

"And then the people began to build fire-escapes. For they said that when the buildings were so large and there were so many rooms and so many families, they must have a way of getting out in case of fire. And from top to bottom of every building—on every side—they put fire escapes, so that no home was without one.

" 'Well,' said Santa Claus, as he drove his reindeer over the roofs of the city that night, to see about his Christmas trip, 'that is something like! Now I know what to do!'

"So when Santa Claus goes to the city homes where there are no chimneys he leaves his reindeer on the roof, and down he goes on the fire-escape to every single home, and in he gets with his pack. For did you ever know any place locked up so tightly but that there was a way for Santa Claus to get in?

"Oh, yes, Santa Claus visits the cities and the villages and the farms. He just has to do a little differently in some homes than in others. But it makes no difference to him what they may build, for, after all, Santa Claus is Santa Claus, and he always makes a way to visit children every Christmas! For he is the children's King and he reigns over Christmas Day—the greatest day of all!"

DECEMBER 29: The Barnyard Christmas

WELL, as it was Christmas time," said daddy, "all the barnyard fowls thought they should play some games, so all joined in. There were the turkey hens, turkey gobblers, peafowls, guinea-hens, roosters, chickens, Mr. and Mrs. Duck and all the little ducks. And after they had finished playing the farmer gave them a regular Christmas time feast which made then full of the joyous Christmas spirit of happiness—as well as of food!"

DECEMBER 30: Ambitions

DO you know what ambition means?" asked daddy.

"I think it means to want to get on," said Jack. "Isn't there a word called ambitious? And when a person is spoken of as ambitious it means that person wants to get on and improve and all."

"Right," said daddy. "That's fine. That saves me all the trouble of explaining, too."

"It was nearing the New Year," daddy said, "and Billie Brownie was

300

going around calling one evening. The Dreamland King promised to help him. So he called on a little boy.

" 'How are you this fine evening?' Billie Brownie asked the little boy, whose name, by the way, was Jasper.

" 'I am thinking of what I am going to do when I am big,' said Jasper. 'I have great ambitions.'

" 'Gracious,' said Billie Brownie, 'that does sound noble.'

" 'Would you like to hear them?' asked Jasper.

" 'Enormously,' said Billie Brownie.

" 'Well,' said Jasper, 'when I grow up I want to be very famous. I want to be praised more than anything. Oh, Billie Brownie, I want to write great stories and books and have every one say that I'm greater than Shakespeare. I want to write great plays and have audiences rise to their feet and cheer and cheer. I want to play in concerts and have signs go up which say that all the seats are sold and that there is only standing room.

" 'I want to be so popular that I'll never have to pay for anything, but others will always be honored to treat me. I want some day to make a great speech and have the policemen called out to keep back the crowds who would hear me. I would like to be a great singer and have crowds stand in the rain waiting in line to get tickets. And I'd like to be a tight-rope walker in a circus and have people admire me.

" 'I'd like to have long hair and have folks think me clever without having to say a word. I'd like to own a big automobile and I'd like to act in a show where all I'd have to do would be to smile and folks would think me grand.'

" 'Well, well,' said Billie Brownie. 'Anything else?'

" 'Yes,' said Jasper, 'I'd like to make a great deal of money and have a fine job and not have to work at all.'

" 'In fact,' said Billie Brownie, 'you'd like to be famous and rich and admired without doing a thing yourself! Well, well, Jasper, your ideas are all mixed up. You haven't ambitions. You're just greedy, I fear. And if I were you, I'd think a while and make a New Year's resolution that I'd be good and kind and work hard and make myself worth while rather than rich. And when you've tried what fun it is to work hard and play hard and be kind, you'll find how happy you are. And happiness is greater than fame. Billie Brownie knows!' "

DECEMBER 31: Little Pitchers

FAIRY GRANT-YOUR-WISHES was calling on a little girl named Janet on New Year's Eve after Janet was in bed and asleep. For the Dreamland King had arranged this.

"I have come to grant your wishes," the Fairy said.

"Then I wish," said Janet, "that my mother and daddy would know that it hurts me dreadfully when they say that 'little pitchers have big ears.' I feel so much in the way then. And when people come to visit and say that 'children should be seen and not heard,' and 'I used to know you when you were so high.' Oh, dear, I wish they wouldn't say such things."

"I'll tell you what I'll do," the Fairy said, "I will ask the Dreamland King to tell your mother and daddy that it hurts you to be told these things. And I will get the Dreamland King to tell as many other people as he can, too. And he will send his messengers right out by the direct route from Dreamland to Grown-up-Land."

THE END

302